The IDG Books Creating Co

We at IDG Books Worldwide made *Creating Cool FrontPage Web Sites* to meet your growing need for quick access to the most complete and accurate computer information available. Our books work the way you do: They focus on accomplishing specific tasks — not learning random functions. Our books are not long-winded manuals or dry reference tomes. In each book, expert authors tell you exactly what you can do with your new technology and software and how to evaluate its usefulness for your needs. Easy to follow, step-by-step sections; comprehensive coverage; and convenient access in language and design — it's all here.

The authors of IDG books are uniquely qualified to give you expert advice as well as to provide insightful tips and techniques not found anywhere else. Our authors maintain close contact with end users through feedback from articles, training sessions, e-mail exchanges, user group participation, and consulting work. Because our authors know the realities of daily computer use and are directly tied to the reader, our books have a strategic advantage.

Our authors have the experience to approach a topic in the most efficient manner, and we know that you, the reader, will benefit from a "one-on-one" relationship with the author. Our research shows that readers make computer book purchases because they want expert advice. Because readers want to benefit from the author's experience, the author's voice is always present in an IDG book.

In addition, the author is free to include or recommend useful software in an IDG book. The software that accompanies each book is not intended to be a casual filler but is linked to the content, theme, or procedures of the book. We know that you will benefit from the included software.

You will find what you need in this book whether you read it from cover to cover, section by section, or simply one topic at a time. As a computer user, you deserve a comprehensive resource of answers. We at IDG Books Worldwide are proud to deliver that resource with *Creating Cool FrontPage Web Sites*.

Brenda McLaughlin
Senior Vice President and Group Publisher

Internet: YouTellUs@idgbooks.com

CREATING COOL™ FRONTPAGE™ WEB SITES

Paul M. Summitt
Mary J. Summitt

CREATING COOL™ FRONTPAGE™ WEB SITES

Paul M. Summitt

Mary J. Summitt

IDG Books Worldwide, Inc.
An International Data Group Company

Foster City, CA ♦ Chicago, IL ♦ Indianapolis, IN ♦ Southlake, TX

Creating Cool™ FrontPage™ Web Sites

Published by
IDG Books Worldwide, Inc.
An International Data Group Company
919 E. Hillsdale Blvd.
Suite 400
Foster City, CA 94404
www.idgbooks.com (IDG Books Worldwide Web Site)

Library of Congress Catalog Card No.: 96-77694

ISBN: 0-7645-3020-8

Printed in the United States of America

10 9 8 7 6 5 4 3 2 1

1B/RY/QZ/ZW/IN

Distributed in the United States by IDG Books Worldwide, Inc.

Distributed by Macmillan Canada for Canada; by Contemporanea de Ediciones for Venezuela; by Distribuidora Cuspide for Argentina; by CITEC for Brazil; by Ediciones ZETA S.C.R. Ltda. for Peru; by Editorial Limusa SA for Mexico; by Transworld Publishers Limited in the United Kingdom and Europe; by Academic Bookshop for Egypt; by Levant Distributors S.A.R.L. for Lebanon; by Al Jassim for Saudi Arabia; by Simron Pty. Ltd. for South Africa; by Pustak Mahal for India; by The Computer Bookshop for India; by Toppan Company Ltd. for Japan; by Addison Wesley Publishing Company for Korea; by Longman Singapore Publishers Ltd. for Singapore, Malaysia, Thailand, and Indonesia; by Unalis Corporation for Taiwan; by WS Computer Publishing Company, Inc. for the Philippines; by WoodsLane Pty. Ltd. for Australia; by WoodsLane Enterprises Ltd. for New Zealand. Authorized Sales Agent: Anthony Rudkin Associates for the Middle East and North Africa.

For general information on IDG Books Worldwide's books in the U.S., please call our Consumer Customer Service department at 800-762-2974. For reseller information, including discounts and premium sales, please call our Reseller Customer Service department at 800-434-3422.

For information on where to purchase IDG Books Worldwide's books outside the U.S., please contact our International Sales department at 415-655-3172 or fax 415-655-3295.

For information on foreign language translations, please contact our Foreign & Subsidiary Rights department at 415-655-3021 or fax 415-655-3281.

For sales inquiries and special prices for bulk quantities, please contact our Sales department at 415-655-3200 or write to the address above.

For information on using IDG Books Worldwide's books in the classroom or for ordering examination copies, please contact our Educational Sales department at 800-434-2086 or fax 817-251-8174.

For authorization to photocopy items for corporate, personal, or educational use, please contact Copyright Clearance Center, 222 Rosewood Drive, Danvers, MA 01923, or fax 508-750-4470.

is a trademark under exclusive license to IDG Books Worldwide, Inc., from International Data Group, Inc.

About the Authors

Paul M. Summitt taught broadcasting at the college and university level for ten years. He has worked in and with radio, television, and film since 1970 and with computers since 1972. Paul enjoys researching his family genealogy (he's the editor of the *Summitt Family Quarterly*) watching movies, playing his guitar, reading science fiction, and discussing quantum realities.

Mary J. Summitt is the owner of VREvolution, a computer-oriented research and publishing concern. She enjoys reading mysteries, researching various topics, watching movies, and discussing quantum realities.

Mary and Paul are both interested in cyberspace, virtual reality, and programming for the Internet. They have recently bought an RV and plan to travel around the country for a while as they explore their own combined quantum reality.

ABOUT IDG BOOKS WORLDWIDE

WINNER
Eighth Annual
Computer Press
Awards 1992

WINNER
Ninth Annual
Computer Press
Awards 1993

IDG BOOKS
WORLDWIDE

Welcome to the world of IDG Books Worldwide.

IDG Books Worldwide, Inc., is a subsidiary of International Data Group, the world's largest publisher of computer-related information and the leading global provider of information services on information technology. IDG was founded more than 25 years ago and now employs more than 8,500 people worldwide. IDG publishes more than 270 computer publications in over 75 countries (see listing below). More than 90 million people read one or more IDG publications each month.

Launched in 1990, IDG Books Worldwide is today the #1 publisher of best-selling computer books in the United States. We are proud to have received eight awards from the Computer Press Association in recognition of editorial excellence and three from *Computer Currents'* First Annual Readers' Choice Awards. Our best-selling *...For Dummies*® series has more than 25 million copies in print with translations in 30 languages. IDG Books Worldwide, through a joint venture with IDG's Hi-Tech Beijing, became the first U.S. publisher to publish a computer book in the People's Republic of China. In record time, IDG Books Worldwide has become the first choice for millions of readers around the world who want to learn how to better manage their businesses.

Our mission is simple: Every one of our books is designed to bring extra value and skill-building instructions to the reader. Our books are written by experts who understand and care about our readers. The knowledge base of our editorial staff comes from years of experience in publishing, education, and journalism — experience which we use to produce books for the '90s. In short, we care about books, so we attract the best people. We devote special attention to details such as audience, interior design, use of icons, and illustrations. And because we use an efficient process of authoring, editing, and desktop publishing our books electronically, we can spend more time ensuring superior content and spend less time on the technicalities of making books.

You can count on our commitment to deliver high-quality books at competitive prices on topics you want to read about. At IDG Books Worldwide, we continue in the IDG tradition of delivering quality for more than 25 years. You'll find no better book on a subject than one from IDG Books Worldwide.

John Kilcullen
President and CEO
IDG Books Worldwide, Inc.

IDG Books Worldwide, Inc., is a subsidiary of International Data Group, the world's largest publisher of computer-related information and the leading global provider of information services on information technology. International Data Group publishes over 276 computer publications in over 75 countries. Ninety million people read one or more International Data Group publications each month. International Data Group's publications include: **ARGENTINA:** Annuario de Informatica, Computerworld Argentina, PC World Argentina; **AUSTRALIA:** Australian Macworld, Client/Server Journal, Computer Living, Computerworld, Computerworld 100, Digital News, IT Casebook, Network World Australia, PC World, Publishing Essentials, Reseller, WebMaster; **AUSTRIA:** Computerwelt Osterreich, Networks Austria, PC Tip; **BELARUS:** PC World Belarus; **BELGIUM:** Data News; **BRAZIL:** Annuário de Informática, Computerworld Brazil, Connections, Super Game Power, Macworld, PC Player, PC World Brazil, Publish Brazil, Reseller News; **BULGARIA:** Computerworld Bulgaria, Networkworld/Bulgaria, PC & MacWorld Bulgaria; **CANADA:** CIO Canada, Client/Server World, ComputerWorld Canada, InfoCanada, Network World Canada; **CHILE:** Computerworld Chile, PC World Chile; **COLOMBIA:** Computerworld Colombia, PC World Colombia; **COSTA RICA:** PC World Centro America; **THE CZECH AND SLOVAK REPUBLICS:** Computerworld Czechoslovakia, Elektronika Czechoslovakia, Macworld Czech Republic, PC World Czechoslovakia; **DENMARK:** Communications World, Computerworld Danmark, Macworld Danmark, PC Privat Danmark, PC World Danmark, PC World Danmark Supplements, TECH World; **DOMINICAN REPUBLIC:** PC World Republica Dominicana; **ECUADOR:** PC World Ecuador; **EGYPT:** Computerworld Middle East, PC World Middle East; **EL SALVADOR:** PC World Centro America; **FINLAND:** MikroPC, Tietoverkko, Tietoviikko; **FRANCE:** Distributique, Golden, Hebdo-Distributique, Info PC, Le Guide du Monde Informatique, Le Monde Informatique, Reseaux & Telecoms; **GERMANY:** Computer Partner, Computerwoche, Computerwoche Extra, Computerwoche Focus, I/M Information Management, Macwelt, PC Welt; **GREECE:** GamePro, Multimedia World; **GUATEMALA:** PC World Centro America; **HONDURAS:** PC World Centro America; **HONG KONG:** Computerworld Hong Kong, PCWorld Hong Kong, Publish in Asia; **HUNGARY:** ABCD CD-ROM, Computerworld Szamitastechnika, PC & Mac World Hungary, PC-X Magazine; **ICELAND:** Tolvuheimur/PC World Island; **INDIA:** Information Systems Computerworld, PC World India, Publish in Asia; **INDONESIA:** InfoKomputer PC World, Komputek Computerworld, Publish in Asia; **IRELAND:** ComputerScope, PC Live!; **ISRAEL:** People & Computers; **ITALY:** Computerworld Italia, Computerworld Italia Special Editions, Macworld Italia, Networking Italia, PC Shopping, PC World Italia, PC World/Walt Disney; **JAPAN:** DTP World, HP Open World Japan, Macworld Japan, Nikkei Personal Computing, Open World Japan, OS/2 World Japan, SunWorld Japan, Windows World Japan; **KENYA:** East African Computer News; **KOREA:** Hi-Tech Information/Computerworld, Macworld Korea, PC World Korea; **MACEDONIA:** PC World Macedonia; **MALAYSIA:** Computerworld Malaysia, PC World Malaysia, Publish in Asia; **MEXICO:** Computerworld Mexico, Macworld, PC World Mexico; **MYANMAR:** PC World Myanmar; **NETHERLANDS:** Computer! Totaal, LAN Magazine, LanWorld Buyers Guide, Macworld, Net Magazine, Totaal! Beurskrant; **NEW ZEALAND:** Absolute Beginner's Guide, Computer Buyer, Computer Industry Directory, Computerworld New Zealand, MTB, Network World, PC World New Zealand; **NICARAGUA:** PC World Centro America; **NIGERIA:** PC World Nigeria; **NORWAY:** Computerworld Norge, Computerworld Privat (Datamagasinet), CW Rapport Norge, IDG's KURSGUIDE, Macworld Norge, Multimediaworld, PC World Ekspress, PC World Nettverk, PC World Norge, PC World's Produktguide, Windows World Spesial; **PAKISTAN:** Computerworld Pakistan, PC World Pakistan; Panama: PC World Panama; **P. R. OF CHINA:** China Computer Users, China Computerworld, China Infoworld, China Telecom World Weekly, Computer & Communication, Electronic Design China, Electronics Today, Electronics Weekly, Game Camp, Game Soft, Network World China, PC World China, Popular Computer Weekly, Software Weekly, Software World, Telecom World; **PERU:** Computerworld Peru, PC World Profesional Peru, PC World Peru; **PHILIPPINES:** Computerworld Philippines, PC World Philippines, Publish in Asia; **POLAND:** Computerworld Poland, Computerworld Special Report, Macworld, Networld, PC World Komputer; **PORTUGAL:** Cerebro/PC World, Computerworld/Correio Informático, Dealer World Portugal, MacIn/PCIn, Multimedia World Portugal; **PUERTO RICO:** PC World Puerto Rico; **ROMANIA:** Computerworld Romania, PC World Romania, Telecom Romania; **RUSSIA:** Computerworld Russia, Mir PK, Sety; **SINGAPORE:** Computerworld Singapore, PC World Singapore, Publish in Asia; **SLOVENIA:** MONITOR; **SOUTH AFRICA:** Computing S.A., InfoWorld S.A., Network World S.A., Software World; **SPAIN:** Computerworld España, COMUNICACIONES WORLD, Dealer World, Macworld España, PC World España; **SWEDEN:** CAP&Design, Computer Sweden, Corporate Computing, MacWorld, Maxi Data, MikroDatorn, Nätverk & Kommunikation, PC/Aktiv, PC World; **SWITZERLAND:** Computerworld Schweiz, Macworld Schweiz, PCtip; **TAIWAN:** Computerworld Taiwan, Macworld Taiwan, PC World Taiwan, Publish Taiwan, Windows World; **THAILAND:** Thai Computerworld, Publish in Asia; **TURKEY:** Computerworld Turkiye, MACWORLD Turkiye, PC World Turkiye; **UKRAINE:** Computerworld Kiev, Computers & Software, Multimedia World Ukraine, PC World Ukraine; **UNITED KINGDOM:** Acorn User, Amiga Action, Amiga Computing, Appletalk, Computing, GamePro, Macworld, Network News, Parents and Computers, PC Advisor, PC Home, PSX Pro UK, The WEB; **UNITED STATES:** Cable in the Classroom, CD Review, CIO Magazine, Computerworld, Computerworld Client/Server Journal, Digital Video Magazine, DOS World, Federal Computer Week, GamePro, InfoWorld, I-Way, JavaWorld, Macworld, Multimedia World, Netscape World Online, Network World, PC Entertainment, PC World, Publish, SunWorld Online, SWATPro Magazine, Video Event, WebMaster; **URUGUAY:** PC World Uruguay; **VENEZUELA:** Computerworld Venezuela, PC World Venezuela; and **VIETNAM:** PC World Vietnam.
7/16/96

Dedication

To Mary: May your dreams be just beginning to come true. — paul

Credits

Acknowledgments

This is our third book with IDG. Our special thanks go out again to **Ellen Camm** for her continued faith in us. To all of those IDG personnel who helped make this book possible, thanks.

A special thanks to **Victor Hirst** of Pittsburg Online who provides access and support for VREvolution's web site. We also want to thank the people at EarthLink and CompuServe who provide access and services.

To **George Meng**, and others at Microsoft, thanks for the help and information we needed in putting this book together.

To the ISPs who support Microsoft FrontPage Server Extensions, thanks for your help, time, and assistance.

To our friends on CyberForum, again, thanks for listening.

To **Mike and Amy**, a computer is like another child. It has to keep growing and expanding or it gets outdated like many adults.

To **Randy**, keep the faith.

To **John Anderson**, thanks for all of your generous technical assistance.

To **John Gwinner**, "you are, and always will be, [our] friend."

(The publisher would like to give special thanks to Patrick J. McGovern, without whom this book would not have been possible.)

Contents at a Glance

Table of Contents

Introduction

In the wake of the explosive growth of the Internet in general and the World Wide Web specifically, individuals and companies that never before had reason to visit, let alone set up housekeeping in cyberspace, have begun to do so. They now recognize and accept the Internet as a viable and important avenue through which they can conduct business and appeal to their customers. The end result of this recognition has been the need for tools that allow individuals with little web experience and knowledge to create and maintain web presence.

One tool that does just that is Microsoft FrontPage. FrontPage is aimed at the ninety-plus percent of the people out there who don't want to learn computer programming to create a web site. This means that if you are a relative beginner to the World Wide Web and web page design, you will still be able to create a web site that will look professional and accomplish your goals.

At the same time, there are tricks and work-arounds that will allow even more advanced web designers to use this product to create intricate and exciting web pages and sites. This means that those of you who know more about web design can still use FrontPage to incorporate highly interactive web pages created using other tools such as Java, JavaScript, Visual Basic, VBScript, Virtual Reality Modeling Language (VRML), ActiveX, and others. So, while we wait for Microsoft to release Internet Studio which is aimed at the web designer/programmer, those of us interested in using the best tools around can still take advantage of Microsoft FrontPage.

Who This Book Is For

More and more corporations are moving toward the Web as a viable marketing tool every day. As this happens, more and more people with little web experience and knowledge are being thrown into the role of creating and maintaining these new corporate sites. At the same time, the number of new computers sold to first-time users is staggering. Almost every one of these new computers comes with at least one Internet access provider pre-loaded onto their machine; the chances are that that provider offers a free web site as part of its monthly service charge.

The combination of Microsoft FrontPage and this book will allow the people we've described to be able to create their own web sites with little difficulty in a minimum amount of time. This book is aimed first at those new users with little or no experience and knowledge of creating web pages. We also have included tips, tricks, and work-arounds so that more advanced users can use FrontPage to add in more advanced web creation techniques.

What This Book Is About

Creating Cool FrontPage Web Sites is intended to guide you through the creation of your web site with as little effort as possible in as short a time as possible. To help us do that, we want to explain a few terms right up front.

When we talk about a web site we are discussing much more than just the HTML pages. A site can include the server software but doesn't have to. A site can be one page or many pages. The one thing a site must be is connected to either the Internet or to an intranet. Every other aspect of the site is pretty much up for grabs. We'll talk more about what a site is in the first few chapters of this book.

It is a good idea to discuss the issue of Internet versus intranet right up front also. While we will devote an entire chapter to this discussion later, for now it is important that you see through much of the hype and disinformation that marketing and sales types have propagated.

The Internet is a global network of networks of computers that communicate using a common language. While individual networks may be controlled by individual entities, no one individual, company, or country owns or controls the whole Internet. The Web sits on top of the Internet, providing an easy-to-use, graphical navigation interface for looking at documents on the Internet. In this book, when we refer to the Internet, it will be designated with an uppercase letter *I*.

An intranet is any network using the TCP/IP protocols, but which is not connected directly to the Internet. This network can consist of as few as two computers or as many as you can imagine. Once set up as an intranet, your network will operate with the same features and services found on the Internet. This includes hypertext pages, client/server applications, and database access.

Part I: Taking Care of the Basics

Part I of this book begins by presenting you with the basics of webs, the FrontPage product, and the FrontPage Personal Web Server.

Chapter 1: What Is a Web Site?

In this chapter you'll learn that a web site is much more than just a bunch of pages linked together. A web site should be viewed as the mixture of all the elements that make up the whole site. A site might include pages, web creation software, server software, web administration software, and any other element that has been used in creating and maintaining the site. This is a holistic method of viewing a web site. Using it will allow you to see how you might make your site more cohesive and comprehensive in the presentation of your message.

Chapter 2: What Is FrontPage?

Microsoft FrontPage is designed to be a client/server, visual web publishing tool to be used by non-programmers. Even so, FrontPage is a product that is robust enough for even professional web developers to use in the creation of some of their most interactive web sites. In this chapter we discuss how the FrontPage architecture fits into the holistic approach we proposed in Chapter 1 and is, therefore, an essential component of a web-based online information service.

Chapter 3: Setting Up the Personal Web Server

This chapter discusses the setup and operation of the FrontPage Personal Web Server. Here, we cover the basics of using the server and how to get the server to meet your needs. Specific and concise information concerning the command line options of the server are provided.

Part II: Learning to Use FrontPage

Part II of this book introduces you to the tools that allow you to create your web site. These tools include the FrontPage Explorer, the FrontPage Editor, and the FrontPage templates, wizards and WebBots.

Chapter 4: Getting to Know FrontPage

In this chapter you'll learn your way around the FrontPage neighborhood as you discover how to use both the FrontPage Explorer and the FrontPage Editor. You'll begin your web design experiences by creating a new web, creating and saving pages, and inserting objects into those pages.

Chapter 5: Formatting and Organizing Web Pages

Here, you'll expand the knowledge and experience you gain in Chapter 4 as you learn to create a To Do List, to format text on your web pages, to modify page properties, and to create and format tables on those pages. You'll also be exposed to the basics of moving, importing, deleting, and linking pages.

Chapter 6: FrontPage Web Templates, Wizards, and WebBots

Templates are sets of pre-designed formats for text and images on which pages and webs can be based.

Wizards create pages and webs by asking you questions about the features you want included on the page or in the web you are creating.

WebBots are usually called *bots*. Bots are used to include dynamic features that are evaluated and executed either when the page author saves the page to the web server or when a user links to the page.

In this chapter, we examine the use of the templates, wizards, and bots that come with FrontPage. We also look at how others may be created by those of you interested in expanding your web design capabilities.

Part III: Putting FrontPage in Action

The two chapters that make up this part of the book deal with using the tools you've learned in the previous section to plan your web site and use forms on your site effectively.

Chapter 7: Defining Your Site's Purpose

In this chapter you will examine what it is you want your web to achieve. In order to determine this, you'll need to know what you want to say and who it is you want to say it to. We'll also continue to help you expand your knowledge and experience using FrontPage to create your webs and pages.

Chapter 8: Creating Forms Using FrontPage

Chapter 8 shows you how to create forms on your pages to gather information about your visitors and their use of your site.

Part IV: Your Page and Beyond

Part IV of this book expands on what you've already learned by looking at the concepts of collaborating in the creation of a web, linking and importing pages into FrontPage webs, and the concept of intranets.

Chapter 9: Using FrontPage to Collaborate

FrontPage improves your ability to collaborate with others in the creation of a web. Multiple authors can be assigned pages they are responsible for and you can use the To Do List to maintain control over who is working on what and when each author completes his assigned tasks. This chapter will also discuss authorizations, permissions, and security for your site.

Chapter 10: Linking and Importing with FrontPage

This chapter discusses and examines how links between pages are created using FrontPage. You'll be exposed to the various methods that can be used for the linking and importing of pages that have been created using other web page authoring tools into your FrontPage-created web.

Chapter 11: Using FrontPage with Intranets

An intranet is any network using the TCP/IP protocols but is not connected directly to the Internet. In this chapter, we'll look through the hype at what you can use an intranet for at your company.

Chapter 12: Getting the Most from FrontPage

This final chapter closes the book by providing a list of some common web design mistakes and how to avoid them, as well as some suggestions of tricks you can use to get the most from FrontPage.

Part V: Appendixes

Appendix A: Resources

This appendix provides a list of the Internet Service Providers that support the Microsoft FrontPage Server Extensions.

Appendix B: Installation Guide

This appendix covers how to install FrontPage, Internet Information Server, and Internet Explorer.

Appendix C: What's on the CD-ROM

This appendix provides you with a list of the directories and subdirectories on the CD-ROM and what is being included in these directories.

Special Elements Used in This Book

There are various special elements throughout this book that have been included to provide added information or refer you to other useful sources of information. These special features are

 You'll see this icon any time we discuss the software that's provided on the *Creating Cool FrontPage Web Sites* CD-ROM or give information about installing the software.

 This icon tells you about other books where you can look for more information on a topic.

 A Note lets you know that there's something here you need to remember, or provides a useful bit of information concerning the topic of discussion.

How to Use This Book

To paraphrase some ancient proverb, the longest journey begins with a first step. The point here is that the journey is linear. It begins at point A and ends at point B.

This book can be used to your benefit by reading it from Page 1 to the end. By the same token, you may get just as much out of it by skipping around, gathering this tip and that until you've read it all.

We suggest that you use it either way, as long as you read it while working with FrontPage. The experience of working with the software will lead you to true knowledge of the product.

Conventions Used in This Book

Some text in this book looks different from the rest of the text or is on a line by itself. This section explains some of the conventions we've used to make these distinctions clearer.

Internet addresses appear in computer font, like this: vrevolution.pitton.com.

Listings of computer code and other things that appear onscreen look like the following line. Notice that things that can change (variables) appear in italic.

```
<A HREF="URL">variable</A>
```

Occasionally, this book's pages are not wide enough to accommodate the number of characters that need to be on a given line of code. To solve this problem, we have used the ↵ symbol to denote that the line continues with the characters that follow this symbol.

The *Creating Cool FrontPage Web Sites* CD-ROM

The CD-ROM that comes with this book includes templates, art work and graphics, and tools that will help you create your web using Microsoft FrontPage. As we suggested earlier, we have listed the entire contents of the CD-ROM in Appendix C of this book.

Web Addresses

We've tried to provide the most up-to-the minute Web addresses and e-mail addresses we could for the people and companies we discuss in this book. Keep in mind that the Web is growing and changing every minute. These URLs may change.

Where to Go From Here

No matter what the reason, you are now embarking on a wonderful journey. That journey is into cyberspace. With the help of Microsoft FrontPage and this book, you are going to stake your claim in the virtual "un-real estate" that exists (?) out there.

Turn the page and begin that journey.

Taking Care of the Basics

PART
I

What Is a Web Site?

Before you delve into this chapter, we want to mention that some of the materials in it may seem rather elementary at first glance. The main purpose of this chapter is to define the terms that will be used in the rest of this book and to make sure you understand what is meant when we use certain words. If you have a good grasp of Internet and Web terminology, you can go ahead and move on to Chapter 2. However, we recommend that you begin here, at the beginning, so that we'll all be on the same wavelength later on.

Because of the hype and misinformation surrounding the Internet, and the World Wide Web in particular, it can be very confusing when someone says he has a web site. The terms *page* and *site* seem to get thrown around without much consideration for what these terms may mean to the people hearing and reading them.

For instance, go to a specific URL address and what do you see there? Is this a web page? Did you actually go somewhere? Was there a physical location involved in traveling on the Web? Click the printer icon of your browser. How many pages printed out? Depending on where you went, what printed out may have been anything from less than a page to many pages. In fact, a web page can be more or less than a printed page in length.

Defining Terms

We discovered, while setting up our site, `http://vrevolution.pitton.com`, and writing our book *Creating Cool Interactive Web Sites* (IDG Books Worldwide, Inc., 1996), that the term web site can cause considerable confusion. Just what is a web site? Is a site different from a page? (What is the meaning of reality?)

In this chapter, we're going to clear up some of the confusion that you may have concerning web sites. We'll begin by defining our terms.

Understanding the web analogy

Yes, we know that you're experienced enough to have heard of, or even traveled around, the World Wide Web; but, think about the word *web* for a moment. Just what does it mean?

Taxonomy

Now, before anyone objects to our use of the word taxonomy to discuss web-related terms, let us explain our use of the word here. A taxonomy is a classification system that usually refers to living things. Numerous books, magazine articles, and Internet gurus have referred to the Internet and the Web as "growing." Some have even gone so far as to refer to the Web as a living and breathing thing. Since the analogy of the Web as a living thing exists in the media already, using the term taxonomy as a metaphor to refer to the classification of words describing the Web and its contents does not appear to be a stretch.

So, we'll now classify Web terminology into a taxonomy that will allow you to better understand what we are talking about when we discuss a web site. A taxonomy also allows for greater latitude in discussion than does a simple glossary of terms. While a glossary is static and finite, a taxonomy, as with the living things it describes, grows and matures. This approach will allow for your understanding of these definitions to grow and mature as you gain knowledge and experience using FrontPage.

The web in insect terminology

Most people think of spider webs, also known as cobwebs, when they think of the word web. Insect-related terms are used extensively in referencing the World Wide Web. People refer to spiders when discussing intelligent agents. The metaphor suggests the image of these spiders crawling the Web in search of information. People also refer to worms, mostly in a negative manner, and ants. Worms are often considered in the same context as viruses. They are considered malicious agents. Ants are groups of web robots whose programming borrows from the world of insects and analyzes usage in the context of multi-robot systems. You can see, therefore, that the insect metaphor is already quite well-established.

The web in network terminology

Another definition of the word web is as a network. Network is used here as in a network of highways, (although, due to our personal work experience in broadcasting, the term network most often conjures up the vision of a chain of television stations). This highway network metaphor has been used in describing the Internet itself. The Internet has been referred to many times as the Information Superhighway and the Information Autobahn.

The web as the fabric of communication

The primary definition of the word web, however, is as a fabric created on or coming from a loom. We believe that this definition is most relevant. Information, or the intended message, is the fabric that is produced on the loom, which we can visualize as the Internet.

So, what is the World Wide Web...and what is a web?

The World Wide Web itself is many things. It is audio data, video data, textual data, and graphical data. It is server software, computer hardware, high-speed data transmission lines, and telephone lines. It is also protocols and conventions, hypertext and multimedia. These are the tools that allow the communication of information.

The Web, therefore, is a communication medium connecting information in the form of presentations to users through the Internet. But, in the same manner as there are many computer networks that make up the Internet, there are many web presentations that make up the Web, called web sites.

A web site, also called just a web, is a collection of documents, hyperlinks, data, and other forms of communication. It is the information that you will put together in an effort to get your message across to the people who visit your site. We'll be using the web authoring tool Microsoft FrontPage to create the pages or documents that will make up these web sites.

How webs are structured

As suggested in the previous section, there are two ways to use the word *web*. The *Web* refers to the World Wide Web, a worldwide hypertext system or communication medium. On the other hand, a *web* or *web site* (with the lower-case designation), is a presentation of information, often consisting of several documents or pages; although not necessarily stored on the same system, these webs are interlinked, and comprise the contents of the World Wide Web.

These webs can be structured in two different ways, which we'll call major webs and minor webs.

A major web

A major web consists of multiple pages interconnected in more than one way. The major web is usually quite large and may consist of a number of minor webs. The major web is identified by the various ways that the user can get to its pages, as seen in Figure 1-1.

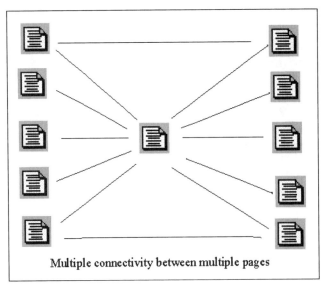

Multiple connectivity between multiple pages

Figure 1-1: In a major web, you can access a page from a variety of different directions.

In other words, other than addressing the URL of a page directly, there are a variety of ways that you can get to any of the various pages that make up a major web. For instance, you might access the page by following a link from a page in a completely different web. This is quite different than the access allowed in a minor web.

A minor web

A minor web consists of multiple pages connected to one main page (see Figure 1-2). This web is typically relatively small in size and it contains a lesser number of interconnected pages. There is basically only one way to get to these pages while browsing the Web: by going through the *home page* of the web itself.

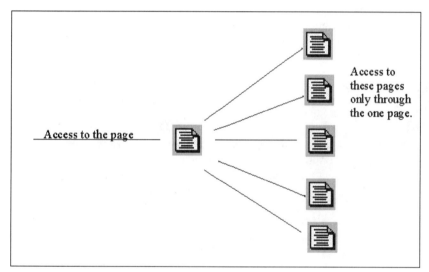

Figure 1-2: In a minor web, access to some pages can only be achieved via very few directions.

In other words, you can only get to some pages in a minor web by working through a sequence of pages.

Keep in mind that each web, whether major or minor, is made up of a number of pages. That brings us to our next question.

What is a web page?

We mentioned earlier in this chapter that a web page can be more or less than a printed page. The truth of the matter is that this entire chapter could be one page on the Web. On the other hand, each physical page of this book could be its own web page, or every paragraph can be its own web page. In fact, web pages are simply documents. These documents can vary in length and it's up to you, as the web designer, to decide how you want the page, and the web, to be broken down into a logical organization of documents and files.

The pages that make up a web can be accessed by the end user in a variety of ways. Currently one of the most prevalent ways of creating web pages is through the use of *HTML* (hypertext markup language). Other methods of displaying and presenting information over the medium of the World Wide Web that may or may not use HTML include VRML, Java, various CGI scripting languages, audio and video, animation, and other forms of multimedia.

HTML

We're not going to explain the workings of HTML here, as our space is limited and understanding HTML isn't necessary to use FrontPage. However, there are many books available if you wish to explore this further. We do, however, want to briefly discuss some of the things that HTML can and can't do.

We suggest that you look at *HTML For Dummies,* by Ed Tittel and Steve James, and *Creating Cool Web Pages with HTML,* by Dave Taylor, for a more in-depth look at HTML.

HTML can be viewed as a computerized version of typography. Typography is the art of printing with type. Typography uses individual letters, often shaped in metal, plastic, or even paper, and uses the forms of these letters to apply ink to paper.

HTML, as we suggested, can be seen as the computerized version of typography. This is especially true with the acceptance into the HTML protocols of the cascading style sheet specification. HTML provides a set of conventions used for publishing documents on the Internet via the Web. Some feel this form of publishing text has the potential for replacing the printed page. As we shall see, however, there are problems associated with this concept.

HTML uses specific codes that are inserted into the document. These codes tell the browser how to interpret the information. The problem is that currently there is no standard for the implementation of this interpretation process.

How HTML is received

HTML and other methods of displaying information to be included in a web page can be seen as methods of communicating. The problem is that the receiver of this communication may not always receive the message (that is the page) in the form that you originally intended. As Figures 1-3, 1-4, 1-5, and 1-6 demonstrate, different browsers (used by different receivers of the information) will display the information differently. (This site can be accessed at http://vrevolution.pitton.com/.)

Figure 1-3: VREvolution's Welcome page as viewed with Quarterdeck Mosaic.

Figure 1-4: VREvolution's Welcome page as viewed with CompuServe Spry AIRMosaic.

Figure 1-5: VREvolution's Welcome page as viewed with Netscape 2.0.

Figure 1-6: VREvolution's Welcome page as viewed with Microsoft Internet Explorer 2.0.

The example shown in the four figures suggests that the sender's control of the presentation of the information isn't uniform. The bottom line is that the same information, as provided in Listing 1-1, was parsed by all four Web browsers, resulting in four different interpretations or displays of the information.

Listing 1-1: TBLCONT.HTM

```
<!DOCTYPE HTML PUBLIC "-//W30/DTD HTML//EN">

<html>
<head>
<title>VREvolution Web Site Main Index</title>
<meta name="GENERATOR" content="Microsoft FrontPage 1.1">
<meta name="FORMATTER" content="Microsoft FrontPage 1.1">
</head>
<body background="images/starmap.gif">
<p align="left"><BGSOUND SRC="images/vre1.wav"><img src="images/
vre_logo.gif" align="bottom"
width="180" height="162"> </p>
<h1>Welcome to http://vrevolution.pitton.com</h1>
<p>You will find the following webs at this site:</p>
<ul>
    <li><a
        href="http://vrevolution.pitton.com/VREvolution/
index.htm">VREvolution

        Company Site</a></li>
    <li><a
        href="http://vrevolution.pitton.com/VR Discussion/
index.htm">Virtual

        Reality Discussion</a></li>
    <li><a
        href="http://vrevolution.pitton.com/VRE_Q-
Sort_Web_Project/index.htm">VRE

        Q-Sort Web Project</a></li>
    <li><a
        href="http://vrevolution.pitton.com/VRMLSpec1/
index.htm">VRML

        Examples and Version 1.0 Specification</a></li>
    <li><a
        href="http://vrevolution.pitton.com/FACTOROT_Support/
index.htm">FACTOROT
```

(continued)

Listing 1-1 *(continued)*

```
Customer Support web</a></li>
    <li><a href="http://vrevolution.pitton.com/fpassist/
">VREvolution's

        FrontPage Assistance web</a></li>
    <li><a
        href="http://vrevolution.pitton.com/marys_web/
index.htm">Mary's

        web</a></li>
    <li><a
        href="http://vrevolution.pitton.com/Pauls_web/
index.htm">Paul's

        web</a></li>
    <li><a
        href="http://ourworld.compuserve.com/homepages/PSummitt/
summitth.htm">The

        Summitt Family Quarterly</a> Newsletter - Online Edi-
tion</li>

</ul>
<blockquote>
    <p align="left"><a href="guestbk.htm">Please Sign our
    Guestbook</a></p>
</blockquote>
<h6 align="center">These pages Copyright &#169;1996,
VREvolution.</h6>

<h6 align="center">This page last updated July 12, 1996 09:14
AM.</h6>

</body>
</html>
```

Our purpose in placing this page on the Web was to communicate information.
With few exceptions, the HTML code in Listing 1-1 is straight HTML 2.0; you
might think it would be interpreted in the same way by each receiver. Unfortunately, as you've seen, the various browsers don't interpret this page the same
and therefore viewers see the page differently.

Recently, there has been some discussion of possible advances in HTML that may solve this problem. Adobe, with the support of Netscape and others, has proposed a set of standardized fonts that would go a long way toward making pages look the same, no matter what browser they are viewed with.

What is a hyperlink?

Now that you've got a general idea of what a page is and what HTML is, our next step is to look at how pages are interconnected. How do you, as a viewer, get from one page to another?

It seems like it was only a few years ago that hypertext and hypermedia were the "in" things to be involved with. Hypertext and hypermedia were cool and multimedia ruled (as our young programmer friend Damion would say).

You can think of *hypertext* as a technique that allows the linking together of information in a free-form manner based on codes embedded in text. In other words, any given word or phrase can be used to take the viewer to another location in the same document, another document within the same web, or another document in another web.

Hypermedia can be thought of as a hypertext-based system that combines text, graphics, video, and audio with more traditional forms of data. Hypermedia is sometimes referred to as multimedia. The Web is sometimes referred to as a hypermedia or multimedia environment because it allows multiple layers of media to be used at the same time within a given page.

A hyperlink is simply a link in a hypertext, hypermedia, or multimedia system that establishes a connection. The first half of the connection is a word, phrase, graphic, or other form of information provided in the system. The second half of the connection is a related grouping of information or further explanation of the original data (not always in the form of another document or file). A text hyperlink object is generally blue in color on your screen by default and will usually be underlined. Figure 1-7, while not in color, demonstrates what these hyperlinks can look like.

Hyperlinks within an HTML document don't necessarily have to connect to another HTML document. They can also connect to a variety of other files and documents that can make the Web (in general) and a web (in particular) come alive. In the next few paragraphs, we introduce you to these various types of files and documents.

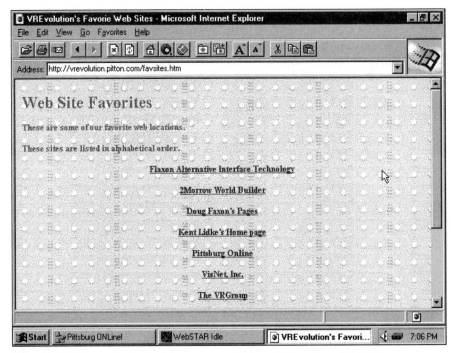

Figure 1-7: The underlined phrases represent hyperlinks to other web sites.

VRML

If you're interested in a 3-D graphics design for your web pages, you'll want to learn more about the *VRML* (the virtual reality modeling language). VRML allows you to create a wide variety of possible objects on your web site. We used VRML to create a 3-D version of the Pittsburg State University Campus shown in Figure 1-8.

We also created VRML worlds within an HTML page using some of the Microsoft extensions to the HTML specification, as with the example shown in Figure 1-9.

Using frames, another extension to the HTML language from Netscape, something similar to the VRML world within an HTML page can be created. An example of such a page is the one shown in Figure 1-10, which was created using Netscape and Live3D.

Each of the previous examples was created using the VRML 1.0 specification. This specification allows for the creation of generally static, three-dimensional objects that the user can examine and navigate around. There are no interactions of behaviors available in this specification. Interactions and behaviors are expected to be present in the new specification, VRML Version 2.0, expected out in August of 1996.

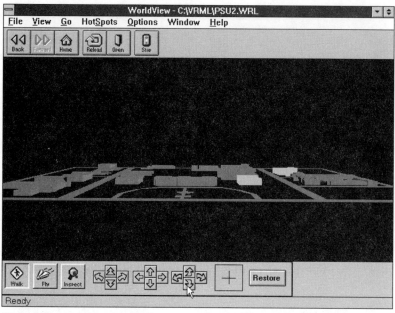

Figure 1-8: People visiting your web site can experience virtual worlds, such as this walk-through of the Pittsburg State University Campus.

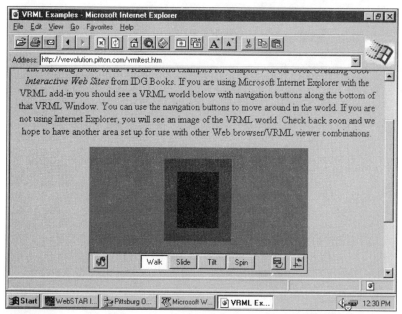

Figure 1-9: A simple VRML example using Microsoft Internet Explorer extensions to the HTML specification.

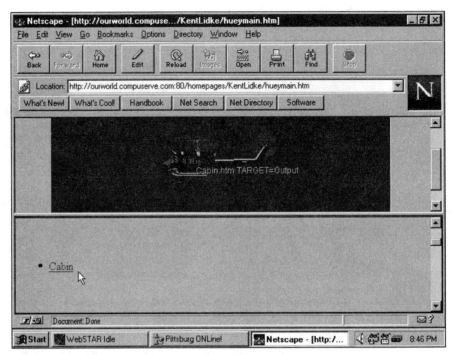

Figure 1-10: Using a browser that reads frames, such as Netscape, HTML information and VRML information can be shown side-by-side.

CROSS-REFERENCE

There is not enough space in this chapter to go into the creation of VRML worlds. We suggest that you refer to our own *Creating Cool 3-D Web Worlds with VRML* from IDG Books Worldwide, Inc. as a good starting point in creating VRML worlds with the Version 1.0 specification.

The VRML Version 2.0 specification is expected to bring *behaviors* and *interactions* to VRML. An example of a behavior would be the movement of a graphic clock's pendulum, while an interaction would be the act of a visitor to that VRML page reaching out and stopping the pendulum. Already there are some preliminary examples of these possibilities. Black Sun Interactive (`http://www.blacksun.com`), as seen in Figure 1-11, allows you to select your own *avatar* (an image that represents yourself) and converse with fellow cybernauts in a 3-D virtual space.

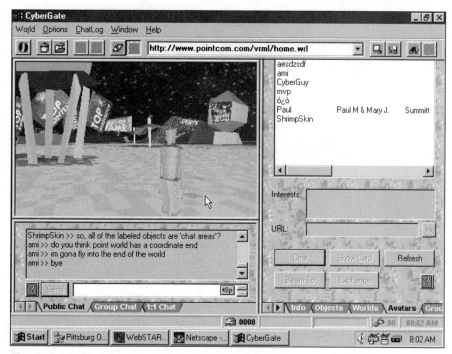

Figure 1-11: Black Sun Interactive provides a VRML plug-in for use with Netscape 2.0 to be used when visiting their web site.

Another example of the possible directions VRML may take can be seen on the SuperScape web page, `http://www.superscape.com`. Figure 1-12 illustrates an example of what these worlds look like.

VRML, in either specification, can add new and interesting vistas to your web site. We'll turn our attention now to some of the other ways your site can be made more interesting.

Java and JavaScript

During the early months of 1991 a small group of employees at Sun Microsystems began work on a project with the goal of developing consumer electronics. By late 1994, the direction of the project had been changed and Java had been born.

Java has been called an extension of the C++ programming language, but Java developers deny this. The developers of Java say that, while they originally began with C++, the C++ language wasn't able to do everything that was needed and was soon abandoned. One of these developers, James Gosling,

Figure 1-12: Superscape provides a plug-in for use with Netscape 2.0 that allows the viewing of their worlds on the Web.

therefore ended up creating and developing a totally new language called Java. Java is designed for fast execution and safe use. Java programs consist solely of classes and their metho

JavaScript (developed primarily by Netscape) resembles Java but it does not include static typing and strong type checking. (Don't worry if you don't understand what static typing and strong type checking are; that's not necessary to create web pages with FrontPage. It might be necessary, however, if you want to go further with FrontPage and add some "cool" custom aspects to your pages). Both JavaScript and Java are secure in that they do not write to the hard disk. JavaScript does, however, support most of the Java expression syntax and basic control flow constructs. Other similarities and differences include

➥ Java is compiled on the server before execution, while JavaScript is interpreted by the client.

➥ Java is object-oriented, while JavaScript is object-based. What this means is that in Java, applets consist of object classes with inheritance. This is contrasted with JavaScript: the JavaScript code uses built-in extensible objects with no classes or inheritance.

⟿ Java applets are separate and distinct from the HTML code, although they are accessed through and from HTML pages. JavaScript code is integrated with and embedded in the HTML code.

⟿ Java uses static binding, whereas JavaScript uses dynamic binding. This means that Java object references must exist at compile time, whereas JavaScript object references are checked at run time.

⟿ Java variable data types must be declared. JavaScript variable data types are not declared.

 We don't have the space here to discuss and explain how to program in either Java or JavaScript. Knowing either of these is not necessary to creating pages using FrontPage. Some cool possibilities for your pages might require using these in conjunction with FrontPage. There are several good books out there that will give you a much broader introduction to Java and provide tutorials on how to use these languages. We suggest, if you are interested in these two languages, that you seek out one of these books.

Much of what can be done with Java and JavaScript can also be done with CGI (Common Gateway Interface) programming or other programming techniques and scripting languages. We'll take a look at these next.

CGI scripting languages

In the past, CGI has been the default standard for programs and applications to interface with your Web server software. CGI supplies the transport mechanism between the data on a server and the person trying to access that site. It works like this: the user's browser sends a request to the server. The server passes the data to the CGI script and the CGI script reformulates it and passes it to the external entity. The external entity returns some data, which the CGI reformulates and sends back to the server. The server then displays it to the user.

CGI programs are actually extensions to the server software, in that they allow for the inclusion of a variety of services that are not specifically part of the server software itself. In Windows, this extension to the server's capabilities through CGI comes in the form of an application programming interface (API). This API allows the use of the various forms of BASIC, C, C++, Perl, QuickBASIC, various SHELL applications, Visual Basic, and other languages to access the server.

Java and JavaScript, therefore, are not your only possibilities for scripting languages when creating content for your site. For information on how to use Visual Basic and the new VBScript (which, again, you don't have to know to use FrontPage), aim your browser at `http://www.microsoft.com/intdev/vbs`. There are several pages available for Perl, C, C++, QuickBasic, and others that include (but are not limited to):

➡ CGI Scripting in C — `http://www.he.net/~searsbe/ScriptingInC.html`

➡ Serge's Sources (sample CGI scripts in C++) — `http://serg.gs.pssr.e-berg.su/docs/src/index.html`

➡ CGI Scripting with PowerBuilder — `http://1page.com/cgi/`

➡ Guavac, a free Java compiler — `http://http.cs.berkeley.edu/~engberg/guavac`

➡ Scripting using C/C++/Perl/ and Pascal — `http://blackcat.brynmawr.edu/~nswoboda/prog-html.html`

➡ Scripting using CGI++2.2 — `http://sweetbay.will.uiuc.edu/CGI%2b%2b/`

➡ Scripting using cgic — `http://www.boutell.com/cgic/`

➡ Scripting using Perl — `http://www-genome.wi.mit.edu/ftp/pub/software/WWW/cgi-docs.html`

➡ Scripting using Perl — `http://www.worldwidemart.com/scripts/`

➡ Scripting using Tcl — `http://www.lbl.gov/~clarsen/projects/htcl/http-proc-args.html`

You can also use such applications as BasicScript from Summit Software Company (no relation to the authors, really) and CmmCGI from Nombas, Inc. in creating CGI applications. You can access the web pages of both of these companies and download evaluation copies of their software. For Summit Software Company, the URL is `http://www.summsoft.com`. For Nombas, Inc. the URL is `http://www.nombas.com`.

Again, we do not have time to go into a full discussion of CGI and its possibilities here. In fact, entire books could be written on the various forms of CGI that are possible. Two very good books that deal with CGI, particularly CGI using Perl, are *Foundations of World Wide Web Programming with HTML and CGI* (IDG Books, 1995) by Ed Tittel, Mark Gaither, Sebastian Hassinger, and Mark Erwin, and *Web Programming Secrets with HTML, CGI, and Perl* (IDG Books, 1996) also by Tittel, Gaither, Hassinger, and Erwin. Remember, a knowledge of CGI is not necessary in the creation of web pages using FrontPage, but many cool applications can be added to pages created with FrontPage using CGI.

The use of CGI scripting, as with HTML, VRML, and Java, is another way to add cool objects to your page beyond the capabilities of FrontPage. But, these are only some components that help to make up the site. Where and when possible in the following pages we will demonstrate how to incorporate these and other methods of adding objects to your FrontPage-created pages.

The server is also part of the web site

While it is not necessary to be running a server in order to use FrontPage, the server software itself is a very important consideration in how a site performs. The server software may open certain possibilities or create handicaps for your site. If you plan on taking advantage of all of the capabilities of the FrontPage software, you will need to make sure that the server that hosts your pages has FrontPage Server Extensions installed. We're not going to tell you which server to use in this book, although we will make some recommendations.

If you're looking for a book that discusses choosing and operating server software in a more detailed manner, we would like to suggest two books: *Setting up an Internet Site For Dummies* (IDG Books Worldwide, Inc., 1996) by Jason Coombs and Ted Coombs, and, of course, our *Creating Cool Interactive Web Sites* (IDG Books Worldwide, Inc., 1996). Either one of these books will give you the necessary background material to select and install your server software.

Careful consideration should be given when selecting, installing, and operating your server software on the necessary platform, or in choosing the ISP that will host your FrontPage webs.

Thinking of Your Web Site Holistically

There is a danger in thinking of your site only in terms of one of the various topics we've discussed so far. A web site actually grows by the correct use of each of these protocols, languages, and specifications. Your site is very much like a good stew. If you add too much or too little water, or too much or too little of any other ingredient for that matter, it can make the stew too weak or too thick. If you add too many graphics on your web, your web will behave very slowly and some visitors might leave, never to return. It's your job to determine just how much of each ingredient is needed. You won't be able to do this properly if you get too enamored of the potatoes or the onions or the beef.

Think of your site in these terms: as a place where balance and equilibrium between the ingredients can help you to create a more dynamic web. We'll turn our attention now to a tool that can assist you in thinking about your site holistically.

Holistic web authoring

It's difficult to think in terms of creating a web site without thinking about creating web pages. Most authoring tools do just that: they create individual web pages. When you want to add a form to accept registrations, you think in terms of the form and not in terms of how that form will fit within your web. The individual page becomes the center of attention and the web as a whole is forgotten.

Thinking holistically of your web, and not just your pages, can improve the way your site looks and the way in which it will be interpreted by visitors. Thinking holistically forces you to look at how these pages fit with one another. Web authoring tools like Front Page are therefore different from page authoring tools.

What is Microsoft FrontPage?

We'll go into far more detail as to what Microsoft FrontPage is and what it can do for you in Chapter 2. Briefly, however, FrontPage is the first client/server visual web authoring tool created for non-programmers. This is an important distinction. We've stated previously that, while we discussed them, you didn't need to know how to program in Java, JavaScript, Visual Basic, or any other CGI or application language in order to create webs and pages with FrontPage. FrontPage is aimed at the ninety percent of the people out there who do not want to learn HTML and these other languages and protocols to create web pages.

We can't stress enough that FrontPage is a web authoring tool. It does not just help you create pages, it helps you to create a web site. With Front Page you can

- ➡ Create high-quality web pages with FrontPage Editor without having to learn HTML.
- ➡ Run your web site right out of the box with FrontPage Personal Web Server.
- ➡ Create both pages and sites automatically using the templates and wizards that help make up FrontPage.
- ➡ Use FrontPage WebBots to add drop-in, interactive functions, thereby eliminating many of the programming tasks that are required by CGI applications.
- ➡ Develop your site using either local or remote authoring teams.
- ➡ Maintain your site with web server administration tools.
- ➡ Use the To Do List to manage, control, and track tasks and contributors in the site creation process.
- ➡ Create a professional-looking site with the FrontPage desktop publishing features.

FrontPage as a holistic web authoring tool

A holistic web authoring tool is one that looks at the web as a whole. While page authoring tools create individual pages, a web authoring tool should involve itself with the creation and maintenance of the web in its entirety.

Microsoft FrontPage does just that. In fact, it allows busy or less technical people to control their webs without having to learn the intricacies of HTML. FrontPage does this by providing a client/server system of web authoring and management tools that take the programming out of creating a web site by making the entire process visual. In addition, FrontPage also helps in and simplifies the task of maintaining complex web sites.

We'll be getting into the use and operation of FrontPage in the following chapters. What might be useful here, before we look at FrontPage as a holistic web authoring tool, is to look briefly at the history of FrontPage.

FrontPage: The beginnings

A small company called Vermeer Technologies, Inc. from Cambridge, Massachusetts, developed FrontPage. During the months that followed the software's release the media discussed what the suggested price for this product was going to be, as well as its competition. Early in 1996, Microsoft bought Vermeer and the FrontPage product. In doing so, they put their own plans for a product code-named Blackbird on hold. By the time the FrontPage product was released in the second quarter of 1996, the price had dropped and integration with Microsoft Office and technologies was planned to enhance the product. These plans for future integration with Office were considered key to the power of this product and to the broadening of the potential audience for it. Although in an early release and with changes still occurring, FrontPage has already proven itself to be one of the best web authoring tools on the market and has received several awards.

Moving On

In this chapter you learned or reviewed definitions of some terminology and concepts relevant to the World Wide Web and webs in general.

You were encouraged, possibly for the first time, to think of your web site holistically instead of by its individual pieces.

You were introduced to the components that make up Microsoft FrontPage as a product and some of the things Microsoft FrontPage can do for you.

You were given a brief glimpse into the history, and future, of Microsoft FrontPage.

In the next chapter we get into a more detailed discussion of what FrontPage is and how it works. We look at the various components of FrontPage briefly and see how they work together to help you produce a professional-looking web.

What Is FrontPage?

Exploring FrontPage

Examining the components

Investigating the tools

Considering the requirements of your site

In the last chapter we touched upon the fact that Microsoft FrontPage is a visual web authoring tool created for non-programmers. We also looked at the fact that, by using FrontPage, you can look at your entire web holistically and therefore create a greater sense of cohesion for your site.

In this chapter you will continue your examination of Microsoft FrontPage. We'll begin this chapter with a look at who FrontPage is intended for, and why.

Who Should Use FrontPage?

FrontPage is a high-powered tool for those who have to maintain both a web site and a web server. Unless you are doing both, this product is not for you.

FrontPage is designed to be a client/server visual web publishing tool for the non-programmer. We'll get back to this client/server concept shortly. Right now we'll concentrate on the idea that FrontPage is a tool for people who don't have any programming training or experience in creating web sites. That would include people such as marketing managers and others who might have the responsibility of running and operating either an in-house intranet-based web or a worldwide Internet-based web or both delegated to them.

Keep in mind, as was suggested in the last chapter, that a web is more than just a collection of document files. A web is a hierarchy of *HyperText Markup Language* (HTML) files, *Virtual Reality Modeling Language* (VRML) files, graphic images, Java applets, text files, video, sound files, and other CGI and scripting applications. By maintaining control over both the web site and the web server with a product such as FrontPage, you are able to operate a web much more easily.

This control is made possible, even for those without training and experience creating webs, by using the drag-and-drop features of the software. FrontPage provides you with step-by-step procedures for the creation of your web site incorporating HTML, VRML, graphic images, video, sound, Java, text files, and more through simple tools and dialog boxes.

At the same time, FrontPage is powerful and robust enough even for the professional web developer. FrontPage makes developing and maintaining a professional-quality web site simple, fast, and easy. Also, for more experienced web designers, there are workarounds and shortcuts that allow you to use more advanced techniques on your site and get a web up faster.

In fact, using FrontPage, anyone, no matter what his or her experience with the Web, can create web pages and then ftp them to their web site using the FrontPage Publishing Wizard. FrontPage and the FrontPage Server Extensions also allow you to update your pages in real time over the Internet.

Looking at FrontPage Features

FrontPage consists of three major components, FrontPage Editor, Explorer and the To Do List, which we'll look at shortly. First, however, we'll take a look at some of the specific features and functionality that are present in FrontPage.

In conjunction with its major components, the following FrontPage functions and features are designed to give you complete control over the web authoring environment:

- **Active-Color Link** allows you to specify the color of your active links.
- **Alignment Toolbar** lets you align paragraphs and images to the left, right, or center by using the Alignment buttons on the toolbar.
- **Alternative Image Representation** allows you to specify that low resolution images should be downloaded and displayed to visitors until higher resolution images can be downloaded.
- **Auto-Fix Backlinks** automatically update all instances of a hyperlink within a given web.
- **Custom Page Templates** can be created directly within FrontPage.
- **Discussion Groups**. FrontPage gives you complete control over discussion groups with the discussion group administration facility.
- **Font Color** allows you to change the color of any text.
- **Font Size Toolbar** makes setting font size easy.

➡ **Frames** are supported by FrontPage, and the software includes a Frame Wizard to help you create frame sets. You can choose from a variety of frame templates or create your own custom frame grid.

➡ **Local Host Check** automatically checks and determines the local host name for a New Web, Open Web, or Copy Web dialog box. This is a safety feature to keep people who don't need to be in your web out.

➡ **Microsoft Office Integration** means that you can update Office documents from within webs. FrontPage shares its spell checker with the Office applications.

➡ **Multi-Homing** allows you to host more than one web domain name on your single web server machine.

➡ **Multi-Level Undo** gives you the capability of undoing up to thirty past actions.

➡ **Page Variables** allow you to set META and HTTP-EQUIV variables within a page for special purposes. For instance, you could set the variable [webmaster] to your name and FrontPage would replace this variable with your name throughout the web.

➡ **Personal Web Server Automatic Start-up** automatically starts FrontPage Personal Web Server if you are not already running the server when you start FrontPage Explorer. This prevents error messages.

➡ **Style Sheets** provide color schemes for pages that can be specified by a separate style page.

➡ **HTML Tables** are fully supported.

➡ **TCP/IP Validity check**. FrontPage Explorer automatically verifies valid TCP/IP operation on startup.

Now that we've got your interest with some of the cool functions and features of FrontPage, we'll look at the major components of FrontPage.

Understanding the Components of FrontPage

We've looked at the features of the software as a whole. Now let's look at the individual components which provide those features: the FrontPage Server Extensions, FrontPage Explorer, FrontPage Editor, and the To Do List.

FrontPage Server Extensions and the Personal Web Server

FrontPage comes with 16-bit and 32-bit versions of its own Personal Web Server. These servers allow FrontPage to operate on the Windows 3.1, Windows 95, and Windows NT platforms.

Besides supporting its own Personal Web Server, FrontPage also operates with other popular server software by providing free server extensions. Microsoft FrontPage Server Extensions exist for most free and commercial web servers on many popular platforms.

FrontPage Server Extensions

A web server must be installed prior to the installation of FrontPage. The FrontPage Server Extensions for various servers are available free from Microsoft by downloading them at `http://www.microsoft.com/frontpage/freestuff/fs_fp_extensions.htm` as shown in Figure 2-1. The server extension must be installed separately from FrontPage. Installation instructions for these server extensions are available from Microsoft in this same location.

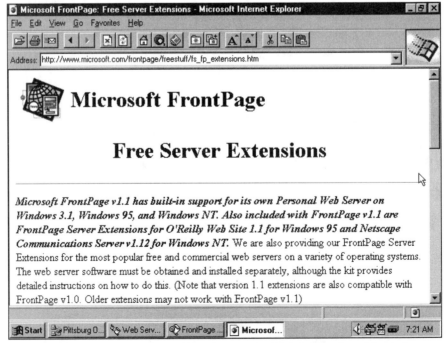

Figure 2-1: The FrontPage Server Extensions are available for free from Microsoft.

Table 2-1 shows the server extensions that are available for use with FrontPage as of May 1996.

Table 2-1	FrontPage Server Extensions
Operating System	**Web Server**
IIP/UX 9.03 (Hewlett-Packard)	Apache
CERN	
NCS	
Netscape Communications Server	
Open Market Web Server	
IRIX 5.3 (Silicon Graphics)	Apache
CERN	
NCSA	
Netscape Communications Server	
Open Market Web Server	
Microsoft Windows 3.1	FrontPage Personal
Microsoft Windows 95	FrontPage Personal
O'Reilly's Web Site 1.1	
Microsoft Windows NT	FrontPage Personal
Microsoft Internet Information Server	
Netscape Communications Server 1.12	
Solaris 2.4 (Sun Workstations, SPARC architecture)	Apache
CERN	
NCSA	
Netscape Communications Server	
Open Market Web Server	
SunOS 4.1.3 (Sun Workstations, SPARC architecture)	Apache
CERN	
NCSA	
Netscape Communications Server	
Open Market Web Server	

In Appendix B you will find instructions for installing FrontPage for use with some of these popular server software products.

Overview of the FrontPage Personal Web Server

Two versions of the Personal Web Server came with the original Vermeer and FTP versions of FrontPage and with the beta versions of Microsoft FrontPage. These two versions are a 16-bit version that will run on Windows 3.1 or Windows for Workgroups 3.11 and a 32-bit version that will run on Windows 95 or on Windows NT (see Figure 2-2). During the installation process, covered in Appendix B of this book, FrontPage automatically installs the correct version for your computer. The release version of FrontPage is specifically for Windows 95 and Windows NT and only comes in the 32-bit version.

Figure 2-2: Microsoft's FrontPage Personal Web Server in the beta version came in both a 16-bit and 32-bit version.

Most of the available documentation for these two server applications is applicable to both, but note that there are some areas of the documentation that are 16-bit specific. These include the sections on Windows CGI, the CGI examples and text cases, notes on using Visual Basic for CGI programs, command line options, and debugging options.

The 32-bit version of Personal Web Server is a porting of the NCSA server version 1.3R for Windows 95 and Windows NT. Sections of the documentation pertaining to HTML, URLs, forms, user access control, and general CGI information apply to both versions of the server. Most of the configuration directives in the documentation are available on both servers, except for those directives beginning with "Shell" or "Win." We go into detail in Chapter 3 concerning these directives as they apply to the FrontPage Personal Web Server. Note that directives beginning with the words "Shell" or "Win" are specific to the 16-bit software. The 32-bit version uses the standard input/output CGI interface as the NCSA web server software. Details concerning this aspect of the server operation can be found in the NCSA documentation at http://hoohoo.ncsa.uiuc.edu.

Both of these software applications support the HTTP and CGI standards. This makes them compatible with existing HTML documents and CGI scripts.

Unfortunately, all modifications to the server itself must be made manually. Personal Web Server does not include a user interface for changing the server configuration such as O'Reilly's WebSite (see Figure 2-3) and Quarterdeck's WebSTAR (see Figure 2-4) provide. There are some modifications that can be made to the server configuration from the FrontPage Explorer. This will be discussed more fully in Chapter 9.

Figure 2-3: O'Reilly's WebSite server software includes a user configuration interface.

Still, the FrontPage Personal Server should run out of the box, with little need for initial configuration. Unless you already have one of the supported server applications, or you require specific abilities provided by some other server application, the FrontPage Personal Web Server should be an acceptable application. It is also possible to run your own intranet using the FrontPage software package on a Windows 95 machine.

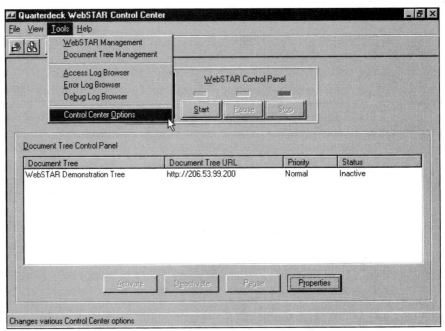

Figure 2-4: Quarterdeck's WebSTAR server software also includes a user configuration interface.

Other features of the FrontPage Personal Web Server are

➥ Small and fast design providing low impact

➥ The ability to handle up to sixteen simultaneous transactions for true multi-threaded operation

➥ Compatibility with most HTTP/0.9 and HTTP/1.0 browsers and proxy servers

➥ Single unified virtual directory structure

➥ Directory indexes allowing for the retrieval of files without FTP

➥ Dual-mode CGI/1.1 script support

➥ Full forms support

➥ Full image mapping support

➥ Limited access security features

➥ WinSock 1.1 compliance

➥ Built-in diagnostic tracing features which aid in the tracking down of problems

➥ Icon animation

You'll be looking in more detail at the FrontPage Pe
Chapter 3. Right now it's time to turn your attention

Overview of FrontPage Explorer

FrontPage Explorer is your tool for creating, viewing, and maintaining your w
site. With FrontPage Explorer, creating a new web is as simple as using a
template or a wizard. Viewing and maintaining a web is also made simple by
easy-to-read graphical displays.

FrontPage Explorer has three views from which you can examine your web: the
Outline view, the Link view, and the Summary view. You will have two views on
your screen at any one time. The Outline view stays on the left side of your
screen and you can toggle the right side of your screen between the Link and
Summary views.

Figure 2-5 shows the Outline and Link views of an earlier version of our
VREvolution web site (http://vrevolution.pitton.com). The address of
this earlier experimental web was Pvrevolution.

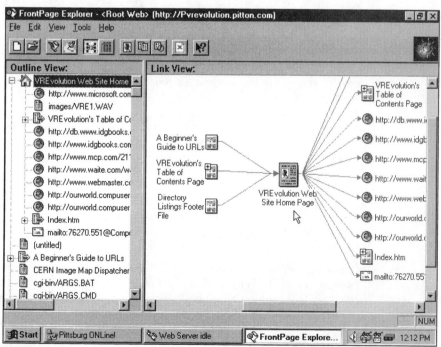

Figure 2-5: The Link view provides an easy to understand graphical display.

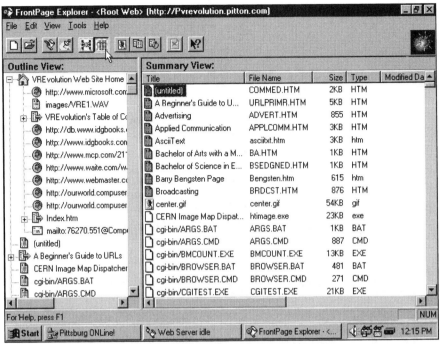

Figure 2-6: Switching to the Summary view is as simple as choosing the Summary view button. The Outline view will always stay on the left side of your screen.

Figure 2-6 shows the Outline and Summary views of this same version of our web.

The larger the web, the more confusing the mixture of links and references can become. The relationships among the pages on a web are easily visualized using the combination of the Explorer views as you graphically isolate individual pages:

➡ The Outline view shows the hierarchical structure of your web. Starting with your home page at the top of the display (in Figure 2-5, our home page is highlighted and designated with a house icon), this view shows each page of the web and which pages are connected.

➡ The Link view shows a graphical display of your web. This display places the selected page, (in Figure 2-5, our home page is selected) at the center of the display. Any links to or from the selected page are displayed graphically with arrows indicating the direction of the link.

➡ The Summary view shows each page or file and lists its properties. These properties include the title, size, date most recently modified, and the author who modified the page.

You can also verify links and assign administrator and author permissions from the Explorer component. We discuss the FrontPage Explorer in more detail in Chapters 4 and 5.

Overview of FrontPage Editor

To actually make changes to your pages' contents you need to use the FrontPage Editor. Whereas FrontPage Explorer is used to create and maintain your web site, FrontPage Editor is the tool you use to create and to perform maintenance on the individual web pages. Although it's useful to know HTML, which is required by most other web page authoring software, it isn't absolutely necessary with FrontPage Editor.

Figure 2-7 provides a look at our home page, which was displayed at the center of the graphical Link view shown in Figure 2-5, in FrontPage Editor.

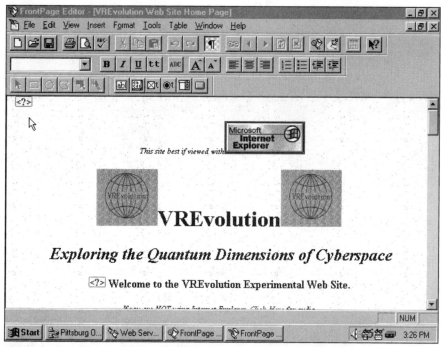

Figure 2-7: Any boxes with question marks in them signify HTML commands that FrontPage doesn't understand.

The FrontPage Editor allows you to simply enter and edit text just as you would in most word processing programs. In this respect, it's very similar in operation to Word for Windows. You can also add images and create links, bookmarks, hotspots, and forms using the FrontPage Editor.

Creating a page is simple using one of the built-in templates or wizards. FrontPage provides several choices of page formats and you can modify any of them to fit your needs. You can also create your own templates.

Although the FrontPage Editor provides, in most cases, a what-you-see-is-what-you-get (WYSIWYG) image of the finished web page, you can't absolutely count on what you see in the FrontPage Editor being identical to what your visitors will see with their browsers. To identify these potential problems, FrontPage Editor will place a box around HTML tags that it doesn't recognize, such as the marquee tag. Also, browsers may interpret the information received on a page differently from what was originally intended by the designer. Compare Figure 2-7, the FrontPage Editor view, with Figure 2-8, which shows the same information when viewed through Microsoft Internet Explorer 2.0.

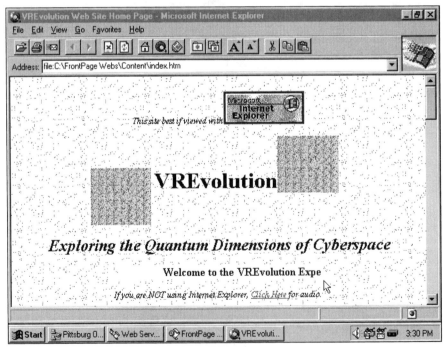

Figure 2-8: As we've seen in Chapter 1, different tools display the same information in different ways.

Still, most of what you see in FrontPage Editor will be what your visitors will see, especially if you use only standard HTML.

What else can you do with FrontPage Editor?

➡ From within the FrontPage Editor you can insert images, in almost any graphical format, onto a page.

➡ You can add hotspots, which are specific areas on an image containing hyperlinks that make the images clickable.

➡ You can insert forms onto pages, making your web more interactive.

➡ You can use WebBots, also called bots, to include dynamic features that are evaluated and executed when the page is saved to the server or when end users link to the page.

We'll have more to say on WebBots in Chapter 6.

An overview of the To Do List

For each web created or maintained by FrontPage, you can create a To Do List. This is a list of the tasks required to complete and maintain the web, such as finishing specific pages, updating information, or replacing old graphics.

When you begin to build a web, such as our VREvolution web shown in Figure 2-9, the To Do List is initially empty.

You can add tasks to this empty To Do List and associate those tasks with specific pages. Some To Do List tasks are also created when you use some of the FrontPage Web Wizards and Web Templates.

The To Do List, in addition to taking you directly to pages associated with tasks you select to complete, will display information about the tasks. This information includes what person (author) is assigned to the task, the date the task was assigned, the priority of the task, and a description of the task. While maintaining a list such as this may just sound like extra work, it actually helps considerably in organizing your work; when working with a group of people on a web site, it can mean the difference between a successful collaboration and failure.

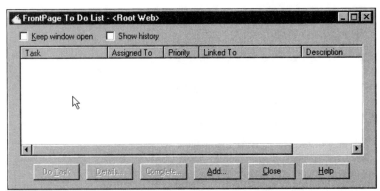

Figure 2-9: When you first start FrontPage, the To Do List for your web is empty.

Using FrontPage

We referred earlier to FrontPage being a client/server application. This means that there are two main parts to FrontPage, the client part and the server part. The FrontPage Explorer and the FrontPage Editor are the client functions and the FrontPage Personal Web Server and the FrontPage Server Extensions for the other servers supported by FrontPage are the server functions.

The FrontPage client consists of the FrontPage Explorer (the tool for creating, viewing, and maintaining your web site), the FrontPage Editor (the tool for creating, viewing, and testing your individual web pages), and the To Do List (the tool to help you keep track of what jobs are left to complete and who is responsible for those jobs). In addition, the client includes the elements created by wizards and templates, as well as WebBots (programming elements used to automate, speed, and ease the construction of the various pages and webs FrontPage can create).

The FrontPage server consists of the Personal Web Server (the 16-bit and 32-bit web servers that fully support HTTP and CGI that comes with the FrontPage package), the FrontPage Server Extensions (the enabling software that allows other servers to work with FrontPage), and the Server Administrator (the tool that allows you to manage the security and access to your server).

To understand what you can do with FrontPage you have to first understand the specific tasks that can be performed using the various components of the client. We'll start with the FrontPage Explorer.

What you can do with FrontPage Explorer

You got an overview of the purpose of FrontPage Explorer earlier. Now we'll show you what specific tasks you can perform using Explorer. We'll go into much more detail on this in Chapters 4 and 5.

Creating new sites

If you are creating a web for the first time, you may want to take advantage of the FrontPage Web Wizards and Web Templates to simplify the task. These two features walk you through the creation of many popular web formats. A Web Wizard will ask you a series of questions that will help you select the features you want for your web site. Web Templates provide pre-defined formats so that you can replace certain placeholders for text and graphics with elements you've created. For a more customized look for your site, you can even build your own templates.

Developing a site at your own pace

FrontPage allows you to create a number of webs and pages and maintain information concerning the pages, including creation or modification date and time, author, and comments. Using the FrontPage Web Copy and Rename Web commands allows you to upgrade and update your web periodically, staging the release of the site without making everything public at the same time. When a part of your web is ready, it's easy to make it public and promote pages into service in stages.

Keeping your site up-to-date

One of the main reasons sites aren't revisited is that they are not updated on a regular basis. Maintaining a web site is a time-consuming task. FrontPage allows multiple authors to develop and maintain sites on local or remote servers. This allows for easier updating with the latest information. You can also easily transport your web site from one server to another via the Internet or a LAN using FrontPage. This makes it simple to use a higher-powered server platform as your web site traffic increases.

Maintaining security

FrontPage increases your opportunities for collaboration by allowing multiple authors to simultaneously update different pages of the same server. If one author tries to overwrite a page that another author has already edited, a warning is issued. All communications between the remote and local sites are safe, secure, and encrypted. Access is controlled with password and IP address user-authentication to keep those without approved access from modifying your pages and information. You can divide your access approvals into three classes: administrators, authors, and end users. The permissions for these three classes can range from full unrestricted access to content viewing only. These permissions are set with simple point-and-click operation. Even *firewalls* (hardware/software combinations on a network that allow the restriction of access in and out of the system) are supported.

Verifying links

FrontPage can be used to verify links, not only to other pages within your web on the same server, but to other pages on other servers in other webs. By using FrontPage, you can assure yourself and your users that your links are good.

What you can do with FrontPage Editor

FrontPage Editor is used to create and perform maintenance on individual web pages by allowing you to take advantage of several features.

Creating pages without knowing HTML

Using FrontPage Editor you can edit pre-existing pages, create new pages, or add text or images to blank pages without having to know HTML. This is one of the main advantages of using the FrontPage Editor.

All of the styles of HTML are available to you. These include both character and paragraph styles, as well as bulleted and numbered lists. Instead of using HTML tags, in FrontPage Editor you format your paragraphs just as you would in Microsoft Word for Windows or any other word processor. FrontPage then automatically generates the HTML code so you never have to see it (unless you want to).

Editor has other features that make page design easier than using HTML code:

➡ When you're in the FrontPage Editor you see the web page displayed in much the same way any web browser would display it.

➡ The FrontPage Editor allows the display of hidden formatting or authoring commands. This maintains your complete control over the page's design and format.

➡ FrontPage contains a built-in spell checker.

➥ You can include information such as graphic files or RTF (Rich Text Format) or ASCII text files on your web site. FrontPage Editor automatically converts the RTF or ASCII file to HTML.

➥ FrontPage Editor automatically converts a wide range of graphic formats to GIF or JPEG.

Creating links and hotspots on the fly

Using FrontPage Editor you can easily create a link to another page, another bookmark, or another web site. You can insert images and then turn those images into clickable image maps. You can link to any file, FTP site, Gopher site, or newsgroup. Linking to a nonexistent page automatically adds the task of creating this nonexistent page to your To Do List.

Adding advanced interactive capabilities

FrontPage provides several interesting and exciting interactive capabilities that can be added to your web site. These capabilities are made possible through the use of WebBots. You won't have to create your own scripts or complicated HTML commands. You simply click your mouse a few times to add navigation bars, discussion groups, full-text search, and registration forms to your site. Some of these WebBots are described in the following list:

➥ **The Search WebBot.** You can add a customizable, interactive full-text search capability to your web using this WebBot. The results of such a search would contain links to the matching documents. The full-text search engine is included with FrontPage.

➥ **The Include WebBot.** By using this WebBot you can maintain a consistent look over your entire web. For instance, the header or footer of your pages can be automatically updated by making only one change.

➥ **The Save Results WebBot** automatically sends the contents of a form to a file in one of several formats. Interactivity of a web site is increased through the use of forms and the ability to collect information and feedback from the people who visit your site. FrontPage provides you with the tools you need to create several different types of forms, such as registration forms and surveys. Specific properties applicable to the specific form fields you may be working with, such as drop-down list boxes, are easily assigned.

➥ **The Discussion WebBot.** You can easily create a threaded, fully interactive discussion group on a web using this WebBot. New messages and replies to existing messages are automatically posted to the web site. Confirmation messages can even be sent after each new message is posted. You can choose to have the messages appear in either chronological or reverse chronological order. Also, all messages are indexed in a separate file for easy retrieval using the Search WebBot.

Creating and customizing forms

Creating and editing forms is easy using FrontPage Editor. You can create text fields, radio buttons, scrolling lists or other form elements in minutes. Dragging the mouse pointer across the screen quickly resizes any text field. You can also edit any form, even if it wasn't created with FrontPage Editor. Chapter 8 discusses form creation in more detail.

Using the FrontPage To Do List

The FrontPage To Do List is where you can create a list of the tasks required to complete a web. The integrated To Do List makes it easy to keep control of the various tasks that are required for the development, operation and maintenance of your web.

A To Do List lets you name, describe, assign, and prioritize all the jobs and tasks that go into creating and maintaining your web. If you are part of a larger organization, you can arrange to have each part of your organization (such as Sales, Marketing, Public Relations, Engineering, Customer Service, Human Resources, and so on) maintain its own part of the web. In this way, you don't have to rely on a single point of contact for all web updates.

Benefits of a Web Authoring Environment

As a client/server web authoring environment, FrontPage provides a number of benefits. FrontPage provides you with the opportunity for remote authoring, a multi-user collaborative Web development process within your organization, and platform independence between the client workstation and the server.

In this section, we'll look a little more closely at the architecture of FrontPage. Figure 2-10 demonstrates graphically what this architecture might look like.

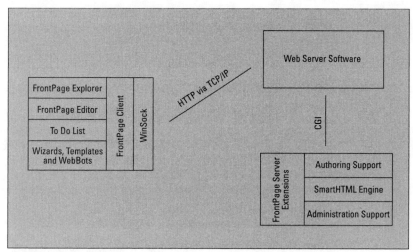

Figure 2-10: This diagram offers a graphical demonstration of the FrontPage architecture.

What are Server Extensions used for?

We've briefly discussed the Server and the extensions. These extensions represent a small number of executables that are installed on the same computer as the server itself. There are three main purposes for these extensions:

➡ They add capabilities to the server software itself that FrontPage requires to perform its job. These functions include such things as the storing of documents, updating the To Do List, and preparing the graphical representation of the documents within a given web.

➡ Server Extensions create a common application program interface (API) among various applications that behave differently on the web. These applications might include the server itself and its relationships with permissions, imagemaps, and configuration information.

➡ Finally, the Server Extensions provide interactive ability to the end user who is browsing the web. These abilities might include full-text search capability, threaded discussion groups, and web registration.

Understanding Server Extension architecture

The extensions listed earlier in this chapter are structured to interface with any standard server software. These extensions are also designed to be easily ported to other hardware and software platforms, creating cross-platform web server compatibility.

In most cases, the Server Extensions are accessed by a server using some version of the Common Gateway Interface (CGI).The way CGI works may be slightly different from one server to another. UNIX web servers generally invoke a CGI extension by forking a new process. Compare that with Windows NT web servers that support a Dynamic Link Library (DLL) variant of CGI. While the Windows NT version incurs less overhead, both approaches get the job done.

The information flow is similar in all versions of CGI. User values and environment parameters are sent to the CGI extension using a block of name or value pairs. The CGI extension then returns a result to the user in the form of an HTML formatted page. This mechanism is sufficiently general: it is non-specific to any one server software so that it allows the necessary communication between the FrontPage client software and the FrontPage Server Extensions.

Server software doesn't always implement the same procedures to do the same things. For example, NCSA Web Server reads a text file on a server to determine permission settings. O'Reilly's WebSite reads the Windows 95 or Windows NT Registry to find the permissions. One of the specific instances in which FrontPage must initiate communication with the server is when it needs to get permissions for administrators, authors, and end users.

As a result of these variances, the FrontPage Server Extensions must be changed to support each individual web server. As much as ninety percent of the Server Extensions' program code can go unchanged between servers, however, since the differences are very slight in most cases.

Communication between the client and the server

The FrontPage client software communicates with the FrontPage Server Extensions installed alongside it for any given site. This communication allows the client to perform authoring and administration functions on that specific web. The client and the server can be located anywhere: at the same location on the same machine, or at different locations around the globe on different types of machines, as long as they are connected by the Internet (or at least an intranet). Even if there is a firewall separating the client from the server, the FrontPage client will use the necessary proxy server to gain access to the web server.

FrontPage can do this because in all cases it uses the same protocol for client/server communication that your web browser and web server use. That protocol is HyperText Transfer Protocol (HTTP). The FrontPage client sends an HTTP POST request to the server. This request contains a URL that identifies a specific executable program in the FrontPage Server Extensions. This program passes along any and all included data as part of the POST.

The server receives the POST and starts the FrontPage Server Extensions. The FrontPage Server Extensions then pass through the data and parameters that were included in the original request. The extensions also process the data and then send any necessary return information or values in the POST reply message.

What's happening in this process is that FrontPage is executing what's called a remote procedure call (RPC) on top of the base-level HTTP POST request structure. The FrontPage client invokes this RPC in the FrontPage Server Extensions and the RPC's results are then returned to the client software. This method is used in tasks such as sending documents to the server for storage.

One reason for sole reliance on the POST request is that many server applications do not implement the PUT request. According to the HTTP specification, PUT is supposed to be used when sending documents to the server software. Since the PUT request is not used by many servers, use of it by FrontPage would interfere with the cross-platform and cross-vendor capabilities of the FrontPage product. FrontPage uses only the POST request for all communication and for requests to the server and Server Extensions.

Implementation of security

There are three areas of concern in security of a web site that are addressed by FrontPage. These three areas are

➡ End user, author, and administrator access control

➡ Access and authoring through a firewall

➡ Client/server communication encryption

End user, author, and administrator access control

FrontPage provides three levels of access, or permissions, to your web. These three levels are

➡ End user access for those who are browsing your web

➡ Author access, which includes permissions to access, update, and maintain the web

➡ Administrative access allowing someone to update end user, author, and administrator permissions

Control over these permissions is achieved by using methods built into the server. Most server applications support *realms*. These realms relate to a specific set of permissions. The server allows access to these realms through the use of either user names and passwords, or lists of IP addresses, or both.

FrontPage makes use of the realms set up by the server by assigning end users to one realm, authors to another realm, and administrators to yet another realm. FrontPage permissions can then be supported using user names and passwords, lists of IP addresses, or both, just as the server itself does. User names, passwords, and IP address masks are then manipulated by FrontPage using simple point-and-click methods.

Access and authoring through a firewall

Sometimes you will need to author a web that is on the other side of a firewall. The FrontPage client might be asked to author against (copy a web to) a server on the other side of the firewall. This could be an outbound situation where you are authoring against an external server outside the firewall. On the other hand, the request could be an inbound one coming from you, where you are authoring against an internal server which is behind a firewall while you are remote from your site.

Don't worry: with FrontPage, you can handle both types of situations. FrontPage allows authors to specify a proxy server (a machine name and optional port number) through which all communication with your web server should be routed. Once this information is provided, FrontPage will ask for the user name and password. This authentication challenge is reflected to the client via the proxy. The user name and password supplied by the author are sent through the proxy back to the server and the author is granted access. All of this happens behind the scenes and, once the author has given FrontPage the proxy server's name, he or she is totally unaware of the operation of this mechanism.

Client/server communication encryption

When you use FrontPage all communications between the client and the server are automatically encrypted. This is a valuable asset. A situation could arise where you might be authoring against a server that's behind a firewall. Non-public data could very well be traveling between the server and the client over the Internet. Encryption provides the protection you and your data need.

This encryption method is also proprietary and difficult to break. It doesn't, however, meet US government requirements for export outside of the United States. As either the Secure HTTP specification proposed by Enterprise Integration Technologies (EIT), the Secure Sockets Layer (SSL) proposed by Netscape Communication Corporation, or some other more standardized process from Microsoft itself become more universally supported by Web server vendors, you can expect the emerging security standards to be incorporated into FrontPage.

The Flexibility of FrontPage as an Authoring Tool

When we looked into the possibility of doing this book one of our first concerns was having to start over from scratch on the rather large web site we developed for our last book.

Our concerns disappeared when we discovered that we could not only create and maintain new webs using FrontPage but could continue the ongoing maintenance required by previously created and installed webs. We also discovered that our more specialized tools for the creation of CGI, VRML, and Java applications could still be used with FrontPage.

Using previously created content with FrontPage

There are a couple of different ways in which previously created content can be incorporated into FrontPage. When FrontPage Server Extensions are installed on a server where pages not created with FrontPage are located, FrontPage Server Extensions automatically gather all information about these pages and prepare them for use with FrontPage.

You can also copy existing webs into the FrontPage content area. You then alert FrontPage to this old material by using the Recalculate Links command from within FrontPage Explorer.

Using FrontPage content with other tools

Just because you've created pages using FrontPage, you're not restricted to using only FrontPage to work with this content. FrontPage stores all pages as HTML and GIF files in organized subdirectories. The FrontPage Server Extensions and other FrontPage-specific files can easily be removed if you wish. Keep in mind that in doing so, any WebBots and imagemaps that you might have included with the web will be disconnected, but the web can be browsed with no problem.

Using content created with other tools in FrontPage

You can use content created with other tools in FrontPage just as easily as you can work with content created in FrontPage. For instance, if you are using some proprietary software that converts text into HTML pages, this externally created material can be added by running the Recalculate Links command from within FrontPage Explorer. This command will search the entire web content area for any new documents and then update FrontPage's file structures as necessary.

Using FrontPage with previously created CGI scripts

Many of the programming features that you might want to add to your web by using CGI can be incorporated in your page using WebBots. There is always the possibility, however, that there might be some task you need to perform for which no WebBot exists. In this case, using custom CGI scripts is not only possible, but practical.

Using FrontPage, it's easy to invoke a CGI script. After you've laid out the form using FrontPage Editor, specify the action to be taken by the form. One of those possible actions is to invoke a custom CGI script from the server. All you do is to provide the URL for the CGI script. You can also make the CGI script into a custom bot. This will make it more configurable and easier to use.

Now that we've looked at what FrontPage is and how the parts work together, we'll turn our attention to what the future might hold for FrontPage.

Future Directions for FrontPage

The integration of FrontPage with Microsoft Office, in particular Word, Excel, and PowerPoint, is almost seamless. FrontPage easily adds and manages Office documents within your web. FrontPage will also automatically start the appropriate application when you open an Office document for editing. You have the capability to automatically retrieve and save Office documents to a remote server via FrontPage.

Microsoft anticipates that in the near future

➡ Office documents themselves will support hyperlinks. FrontPage will then recognize those hyperlinks and show Office documents as interior nodes of a given web in the Link view of FrontPage Explorer.

➡ You'll be able to see the hyperlinks from the Office document. FrontPage will display Office documents using their native icons.

➡ Future releases of FrontPage will allow the use of customized WebBots and the FrontPage Developer's Kit will allow programmers to create these WebBots. Currently the FrontPage Developer's Kit supports the creation of custom wizards and templates.

As HTML changes you can expect Microsoft to continue to keep FrontPage in line with the enhancements and extensions that prove popular. You can also expect to see these changes:

➡ Access to popular databases will be provided in future versions of the software.

➡ By the end of 1996, Microsoft has promised support for Macintosh computers from both the server and the client end.

➡ FrontPage will be enhanced to allow you to add ActiveX controls to your web.

➡ FrontPage will provide support for secure HTTP and SSL security and authentication.

You can also look forward to international versions of FrontPage.

Moving On

In this chapter we've looked at several different aspects of FrontPage and its various components. Some of the things we have looked at include how you can

⟹ Develop and maintain your own web and web site using FrontPage.

⟹ Develop high-quality, professional looking web pages without having to know anything about HTML.

⟹ Run your own web server right out of the box using FrontPage Personal Web Server.

⟹ Create web pages and entire web sites using the FrontPage templates and wizards.

⟹ Add drop-in interactive functions and eliminate programming tasks using WebBots.

⟹ Utilize a team of both remote and local authors to maintain and develop your web site.

⟹ Create professional-looking results with desktop publishing features.

⟹ Maintain your web site with the FrontPage web server administration tools.

⟹ Maintain, manage, and track contributors, authors, and tasks with the To Do List.

In Chapter 3 we delve into details of the FrontPage server installation process.

Setting Up the Personal Web Server

3

In Chapter 2 we began a discussion of the FrontPage Personal Web Server and its capabilities. In this chapter, we will get much more in depth as we explore the use and operation of this important part of the FrontPage product.

The FrontPage Personal Web Server is capable of running right out of the box. If you are a less advanced user, you can install FrontPage according to the instructions in Appendix B and accept the default settings; in that case, you may wish to simply skip the bulk of this chapter and move on to Chapter 4. However, even less experienced users would benefit from reading the first part of this chapter to better understand the basic role of the server in their web site. Much of the information in this chapter is for those who wish to customize the Personal Web Server and set it up for more advanced uses.

We will begin by going over in detail just what the FrontPage Personal Web Server is and what it does. We will then look at how to install both the 16-bit and 32-bit versions of this software and what you need to do to make sure that the server is configured properly for your site. This will require getting into the details of command line options for this product. We'll conclude this chapter by discussing use of the Windows CGI interface with the FrontPage Personal Web Server.

If you are not using the FrontPage Personal Web Server but instead have installed the FrontPage Server Extensions for another server, (such as the O'Reilly WebSite, Netscape Commerce Server, or Microsoft Internet Information Server) you can skip this chapter and move on to Chapter 4. However, if you will be using the FrontPage Personal Web Server, or if you're not sure which server you should use, read on.

An Overview of the Personal Web Server

FrontPage is a client/server application. In this chapter, we'll be looking at the server side of this application, the Personal Web Server. Any server allows you to provide information, in the form of files, to other users on the Internet or on your intranet.

Basically, the server software allows for the posting and retrieval of files between the computer containing the server software and the computer containing the client software. As a result, using the FrontPage Personal Web Server you can make changes to your web sites on-the-fly and they will be ready for viewing by people visiting your site immediately after the change. This can be of great value in keeping your site up-to-date.

Why do you need a server?

Taking advantage of the power of HTML pages and webs requires the use of a running server. It doesn't matter if that server is on the Internet, on a local area network (LAN), or on your own computer. While you could use FrontPage without a server, you'd be giving up many of its most powerful features. In this scenario you would lose the use of several features of the FrontPage Explorer and end up being able to fully use only the FrontPage Editor and its functions.

If you already have a server installed, don't worry; Microsoft has made available freely downloadable Server Extensions for most servers to make your server fully compatible with FrontPage. If there are no Server Extensions available for your server, you can use the Personal Web Server until those extensions do become available. Most servers all provide the same basic services. Some are more stable than others and some have different user interfaces; you may feel one is more useful than the others. Choice of a server is personal and will vary among webmasters.

After it's installed, you can use the Personal Web Server to operate FrontPage on your computer, to set up an intranet for your organization, or to run a World Wide Web site. The Personal Web Server, while not as powerful as some other servers, is a "real" server and is fully capable of providing any of the above-mentioned services. You can, however, run FrontPage using any of the servers for which Microsoft provides Server Extensions, or you can use the FrontPage Personal Publisher to translate the webs you create for use on unsupported servers.

The different versions of the Personal Web Server

Two versions of the Personal Web Server come with the Vermeer and FTP versions of FrontPage and the beta version of Microsoft FrontPage: a 16-bit version that will run on Windows 3.1 or Windows for Workgroups 3.11, and a 32-bit version that will run on Windows 95 or Windows NT. During FrontPage setup and installation, which are discussed in Appendix B, FrontPage automatically installs the correct version of the Personal Web Server for your computer's operating system. The release version of Microsoft FrontPage contains only the Windows 95 and Windows NT version of the server software.

Most of the documentation for these two versions of this server is applicable to both. There are some areas, however, where the documentation is 16-bit specific. The sections on Windows CGI, the CGI examples and text cases, notes on using Visual Basic for CGI programs, command line options, and debugging options are all 16-bit specific.

Keep in mind that the 32-bit version of the Personal Web Server, the version we will mainly focus on in this chapter, is a port of the NCSA server version 1.3R for Windows 95 and Windows NT. Sections of the documentation for that server software pertaining to HTML, URLs, forms, user access control, and general CGI information apply to both the 16-bit and the 32-bit versions of the Personal Web Server.

Most of the configuration directives we will be discussing in this chapter are available on both servers, except for those directives beginning with "Shell" or "Win." Those directives are specific to the 16-bit software; we won't be going into any depth on them. The 32-bit version uses the standard input/output CGI interface as the NCSA server. Details concerning this aspect of the server operation can be found in the NCSA documentation at `http://hoohoo.ncsa.uiuc.edu`. We'll discuss these issues briefly toward the end of this chapter.

Both the 16-bit and the 32-bit version of the FrontPage Personal Web Server applications support the HTTP and CGI standards. This makes them compatible with existing HTML documents and CGI scripts.

Although this all sounds very technical, don't worry. You won't need most of this information unless you decide to modify the entries to the Personal Web Server, which most people won't ever need to do.

Personal Web Server features

It is expected that, with minor changes, the FrontPage Personal Web Server will run out of the box.

Once installed, the Personal Web Server offers you standard server features also offered on many server software platforms, including

- Small and fast design providing low impact
- The ability to handle up to 16 simultaneous transactions for true multi-threaded operation
- Compatibility with most HTTP/0.9 and HTTP/1.0 browsers and proxy servers
- A single unified virtual directory structure
- Directory indexes allowing for the retrieval of files without FTP
- Dual-mode CGI/1.1 script support (that is, it supports standard CGI and WinCGI specifications)
- Full forms support
- Full image mapping support
- Limited access security features
- WinSock 1.1 compliance
- Built-in diagnostic tracing features helping with the tracking down of problems
- Icon animation

While the Personal Web Server is feature-rich, it is unfortunate that most modifications to the server itself must be made manually. The Personal Web Server does not include a user interface for changing the server configuration. However, there are some modifications that can be made from within the FrontPage Explorer interface that we discuss in a later chapter.

Hardware and software requirements

The release version of Microsoft FrontPage comes with only the 32-bit version of its own Personal Web Server that permits FrontPage to operate on the Windows 95 and Windows NT platforms. Minimum operating system requirements include

- A 486 CPU
- Windows 95 or Windows NT Workstation version 3.51 or later operating system

➡ 16MB (megabytes) of RAM

➡ 15MB of hard disk space

➡ One 3.5 inch high-density disk drive

➡ A VGA or higher resolution video adapter

➡ A Microsoft mouse or a compatible pointing device

Keep in mind that these are minimum requirements. Although FrontPage works fine with these minimums, your system will work most efficiently with additional upgrades such as a Pentium or better CPU, more memory, and an SVGA 256-color video adapter.

Installing the Personal Web Server

The FrontPage Personal Web Server is installed automatically during the installation of the FrontPage software.

General instructions for installation and setup of FrontPage are provided in Appendix B of this book. There you learn how to install the FrontPage components and any necessary Server Extensions. You'll also learn how to run the Server Administrator to set FrontPage up to work with the server you've decided to use. In this section of Chapter 3 we are going to discuss setup and operation of the Personal Web Server in detail.

During the installation of the FrontPage software you were asked to make the choice to install the FrontPage Personal Web Server. At that point you specified the main Server Configuration file. By default, this file should be named **C:\FrontPage Webs\Server\conf\httpd.cnf**. If you changed any of the defaults during installation, you'll have to adjust what follows for the program directory you entered. If you didn't choose to install the FrontPage Personal Web Server when you installed FrontPage, you will need to reinstall, selecting that option.

Overview of the Personal Web Server Configuration

Keep in mind that the FrontPage installation program configures all the necessary settings for the Personal Web Server. It shouldn't be necessary for you to change any of the configuration files we are going to discuss here. However, if you are an advanced user and wish to go beyond the basic configuration, you may want to take advantage of the information that follows.

There are a few simple rules that apply to all of the configuration files:

➡ Use the UNIX-style forward slash (/) in all configuration path names, as opposed to the Windows-style back slash (\).

➡ Filenames are not case sensitive.

➡ Lines that begin with the # character are ignored. The # character must be the first character on a comment line and comments must always be on a line by themselves.

➡ Only one directive can be on any given line.

➡ All extra white space is ignored.

There are four different configuration files that we'll be discussing here:

➡ The Server Configuration file

➡ The Global Access Configuration file

➡ The Server Resource Map Configuration file

➡ The MIME Types Configuration file

Using Directives

Before we get into detail about the various configuration files, you need to understand what a directive is. A *directive* is a keyword that a server recognizes. The directive tells the server what to do with the specified information. There can be only one keyword per line in a configuration file. This keyword is followed by one space and then data. This data is always specific to the keyword. This results in a syntax which looks like the following:

```
Directive data
```

Remember that extra spaces or tabs are always ignored. If you want to put a space within the data without separating it from any subsequent arguments, you use a \ character before the space.

FrontPage Configuration Files

The FrontPage installation process creates a subdirectory called **conf**\. Three configuration files are created inside this subdirectory. These three files are **access.cnf**, **httpd.cnf**, and **srm.cnf**. We'll go through these configuration files step-by-step so that you understand how to manipulate the various commands. We'll begin with the Server Configuration file itself.

Explicit directives for the configuration file

Look inside the \conf\ subdirectory and find **httpd.cnf**. Take a look at this file using *NotePad*, *WordPad*, *Write*, or your word processor. We've also provided the contents of the file for you to look at in Listing 3-1.

Listing 3-1: httpd.cnf

```
#----------------------------------------
#
#   HTTPD.CNF
#
# Main server configuration for the FrontPage Personal Web Server
#
# This is the main server configuration file. It is best to
# leave the directives in this file in the order they are in, or
# things may not go the way you'd like.
#
# Do NOT simply read the instructions in here without ⊃
understanding
# what they do, if you are unsure consult the online docs.
#
# Server configuration commands are similar to those for the NCSA
# server version 1.3R.  If you have questions please see the ⊃
online
# documentation at http://hoohoo.ncsa.uiuc.edu
#
# NOTE: path defaults are relative to the server's installation
#       directory (ServerRoot). Paths should be given in Unix
#       format (using '/').
#
#----------------------------------------


# ServerRoot: The directory the server's config, error, and ⊃
log files
# are kept in. This should be specified on the startup command ⊃
line.
#
# Format: ServerRoot <path>
#
ServerRoot VSERVER/


# Port: The port the standalone listens to. 80 is the network ⊃
standard.
#
```
(continued)

Listing 3-1 *(continued)*

```
Port VPORT

# Timeout: The timeout applied to all network operations. It's ⊃
the
# maximum time for a network send or receive, and the maximum ⊃
time that
# a CGI script is allowed to take.  The default is 20 minutes ⊃
(1200 seconds).
#
# Format: Timeout nn    (seconds)
#
# Timeout 1200

# ServerAdmin: Your address, where problems with the server ⊃
should be
# e-mailed.
#
# Format: ServerAdmin <email addr>
#
# ServerAdmin www-admin

# ErrorLog: The location of the error log file. If this does ⊃
not start
# with / or a drive spec (recommended!), ServerRoot is ⊃
prepended to it.
#
# Format: ErrorLog <path/file>
#
# ErrorLog logs/error.log

# TransferLog: The location of the transfer log file. If this ⊃
does not
# start with / or a drive spec (recommended!), ServerRoot is ⊃
prepended to it.
#
# Format: TransferLog <path/file>
#
# TransferLog logs/access.log

# ServerName allows you to set a host name which is sent back ⊃
to clients for
```

```
# your server if it's different than the one the program would ⊃
get (i.e. use
# "www" instead of the host's real name). Make sure your DNS ⊃
is set up to
# alias the name to your system!
#
# Format: ServerName <domain name>
#
# no default

# Command line template for CGI WinExec
# Uncomment next line for shorter form of command line
ShellWinCmdTempl ~p ~v ~a
```

The Server Configuration file recognizes a variety of directives. We will step through the directives present in this example file, and then look at other directives that you might want to use and why you might want to use them. We'll begin with setting the ServerRoot.

ServerRoot

As you read the Server Configuration file, the first command that you will come across is the ServerRoot directive. This part of the configuration file reads

```
# ServerRoot: The directory the server's config, error, and ⊃
log files
# are kept in. This should be specified on the startup command ⊃
line.
#
# Format: ServerRoot <path>
#
# ServerRoot VSERVER/
```

Purpose.   The ServerRoot directive sets the subdirectory in which the FrontPage Personal Web Server exists. When the Personal Web Server starts up, it expects to find the Server Configuration file **httpd.cnf** in the ServerRoot subdirectory. Other Server Configuration directives also use this subdirectory as a reference point to set relative paths for the locations of other files. This is, therefore, a very important directive to set.

Syntax.

```
ServerRoot dir
```

In the example in Listing 3.1, *dir* is the *absolute path* of a directory on your server machine. In an operating system based on a hierarchical file structure system, such as Windows 95, the full path to a file beginning at the root directory is called the absolute path. On our computer, for example, the absolute path for our httpd.cnf file is

```
c:\FrontPage Webs\server\conf\httpd.cnf
```

Keep in mind, however, that you need to specify the paths in UNIX format, so this absolute path should read

```
c:/FrontPage Webs/server/conf/httpd.cnf
```

Default.

If you don't specify or modify the ServerRoot, FrontPage will automatically assume

```
ServerRoot /usr/local/etc/httpd
```

or something similar. In our case, FrontPage set the ServerRoot directive to

```
ServerRoot c:/frontpage\ webs/server/
```

Examples.

In the example in Listing 3.1,

```
ServerRoot /usr/local/etc/httpd
```

sets the ServerRoot to the subdirectory \usr\local\etc\httpd.

Port

The next directive in the Server Configuration file is Port, which is shown in the example configuration file like this:

```
# Port: The port the standalone listens to. 80 is the network ⤶
standard.
#
Port VPORT
```

Purpose. The Port directive sets what port, or what communications channel, the FrontPage Personal Web Server listens to for clients.

Syntax.

```
Port number
```

The variable *number* can be anything from 0 to 65,536. The normal port for a web server is Port 80. This is the port that a URL specifying http:// service will default to. Most other ports below 1024 are reserved for other uses. Only one Port directive is allowed in your Server Configuration file.

Default. If you fail to specify a Port, the FrontPage installation program automatically sets the Port directive as 80.

Examples.

```
Port 8080
```

The server would listen to port 8080 if the directive was set to this. Experimental servers are often run on port 8080 by loose convention. This experimental server would then be accessed with the URL

```
http://www.whateversite.com:8080/
```

TimeOut

The next directive in the Server Configuration file is the TimeOut directive. The entry in the file reads

```
# TimeOut: The timeout applied to all network operations. It's ⊃
the
# maximum time for a network send or receive, and the maximum ⊃
time that
# a CGI script is allowed to take.  The default is 20 minutes ⊃
(1200 seconds).
#
# Format: Timeout nn     (seconds)
#
# TimeOut 1200
```

Purpose. This directive sets the maximum amount of time that the Personal Web Server will wait for any network communication, whether it consists of a read or a write operation. This would include the amount of time that the server will wait for a client to start communication after the initial connection. Network writes are 4K in size and are individually timed.

Syntax.

```
TimeOut Time
```

The variable *Time* represents the amount of time in seconds that the server will wait for the connection. Only one TimeOut directive is allowed in the Server Configuration file.

Default. If you don't specify a TimeOut, the Personal Web Server assumes

```
TimeOut 30
```

This would provide a time out of 30 seconds.

You'll notice that, in the example file in Listing 3-1, the TimeOut directive is commented out. This was also the case in our FrontPage installation Server Configuration file. This results in our FrontPage Personal Web Server installation defaulting to a time out of 30 seconds.

Example.

```
TimeOut 60
```

This directive would provide a time out of 60 seconds. You may want to try this if you have a slow connection.

ServerAdmin

The next directive in the Server Configuration file is the ServerAdmin directive. This is how it reads in the file itself:

```
# ServerAdmin: Your address, where problems with the server ⤶
should be
# e-mailed.
#
# Format: ServerAdmin <email addr>
#
# ServerAdmin www-admin
```

Purpose. This directive provides the server with your e-mail address; the address can then be provided to visitors so that they can report trouble or error conditions that might exist with your site.

Syntax.

```
ServerAdmin address
```

The variable *address* represents an e-mail address accessible from the Internet. Only one ServerAdmin directive is allowed in your Server Configuration file.

Default. The FrontPage installation process will not insert your e-mail address for you. You'll notice that the example file in Listing 3-1 comments out the ServerAdmin directive. There is no default e-mail address. The result is that, if you fail to specify a ServerAdmin, the Personal Web Server will print no address for reporting errors. This can be extremely frustrating to web site visitors who have problems at your site.

Example.

```
ServerAdmin 76270.551@Compuserve.com
```

This example demonstrates how errors with our web site are directed toward our CompuServe e-mail address.

ErrorLog

The next directive in the Server Configuration file is the ErrorLog directive. This directive reads as follows:

```
# ErrorLog: The location of the error log file. If this does ⊃
not start
# with / or a drive spec (recommended!), ServerRoot is ⊃
prepended to it.
#
# Format: ErrorLog <path/file>
#
# ErrorLog logs/error.log
```

Purpose. The ErrorLog directive tells the Personal Web Server where to log any errors it runs into. The types of errors that would be logged to this file include

➡ Clients that may time out during a connection

➡ Any CGI scripts that would produce no output

➡ Any **#haccess.cnf** files that might be attempting to override things that they don't have the necessary permission to override (We'll be explaining **#haccess.cnf** files later in this chapter.)

➡ Any server errors that would produce a segmentation violation or a bus error

➡ Any user authentication problems that might occur

Syntax.

```
ErrorLog File
```

The variable *File* represents the name of the file where the errors will be logged. This can either be a full path name or a partial path name relative to the ServerRoot. Only one ErrorLog directive is allowed in any Server Configuration file.

Default. If no ErrorLog is specified, the Personal Web Server assumes

```
ErrorLog logs/error_log
```

Notice that both the example file in Listing 3-1 and the actual configuration file comment this out, thereby accepting the default.

Examples.

```
ErrorLog /temp/weberror.log
```

This directive would log any server errors to the file weberror.log in the \temp\ subdirectory relative to the ServerRoot directory.

```
ErrorLog NUL:
```

This statement effectively turns off all error logging. We don't recommend that you do this: You need to be able to see any errors that might be occurring with your web site and server.

TransferLog

The next directive in the Server Configuration file is the TransferLog directive. This information is

```
# TransferLog: The location of the transfer log file. If this ⤵
does not
# start with / or a drive spec (recommended!), ServerRoot is ⤵
prepended to it.
#
# Format: TransferLog <path/file>
#
# TransferLog logs/access.log
```

Purpose.   The purpose of the TransferLog directive is to allow you to specify where the Personal Web Server will record all client accesses, or visits, to your web site. The Personal Web Server provides this log in a format known as Common Log Format. This format is used by most web server applications, including those from both NCSA and CERN.

Syntax.

```
TransferLog File
```

The variable *File* represents the name of the file where the Personal Web Server will log all transfers and accesses. This variable can be either a full path name or a partial path name relative to the ServerRoot. Only one TransferLog directive is allowed in any Server Configuration file.

Default.   If you don't specify a TransferLog directive, the Personal Web Server will assume

```
TransferLog logs/access_log
```

You'll notice that in both the example configuration file in Listing 3-1 and in your personal installation configuration file, the TransferLog directive is commented out, thereby accepting the default.

Examples.

```
TransferLog /temp/waccess.log
```

This directive would log all accesses to your web in the **waccess.log** file in the **\temp** subdirectory relative to your ServerRoot.

```
TransferLog NUL:
```

This directive turns off access logging. We don't recommend you do this. Should your server experience problems, you'll need this access log file to help you determine what went wrong and how it can be corrected.

ServerName

The next directive in the Server Configuration file is the ServerName directive. In the Server Configuration file, this section reads

```
# ServerName allows you to set a host name which is sent back ⊃
to clients for
# your server if it's different than the one the program would ⊃
get (i.e. use
# "www" instead of the host's real name). Make sure your DNS ⊃
is set up to
# alias the name to your system!
#
# Format: ServerName <domain name>
#
# no default
```

Purpose.

The ServerName directive tells the Personal Web Server what name it should send back to users when it creates redirection URLs. You'll need to use this directive if *gethostbyname* does not work on your local host, or if the hostname returned should be a Domain Name System (DNS) alias. The name for your server must be a valid DNS-recognized name.

Syntax.

```
ServerName FULLNAME
```

The variable *FULLNAME* represents the full hostname and domain name that you want returned as the server address. Only one ServerName directive can be included in a given Server Configuration file.

Default.

There is no default. If there is no ServerName specified, the Personal Web Server will find it by using system calls.

Examples.

```
ServerName www.VREvolution.com
```

This sets the server's hostname as www.VREvolution.com, instead of vrevolution.pitton.com, as is returned using the gethostbyname system call.

ShellWinCmdTempl

The final directive in the Server Configuration file is the ShellWinCmdTempl directive. The final lines in the example Server Configuration file in Listing 3-1 read

```
# Command line template for CGI WinExec
# Uncomment next line for shorter form of command line
ShellWinCmdTempl ~p ~v ~a
```

Purpose.   This directive specifies a special formatting string that controls the composition of the command line used in the Personal Web Server's call to WinExec() to start up a script execution. Basically, what that means is that it controls how the command line that's sent by the Personal Web Server to WinExec() to start a CGI script execution environment will look.

Syntax.

```
ShellWinCmdTempl format-string
```

The variable *format-string* represents a template for the WinExec() command line. This variable can consist of anything that would be legal inside a Windows command line, plus certain special sequences that allow for specific substitutions. Those special sequences are shown in Table 3-1.

Table 3-1   Sequences That Allow for Specific Substitutions

Variable	Description
~s	This variable represents the executable file that is to be run, as specified by ShellExec.
~x	This variable represents the shell exec option or options that are specified by ShellExecOption or ShellExecOptionDeb (if script tracing is active).
~p	Here, the variable represents the tempfile that contains the shell startup jacket procedure. This defines the environmental variables that will start the actual script.
~l	Represents the tempfile containing the POST content, if there is any, that was supplied by the client.
~o	This variable represents the tempfile where the Personal Web Server expects to find the output of the executed script.

Remember that only one ShellWinCmdTempl directive is allowed in any given Server Configuration file.

Default. If there is no ShellWinCmdTempl specified in the Server Configuration file, the FrontPage Personal Web Server will assume

```
ShellWinCmdTempl ~s ~x ~p ~o
```

Examples.

```
ShellWinCmdTempl ~s ~x ~p -i ~i -o ~o
```

This example represents a hypothetical shell that would use -i and -o for input and output files instead of command line redirection.

Now that we've looked at the directives that are required to be present, in some manner, in the Server Configuration file, we will look at other optional directives that you might need to include.

Optional directives for the Server Configuration file

The following are some of the directives that the Personal Web Server's Server Configuration file recognizes. These directives are listed in alphabetical order. These directives are allowed in the configuration file, but are not explicit or required.

AccessConfig

Purpose. The AccessConfig directive tells the FrontPage Personal Web Server where it can find the Global Access Configuration file (ACF). By default, the Global ACF is a file found in your server's \conf\ subdirectory. This file controls access to any and all files within your document tree. The Personal Web Server requires that there be a Global ACF or the server will not work.

Syntax.

```
AccessConfig      filename
```

The variable *filename* represents the name of the Global ACF. This variable can be written either as a full path name, or as a partial path name relative to ServerRoot.

Default. If no AccessConfig is specified in the Server Configuration file, then the Personal Web Server assumes

```
AccessConfig        conf/access.cnf
```

In our example Server Configuration file provided in Listing 3-1, no AccessConfig directive was specified. The result is that the FrontPage Personal Web Server looks for the access configuration in the file

```
conf\access.cnf
```

as located under the ServerRoot directive.

Examples.

```
AccessConfig        conf/access-global
```

In this example, the Personal Web Server would look for the access configuration in the file access-global that it would find in the **\conf** subdirectory, as specified under the ServerRoot directive.

```
AccessConfig        httpd/admin/access
```

In this example, the Personal Web Server will look for the access configuration in the file **access**. This file will be found in the **\admin** subdirectory under the **\httpd** subdirectory.

ResourceConfig

Purpose. This directive tells the FrontPage Personal Web Server where it will find the Resource Configuration file.

Syntax.

```
ResourceConfig    Filename
```

The variable *Filename* is the name given to the Resource Configuration file. This can either be a full path name or a partial path name relative to the ServerRoot.

Only one ResourceConfig directive can be present in any given Server Configuration file.

Default. If no ResourceConfig directive is found in the Server Configuration file, the FrontPage Personal Web Server assumes

```
ResourceConfig    conf/srm.cnf
```

In our example Server Configuration file provided in Listing 3-1, no ResourceConfig directive was specified. The result is that the FrontPage Personal Web server looks for the resource configuration in the file

```
conf\srm.cnf
```

This file is located under the ServerRoot directive.

Examples.

```
ResourceConfig    conf/resources
```

In this example, the Personal Web Server would look for a Resource Configuration file named resources in the **\conf** subdirectory as specified in the ServerRoot directive.

```
ResourceConfig    httpd/admin/resources
```

In this example, the Personal Web Server would look for a Resource Configuration file named **resources** in the **\admin** subdirectory under the **\httpd** subdirectory.

TypesConfig

Purpose. This directive tells the FrontPage Personal Web Server where it will find the typing configuration file. This file allows the Personal Web Server to map the various filename extensions of MIME types to their various HTTP/1.0 clients.

 You shouldn't need to edit this file at all. It is highly recommended that you use the AddTypes directive instead.

Syntax.

```
TypesConfig        Filename
```

The variable *Filename* represents the name of the types configuration file. This can be represented either as a full path name or as a partial path name relative to ServerRoot.

Only one TypesConfig directive can be present in any given Server Configuration file.

Default.   If no TypesConfig directive is specified in the Server Configuration file, the FrontPage Personal Web Server assumes

```
TypesConfig        conf/mime.typ
```

Examples.

```
TypesConfig        conf/mine-types
```

In the above example, the FrontPage Personal Web Server will look for a types configuration file named **mime-types** in the **\conf** subdirectory under the ServerRoot directive.

```
TypesConfig        httpd/admin/types-local
```

In this example, the Personal Web Server will look for a types configuration file named **types-local** under the **\admin** subdirectory under the **\httpd** subdirectory.

Now that you've seen the various directives that are used in the Server Configuration file with the FrontPage Personal Web Server, we'll turn to the Access Configuration file and the various directives that are used in this instance.

Access Configuration with the Personal Web Server

Before we get into detail with the **access.cnf** file, we need to look at the methods that the FrontPage Personal Web Server allows you to use to control certain aspects of the directories in which you are placing your webs. These aspects include the various security features that will allow you to restrict access to some or all of your web site. All of these methods are available through access and through server features.

The first method is that of global access. Here, you can allow or restrict access to certain directories, thereby admitting or denying hosts and/or users to those directories. This is accomplished with the Global Access Configuration File (ACF). The ACF is a file found in your server's **\conf** subdirectory. This file is specified by the Server Configuration directive AccessConfig. The file controls access to any and all files within your document tree. The Personal Web Server requires that there be a Global ACF or the server will not work.

The second method is through various server features controlling per-directory access. You can make certain directories more secure by disabling some server functions to those specific directories. This is possible by creating per-directory Access Configuration files. Within the various subdirectories are files that are specified by the AccessFileName directive in the Resource Configuration file. These files are normally called **#haccess.ctl**. These files control the access to the subdirectory that they are in, as well as any subdirectories under this subdirectory. These per-directory ACFs are completely optional. You can even restrict their use or, if you want, completely forbid their use under the Global ACF.

Now that you have a general understanding of how the FrontPage Personal Web Server grants and restricts access, you need to examine the contents of the Access Configuration File. Listing 3-2 provides the default listing for **access.cnf** as installed by the FrontPage installation process using the default settings.

Listing 3-2: access.cnf

```
#-----------------------------------------
#
#   ACCESS.CNF
#
# Global access configuration for the FrontPage Personal Web ⊃
Server
#
# This is the server global access configuration file. It is ⊃
best to
# leave the directives in this file in the order they are in, or
# things may not go the way you'd like.
#
# Do NOT simply read the instructions in here without ⊃
understanding
# what they do, if you are unsure consult the online docs.
#
# Server configuration commands are similar to those for the NCSA
# server version 1.3R.  If you have questions please see the ⊃
online
# documentation at http://hoohoo.ncsa.uiuc.edu
#
#-----------------------------------------
#
# The following access configuration establishes unrestricted access
# to the server's document tree. There is no default access config, so
# _something_ must be present and correct for the server to ⊃
operate.
```

```
#
# This should be changed to whatever you set ServerRoot to.
#
<Directory c:/frontpage\ webs/server>
Options Indexes
</Directory>

### This should be changed to whatever you set DocumentRoot to.
#
#
#<Directory c:/frontpage\ webs/content/>
### This may also be "None", "All", or "Indexes"
#
#Options Indexes
#
### This controls which options the #HACCESS.CTL files in ↵
directories can
### override. Can also be "None", or any combination of ↵
"Options", "FileInfo",
### "AuthConfig", and "Limit"
#
#AllowOverride All
#
### Controls who can get stuff from this server.
#
#<Limit GET>
#order allow,deny
#allow from all
#</Limit>
#
#</Directory>

# You may place any other directories you wish to have access
# information for after this one.
```

As the configuration file itself suggests, it is best to leave the various configuration commands in the order that they are presented in the configuration file. We recommend that you follow this commandment exactly. We also suggest that you not make random modifications until you are sure of what you want to do. We'll examine **access.cnf** in detail.

Look carefully at Listing 3-2. You'll discover that everything is commented out, and therefore ignored, except for the following.

```
<Directory c:/frontpage\ webs/server>
Options Indexes
</Directory>
```

The only directive present in the example Access Configuration file is the Directory directive.

Required directives in the Access Configuration file

There are two directives that are required in the Access Configuration file. These two are Directory and Options. You will find default settings for them in Listing 3-2.

Directory

Purpose. This directive is a sectioning directive. A sectioning directive is an access control directive that requires that specific information apply to all directives within that section. These directives are formatted very much like HTML tags.

The Directory directive controls which directory the access control directives apply to. The Directory directive only applies to the Global ACF. All directives in the Global ACF, therefore, have to be contained in the Directory section.

Syntax. Since sectioning directives are formatted in the same manner as HTML tags, they have opening and closing versions. The opening directive would be

```
<Directory directory>
```

The variable *directory* is the absolute path name for the directory that you're protecting. The closing directive would be

```
</Directory>
```

Examples.

```
<Directory /httpd/cosmos>
```

```
Options None
</Directory>
```

The Options directive contained within the above Directory section will only apply to the server directory **\httpd\cosmos**.

In our example Access Configuration file, the Directory section contains

```
<Directory c:/frontpage\ webs/server>
Options Indexes
</Directory>
```

The directive contained within this Directory section, Options and its parameter Indexes, applies only to the server directory **\webs\server** as defined by the ServerRoot directory.

Options

Purpose. This directive controls which server features are available within a given subdirectory. The Options directive applies to both the Global ACF and any per-directory ACFs that you may require.

Syntax.

```
Options opt1 opt2 ... optx
```

The variables *opt1* through *optx* can represent one of the following:

➥ None, where no features are enabled for this specific subdirectory.

➥ All, where all features are enabled for this specific subdirectory.

➥ Indexes, where the server allows users to request indexes in this specific subdirectory. If you disable this option, you are only disabling the server-generated indexes. This doesn't prevent the server from sending a precompiled index file that you might have located within this subdirectory. The name of this precompiled index file will depend on the DirectoryIndex directive.

Default. If no Options are given for a specific subdirectory or any of the parent directories, the FrontPage Personal Web Server will assume

```
Options All
```

Examples.

```
Options Indexes
```

In this example, as in our example Access Configuration file in Listing 3-2, the server will allow users to index the specified subdirectory.

Optional directives used in the Access Configuration file

The following alphabetical list of directives includes some of those that the Personal Web Server Access Configuration file recognizes. These directives are some of the more useful optional directives that you might wish to use in the Access Configuration file.

AddDescription

Purpose.   The AddDescription directive tells the FrontPage Personal Web Server how to describe a file or a file type when the server is generating a directory index.

Syntax.

```
AddDescription   "text_field"   fileident
```

or

```
AddDescription   `text_field`   fileident
```

Here, the variable *fileident* is either a filename extension, such as .htm or .txt, a filename, or a full real path name to a file on your computer. The variable *text_field* must be surrounded by either quotes, as in the first example, or backtics (accent grave characters) and is a short description of the file. It is generally preferable for this description to be less than one line.

The backtic form is provided so that you can put hyperlinks into your descriptions if you want. You can use as many AddDescription directives as you like. This directive only applies to per-directory ACFs when used in Access Configuration files.

Default.   There are no default descriptions in the FrontPage Personal Web Server Access Configuration files.

Examples.

```
AddDescription     "Current Clients" Construction
```

In the Personal Web Server index of Construction's directory a line is included that reads

```
Construction: Current Clients (12000 bytes)
```

AddIcon

Purpose. The purpose of the AddIcon directive is to tell the FrontPage Personal Web Server what kind of icon it needs to show for a specific type of file in any given directory index.

Syntax.

```
AddIcon icon     name1   name2   ...
```

Here, the variable *icon* represents a virtual path to an image file that should be shown for files that match a given pattern. This pattern is specified in the variables *namex*. The variables *namex* is either a file extension, such as .htm or .txt, a partial filename, or a complete physical path name. You can use as many AddIcon directives as you want in the Access Configuration files. This directive applies equally to both Global and per-directory ACFs.

Default. There are no default icons assumed by the FrontPage Personal Web Server.

Examples.

```
AddIcon /icons/image.xbm .gif .jpg .xbm
```

In this example, when the FrontPage Personal Web Server is indexing a specific directory and finds a file with the extension of **.gif**, **.jpg**, or **.xbm**, it will reference **\icons\image.xbm** as the image that needs to be shown next to the filename.

AddType

Purpose. The AddType directive allows you to add entries to the Personal Web Server's default typing information without editing the typing configuration file. This is the preferred method of adding types. The use of this directive will override any conflicting entries in the TypesConfig file.

Syntax.

```
AddType type/subtype        extension
```

Here, the variable *type/subtype* represents the MIME type for the document. The variable *extension* represents the filename extension to map to this particular type. This can either be a filename extension, a full path name, or a filename.

You can use as many AddType directives as you want. This directive applies to both Global and per-directory ACFs.

Default.

The default types for the Personal Web Server are found in the Types Configuration file. We'll be discussing this file in more detail later in this chapter.

Example.

Here's an example which we recommend that you enter:

```
AddType x-world/x-vrml    wrl
```

Adding this to your Access Configuration file will allow your server to serve Virtual Reality Modeling Language (VRML) worlds to your users over the World Wide Web.

Allow

Purpose.

This directive determines which hosts can have access to any given directory with a specific access method. The Allow directive is only available inside the Limit directive. We discuss that directive later in this section.

Syntax.

```
allow from host1 host2    ...        hostx
```

The variables *hostx* represent one of the following:

- ➡ A domain name such as .AOL.com; host names must end in this to be allowed

- ➡ A full host name

- ➡ An IP address of a host

> ➡ A partial IP address including the first 1 to 3 bytes of an IP address for subnet restriction

> ➡ The keyword *all*, where all means that all hosts will be allowed

Default. There are no defaults for this directive in the Personal Web Server.

Examples.

```
<Limit /webs/content>
order allow,deny
allow from all
deny from .AOL.com
</Limit>
```

In this example the FrontPage Personal Web Server evaluates the Allow directive first. In this directive, all hosts are allowed access to **\webs\content**. The Personal Web Server then evaluates the Deny directive and denies those clients from `.AOL.com`.

AllowOverride

Purpose. The AllowOverride directive controls and specifies which access control directives can be overruled by any per-directory ACF that you might put in place. You can place this particular directive only in the Global ACF.

Syntax.

```
AllowOverride    or1    or2    ...    orx
```

Here the variables *or1* through *orx* represent one of the following:

> ➡ **All.** There is no restriction on the use of per-directory ACFs in this directory.

> ➡ **AuthConfig** allows the use of the AuthName, AuthType, AuthUserFile, and AuthGroupFile directives in this directory.

> ➡ **FileInfo** allows the use of the AddType directive in this directory.

> ➡ **Limit** allows the use of the Limit sectioning directive in this directory.

> ➡ **None.** No per-directory ACFs are allowed in this directory.

> ➡ **Options** allows the use of the Options directive in this directory.

Default. If there is no AllowOverride directive present for any given subdirectory or directory, the FrontPage Personal Web Server assumes

```
AllowOverride    All
```

Example.

```
AllowOverride    Limit  Options
```

In this example, any per-directory ACFs in this directory will only be allowed to use the Limit sectioning directive and the Options directive.

AuthGroupFile

Purpose. The AuthGroupFile directive determines the file that contains the list of user groups which are checked during user authentication. This directive applies to both Global and per-directory ACFs. You must use this directive in the company of AuthName, AuthType, and AuthUserFile directives. If you don't use these four directives together, user authentication will not work properly.

Syntax.

```
AuthGroupFile    path
```

The variable *path* represents the absolute path of the group file to be used in a specific subdirectory or directory.

Default. There is no default for AuthGroupFile in the Personal Web Server.

Examples.

```
AuthGroupFile    c:/httpd/conf/htgroup.ctl
```

This example sets the authorization group file for this specific directory to **c:\httpd\conf\htgroup.ctl**.

AuthName

Purpose. The AuthName Directive is used to set the name of the authorization realm for a particular directory. The realm is the name sent by the server to users that tells the users what user name and password the user needs to send in order to enter this directory on the server.

This directive applies to both Global and per-directory ACFs. This directive must be used in conjunction with AuthType, AuthUserFile, and AuthGroupFile directives. If these files are not used in conjunction with one another, user authentication will not work properly.

Syntax.

```
AuthName    name
```

The variable *name* represents a short name describing the authorization realm. This variable can contain spaces.

Default. There are no default AuthName directives in the Personal Web Server.

Example.

```
AuthName  VRE
```

This example sets the authorization name of a specific subdirectory to VRE.

AuthType

Purpose. The AuthType directive is used to set the type of authorization needed for access to a specific subdirectory. This directive applies to both Global and per-directory ACFs. It must be used in conjunction with AuthName, AuthUserFile, and AuthGroupFile directives for user authentication to work correctly.

Syntax.

```
AuthType  type
```

Here, the variable *type* represents the authentication type to be used in a specific subdirectory. The only authentication type currently implemented is Basic.

Default. There is no default AuthType in the Personal Web Server.

Examples.

```
AuthType  Basic
```

This example sets the authorization type for a specific subdirectory to Basic.

AuthUserFile

Purpose.   The purpose of the AuthUserFile directive is to set the file that will be used to list users and passwords for user authentication. This directive applies both to Global and to per-directory ACFs. This directive must be used in conjunction with AuthName, AuthType, and AuthGroupFile directives in order for user authentication to work properly.

Syntax.

```
AuthUserFile     path
```

The variable *path* in this example represents the absolute path of a user file created with the htpasswd program.

Default.   There is no default AuthUserFile in the FrontPage Personal Web Server.

Examples.

```
AuthUserFile     c:/httpd/conf/htpasswd.ctl
```

This example sets the authorization user file for a specific directory to **c:\httpd\conf\htpasswd.ctl**.

DefaultIcon

Purpose.   The DefaultIcon directive specifies what icon is to be used in automatically generated directory listings where no icon information is present.

Syntax.

```
DefaultIcon     location
```

The variable *location* is the virtual path to the icon on the Personal Web Server.

Note that only one DefaultIcon directive should ever appear in the Access Configuration file.

Default.   If there is no DefaultIcon directive present in the Access Configuration file, the Personal Web Server doesn't assume anything.

Examples.

```
DefaultIcon     /icons/unknown.xbm
```

This example causes a file with no icon to be shown with the icon located at **\icons\unknown.xbm** in any automatically generated directories.

Deny

Purpose. The Deny directive is used to determine which hosts are given access to specific subdirectories with a specific method. This directive is only available within the confines of the Limit directive's sections.

Syntax.

```
deny from host1  host2  ...      hostx
```

The variables *hostx* represent one of the following:

➥ A domain name such as .pitton.com. This must include the leading dot.

➥ A fully qualified host name.

➥ A full IP address of a host.

➥ A keyword such as *all.* If you use the keyword *all,* all hosts will be denied

Default. There are no defaults for Deny in the Personal Web Server.

Examples.

```
<Limit /web/content>
order   deny,allow
deny from all
allow from .pitton.com
</Limit>
```

In this example the Personal Web Server will evaluate the Deny directive first for the **\web\content** subdirectory. Consequently, everyone is denied access to **\web\content**. The Personal Web Server then evaluates the Allow directive. As a result of this evaluation, the server will then allow clients from .pitton.com access to this subdirectory.

IndexIgnore

Purpose. The IndexIgnore directive tells the FrontPage Personal Web Server which files it should ignore when generating an index of a specific directory.

Syntax.

```
IndexIgnore        ext1 ext2 …
```

Here, the variables *extx* are file extensions or filenames which should be ignored when generating a directory. When the Personal Web Server looks in a specific directory it tries to match each of the strings represented by this variable to the right-hand side of the entry's string. If it matches, the server ignores that entry in this specific directory index.

Default.   The only entry ignored by default is '.'.

Examples.

```
IndexIgnore README README.HTML .htaccess # ~
```

In this example, the FrontPage Personal Web Server will ignore all files named **README**, **README.HTML**, and any **.htaccess** files when indexing a specific directory. The server will also ignore emacs autosave files and emacs backup files.

Limit

Purpose.   The Limit directive is another sectioning directive. It controls which clients can access a given subdirectory. It applies to both Global and per-directory ACFs.

Syntax.   The syntax for the opening of the Limit directive would read

```
<Limit method1 method2 … methodx
```

Here the variables *methodx* represent one of the following:

➡ GET allows clients to retrieve documents and execute scripts.

➡ PUT is not implemented in the FrontPage Personal Web Server. This command allows for the placing of documents or files onto the server.

➡ POST allows clients to submit data using Mosaic forms and any other POST-based operations.

The syntax for the closing of the Limit directive would read

```
</Limit>
```

Only four directives are allowed inside Limit sections. Those four directives are Order, Deny, Allow, and Require.

Examples.

```
<Limit GET>
order deny, allow
deny from all
allow from .bargle.com
require group chuckers
</Limit>
```

In this example, the only clients allowed to use the GET method in this specific subdirectory must be from .bargle.com. They must also authenticate to the chuckers group.

Order

Purpose. This directive affects the order in which the Deny and Allow directives are evaluated within the Limit section. This directive is only available within Limit sections.

Syntax.

```
order   array
```

The variable *array* should be one of the following

➡ Deny,allow. In this case, the Deny directive will be evaluated before the Allow directive.

➡ Allow,deny. Here the Allow directive will be evaluated before the Deny directive.

Default. In the event that no Order directive is listed, the Personal Web Server assumes

```
order   deny,allow
```

Example.

```
<Limit /webs/content>
order deny,allow
deny from all
allow from .pitton.com
</Limit>
```

In this example, the Personal Web Server will evaluate the Deny directive first. As a result, no one will be allowed access to **webs****content**\. The Personal Web Server then evaluates the Allow directive. In response to this evaluation, the Personal Web Server determines whether to allow clients from .pitton.com access to the **webs****content**\ subdirectory.

ReadmeName

Purpose.

This directive determines what file the Personal Web Server will look for when indexing a subdirectory. This file is used to add a paragraph to the end of the index that is generated automatically. This paragraph gives a general description of what's in the specific subdirectory.

The ReadmeName directive applies to both Global and per-directory ACFs.

Syntax.

```
ReadmeName          name
```

The variable *name* is the name of the file the Personal Web Server is to look for when it is trying to find the description file. The Personal Web Server will first look for *name.htm*. If it finds this file, it will display the HTML inlined with its own index. If it finds just *name*, then this file will be included as plain text.

Only one ReadmeName directive can appear in any given Access Configuration file.

Default.

If there is no ReadmeName directive present, the FrontPage Personal Web Server assumes nothing.

Examples.

```
ReadmeName          README
```

In this example, when the FrontPage Personal Web Server begins to generate an index for any specified subdirectory, it will look for **README.htm** in that subdirectory first and will insert this file, if it is found. If it isn't found, the Personal Web Server will then look through the subdirectory again for a file named **README**. If this file is found it will be inserted. If neither of these is found, nothing will be inserted.

Require

Purpose. The Require directive affects which authenticated clients can access a specified subdirectory with a given method. This directive is only available within Limit sections.

Syntax.

```
Require entity en1 en2 ... enx
```

The variables *enx* are entity names, separated by spaces.

The variable *entity* represents one of the following:

➡ **User.** Only named users can access this specified subdirectory with the given methods.

➡ **Group.** Only users in the named groups can access this specified subdirectory with the given methods.

➡ **Valid-user.** All users defined in the AuthUserFile are allowed access to the specified subdirectory upon providing a valid password.

Default. No default applies for the Require directive in the FrontPage Personal Web Server.

Examples.

```
<Limit GET PUT>
order deny,allow
deny from all
allow from .pitton.com
require user Summitt
require group VRE
</Limit>
```

In this example the Personal Web Server will evaluate the Deny directive first for the specified subdirectory. As a result, everyone is denied access to this subdirectory. The Personal Web Server then evaluates the Allow directive and allows clients from .pitton.com. Through user authentication in this example, the Personal Web Server now only allows those users who are named Summitt or are in the group VRE.

Resource Configuration with the Personal Web Server

You've now looked at the various directives that are used in both the server and the Access Configuration files with the FrontPage Personal Web Server. The third and last configuration file you should learn about is the Resource Configuration file and the various directives that are used with it.

When you installed FrontPage and the Personal Web Server, a subdirectory called **\conf** was created where the various configuration files were installed. Using the Windows Explorer, open this subdirectory now and take a look at the contents.

Down near the bottom of this subdirectory should be two files, **srm.cnf** and **srm.org**. The **.org** file is the template for the Resource Configuration file; you shouldn't edit this file. Instead, use it only for reference.

If you open **srm.cnf** you will see something similar to Listing 3-3.

Listing 3-3:   SMR.CNF - Server Resource Configuration file for the FrontPage Personal Web Server

```
# -FrontPage- version=1.1
#--------------------------------------------------
#
#   SRM.CNF
#
# Server resource configuration for the FrontPage Personal Web ⊃
Server
#
# The settings in this file control the document layout and ⊃
name specs
# that your server makes visible to users. The values in the ⊃
comments
# are the defaults built into the server.
#
# Server configuration commands are similar to those for the NCSA
# server version 1.3R.  If you have questions please see the ⊃
online
# documentation at http://hoohoo.ncsa.uiuc.edu
#
# NOTE: path defaults are relative to the server's installation
```

```
#       directory (ServerRoot). Paths should be given in Unix
#       format (using '/').
#
#———————————————————————————————————
#
# DocumentRoot: The directory out of which you will serve your
# documents. By default, all requests are taken from this ↵
directory, but
# aliases may be used to point to other locations.
#

DocumentRoot c:/frontpage\ webs/content
# DirectoryIndex: Name of the file to use as a pre-written HTML
# directory index. This document, if present, will be opened ↵
when the
# server receives a request containing a URL for the ↵
directory,  instead
# of generating a directory index.
#
# DirectoryIndex index.htm

# AccessFileName: The name of the file to look for in each ↵
directory
# for access control information. This file should have a name ↵
which is
# blocked from appearing in server-generated indexes!
#
# AccessFileName #haccess.ctl

# ==========================
# Aliasing and Redirection
# ==========================
#
# Redirect allows you to tell clients about documents which ↵
used to exist in
# your server's namespace, but do not anymore. This allows ↵
you to tell the
# clients where to look for the relocated document.

#
# Format: Redirect fakename url
#
```

(continued)

Listing 3-3 *(continued)*

```
# Aliases: Add here as many aliases as you need, up to 20. One useful
# alias to have is one for the path to the icons used for the server-
# generated directory indexes. The paths given below in the AddIcon
# statements are relative.
#
# Format: Alias fakename realname
#


# ScriptAlias: This controls which directories contain DOS server
#              scripts.
#
# Format: ScriptAlias fakename realname
#

#ScriptAlias /cgi-dos/ c:/frontpage\ webs/content/cgi-dos/
# WinScriptAlias: This controls which directories contain Windows
#                 server scripts.
#
# Format: WinScriptAlias fakename realname
#

#WinScriptAlias /cgi-win/  c:/frontpage\ webs/content/cgi-win/
# ===========================
# MIME Content Type Control
# ===========================
#
# DefaultType is the default MIME type for documents which the ⊃
server
# cannot find the type of from filename extensions.
#
# DefaultType text/html
DefaultType text/plain

# AddType allows you to tweak MIME.TYP without actually ⊃
editing it, or to
# make certain files to be certain types.
#
# Format: AddType type/subtype ext1
#

# ReadmeName is the name of the README file the server will look for by
# default.  The server will first look for name.htm, include it
```

```
if found,
# and it will then look for name.txt and include it as ⊃
plaintext if found.
# NOTE: Do not include an explicit extension, it is an error.
#
# Format: ReadmeName name
#
ReadmeName #readme


# ============================
# AUTOMATIC DIRECTORY INDEXING
# ============================
#
# The server generates a directory index if there is no file ⊃
in the
# directory whose name matches DirectoryIndex.
#
# FancyIndexing: Whether you want fancy directory indexing or ⊃
standard
#
# FancyIndexing on

# IconsAreLinks: Whether the icons in a fancy index are links as
# well as the file names.
#
# IconsAreLinks off

# AddIcon tells the server which icon to show for different ⊃
files or filename
# extensions. In preparation for the upcoming Chicago version, ⊃
you should
# include explicit 3 character truncations for 4-character ⊃
endings. Don't
# rely on the DOS underpinnings to silently truncate for you.
#
AddIcon /icons/text.gif      .html    .htm    .txt    .ini
AddIcon /icons/image.gif     .gif     .jpg    .jpe    .jpeg   ⊃
.xbm    .tiff   .tif    .pic    .pict    .bmp
AddIcon /icons/sound.gif     .au      .wav    .snd
AddIcon /icons/movie.gif     .mpg     .mpe    .mpeg

AddIcon /icons/binary.gif  .bin  .exe  .bat  .dll
AddIcon /icons/back.gif    ..
AddIcon /icons/menu.gif      ^^DIRECTORY^^              (continued)
```

Listing 3-3 *(continued)*

```
AddIcon /icons/dblank.gif        ^^BLANKICON^^


# DefaultIcon is which icon to show for files which do not have ↩
an icon
# explicitly set.
#
DefaultIcon /icons/unknown.gif


# AddDescription allows you to place a short description after a ↩
file in
# server-generated indexes. A better place for these are in
inidividual
# "#haccess.ctl" files in individual directories.
#
# Format: AddDescription "description" filename
#


# IndexIgnore is a set of filenames which directory indexing ↩
should ignore
# Here, I've disabled display of our readme and access control ↩
files,
# plus anything that starts with a "~", which I use for ↩
annotation HTML
# documents. I also have disabled some common editor backup ↩
file names.
# Match is on file NAME.EXT only, and the usual * and ? ↩
meta-chars apply.
#
# WARNING: Be sure to set an ignore for your access control ↩
file(s)!!
#
# Format: IndexIgnore name1 name2...
#
IndexIgnore  ~* *.bak *.{* #readme.htm #haccess.ctl


#


## END ##
Alias /icons/ c:/frontpage\ webs/server/icons/
WinScriptAlias /cgi-bin/imagemap/ c:/frontpage\ webs/content/ ↩
cgi-bin/imagemap.exe/
WinScriptAlias /cgi-bin/htimage/ c:/frontpage\ webs/content/ ↩
```

```
cgi-bin/htimage.exe/
WinScriptAlias /_vti_bin/_vti_adm/ c:/frontpage\ webs/content/ ⏎
_vti_bin/_vti_adm/
WinScriptAlias /_vti_bin/_vti_aut/ c:/frontpage\ webs/content/ ⏎
_vti_bin/_vti_aut/
WinScriptAlias /_vti_bin/ c:/frontpage\ webs/content/_vti_bin/ ⏎
WinScriptAlias /cgi-bin/ c:/frontpage\ webs/content/cgi-bin/
```

We'll now examine the Resource Configuration file in detail. First we look at the directives that are explicitly used in the FrontPage Personal Web Server example configuration file. After that, we'll examine other directives that are recognized by the configuration file. In some cases, we will be discussing directives that have already been previously discussed in relation to the other configuration files. Rather than make you turn back and look up these directives in the previous parts of this chapter, the directive will be discussed again. Any modifications to the directive for use in this configuration file will be pointed out.

Directives used explicitly in the Personal Web Server configuration file

The first directive you come across in Listing 3-3 that is not commented out is DocumentRoot.

DocumentRoot

Purpose.   The DocumentRoot directive tells the Personal Web Server where it will find the subdirectory that contains the files it should serve to the Internet. If you need to access server files that reside outside of this subdirectory structure, you can use the Alias directive which is discussed in this chapter, or you can create symbolic links. This is a very important directive because it affects how you access files on your server.

Syntax.

```
DocumentRoot      dir
```

The variable *dir* is the absolute path of the directory from which you want documents to be served. Only one DocumentRoot directive is allowed in any given configuration file.

Default. If no DocumentRoot directive is specified in any configuration file, the FrontPage Personal Web Server assumes

```
DocumentRoot /usr/local/etc/httpd/htdocs
```

Examples.

```
DocumentRoot  /home/web
```

In this example, the DocumentRoot is set to the subdirectory **\home\web**.

```
DocumentRoot c:/frontpage\ webs/content
```

In this example, taken from the Personal Web Server example Resource Configuration file in Listing 3-3, the DocumentRoot is set to the **\content** subdirectory of the FrontPage directory structure.

DefaultType

The next directive that is not commented out is the DefaultType directive.

Purpose. When the FrontPage Personal Web Server can't determine a file's type through normal methods, the software types it as defined in the DefaultType directive.

Syntax.

```
DefaultType      type/subtype
```

Here, the variable *type/subtype* represents the MIME-like type. Only one DefaultType directive should appear in any given configuration file.

Default. If no DefaultType directive is found in the configuration files, the Personal Web Server assumes

```
DefaultType      text/html
```

Examples.

```
DefaultType      application/octet-stream
```

In this example, when the FrontPage Personal Web Server encounters a file with an unknown extension, it returns that file as type application/octet-stream.

```
DefaultType text/plain
```

In this example, which is found in the FrontPage Personal Web Server example Resource Configuration file in Listing 3-3, when the server encounters a file with an unknown extension, it returns that file as type text/plain.

ReadmeName

The next directive encountered in the example Resource Configuration file is the ReadmeName directive. The ReadmeName directive was also recognized by the Access Configuration file. We'll look at it again here in the context of Resource Configuration.

Purpose.   This directive determines what file the Personal Web Server will look for when automatically generating an index for a subdirectory, to add a paragraph at the end. This paragraph is used to give a general description of what's in the specific subdirectory.

Syntax.

```
ReadmeName        name
```

Here, the variable *name* is the name of the file the Personal Web Server is to look for when it is trying to locate the description file. The Personal Web Server will first look for *name.htm*. If it finds this file, it will display the HTML inlined with its own index. If it finds just *name*, then this file will be included as plain text.

Only one ReadmeName directive can appear in any given configuration file.

Default.   If there is no ReadmeName directive present, the FrontPage Personal Web Server assumes nothing.

Examples.

```
ReadmeName        README
```

In this example, when the FrontPage Personal Web Server begins to generate an index for any specified subdirectory it will look for **README.htm** in that subdirectory first. It will insert this file if it is found. If the file isn't found, the Personal Web Server will then look through the subdirectory again for a file named **README**. If this file is found it will be inserted. If neither is found, nothing will be inserted.

```
ReadmeName #readme
```

In this example, which is found in the FrontPage Personal Web Server example Resource Configuration file in Listing 3-3, when generating an index for a specific subdirectory, the server software will look for **#readme.htm** in that subdirectory first. If it finds this file, it will insert it into the current file. If **#readme.htm** is not found, the Personal Web Server will then look for **#readme**. If it finds this file, this file will be inserted into the current file. As in the previous example, if neither is found, nothing will be inserted.

AddIcon

The next directive that's not commented out in the example Resource Configuration file in Listing 3-3 is the AddIcon directive. This directive was also discussed in the Access Configuration section of this chapter.

Purpose.   The purpose of the AddIcon directive is to tell the FrontPage Personal Web Server what kind of icon it needs to show for a specific type of file in any given directory index.

Syntax.

```
AddIcon icon       name1    name2   ...
```

The variable *icon* represents a virtual path to an image file that is to be shown for files that match a given pattern, as specified in the variables *namex*. The variable *namex* is either a file extension, such as **.htm** or **.txt**, a partial filename, or a complete physical path name. You can use as many AddIcon directives as you want in any specific configuration file.

Default.   There are no default icons assumed by the FrontPage Personal Web Server.

Examples.

```
AddIcon /icons/image.xbm .gif .jpg .xbm
```

In this example, when the FrontPage Personal Web Server is indexing a specific directory and finds a file with the extension of **.gif**, **.jpg**, or **.xbm**, it will reference **\icons\image.xbm** as the image to be shown next to the filename.

```
AddIcon /icons/text.gif      .html    .htm    .txt     .ini
AddIcon /icons/image.gif     .gif     .jpg    .jpe    ⤴
.jpeg   .xbm    .tiff   .tif    .pic    .pict     .bmp
AddIcon /icons/sound.gif     .au      .wav    .snd
```

```
AddIcon /icons/movie.gif    .mpg    .mpe    .mpeg
AddIcon /icons/binary.gif  .bin  .exe  .bat  .dll
AddIcon /icons/back.gif     ..
AddIcon /icons/menu.gif     ^^DIRECTORY^^
AddIcon /icons/dblank.gif        ^^BLANKICON^^
```

In these examples, which are found in the FrontPage Personal Web Server example Resource Configuration file in Listing 3-3, all files with the extensions **.html**, **.htm**, **.txt**, and **.ini** are assigned the **text.gif** icon. All files with the extensions **.gif**, **.jpg**, **.jpe**, **.jpeg**, **.xbm**, **.tiff**, **.tif**, **.pic**, **.pict**, and **.bmp** are assigned the **image.gif** icon. All files with the extensions **.au**, **.wav**, and **.snd** are assigned the icon **sound.gif**. All files with the extensions **.mpg**, **.mpe**, and **.mpeg** are assigned the **movie.gif** icon. All files with the extensions **.bin**, **.exe**, **.bat**, and **.dll** are assigned the icon **binary.gif**. One directory up from the given subdirectory is assigned the icon **back.gif**. Any directories under the current directory are assigned the icon **menu.gif**. Finally, anything not specifically designated receives the **dblank.gif** icon.

DefaultIcon

The next uncommented directive in the example Resource Configuration file is the DefaultIcon directive. This directive was also discussed in the Access Configuration file section of this chapter.

Purpose.   The DefaultIcon directive specifies which icon is to be used in automatically generated directory listings where no icon information is present.

Syntax.

```
DefaultIcon      location
```

Here, the variable *location* is the virtual path to the icon on the Personal Web Server.

Note that only one DefaultIcon directive should ever appear in any given configuration file.

Default.   If there is no DefaultIcon directive present in the Resource Configuration file, the Personal Web Server doesn't assume anything.

Examples.

```
DefaultIcon      icons/unknown.xbm
```

This example causes a file with no icon to be shown with the icon located at **\icons\unknown.xbm** in any automatically generated directories.

```
DefaultIcon icons/unknown.gif
```

This example, which is taken from the FrontPage Personal Web Server example Resource Configuration file in Listing 3-3, causes a file with no icon to be shown with the icon located in the **\icons** subdirectory with the name **unknown.gif**.

IndexIgnore

The next uncommented directive in the example Resource Configuration file is the IndexIgnore directive. This directive also pertains to the Access Configuration file.

Purpose.   The IndexIgnore directive tells the FrontPage Personal Web Server which files to ignore when generating an index of a specific directory.

Syntax.

```
IndexIgnore        ext1 ext2 …
```

Here, the variables *extx* are file extensions or filenames which should be ignored when generating a directory. When the FrontPage Personal Web Server looks in a specific directory, the server tries to match each of the strings represented by this variable to the right-hand side of the entry's string. If it matches, the server ignores that entry in this specific directory index.

Default.   The only entry ignored by default is '.'.

Examples.

```
IndexIgnore README README.HTML .htaccess # ~
```

In this example, the FrontPage Personal Web Server will ignore all files named **README**, **README.HTML**, and any **.htaccess** files while indexing a specific directory. The server will also ignore emacs autosave files and emacs backup files.

```
IndexIgnore  ~* *.bak *.{* #readme.htm #haccess.ctl
```

In this example, which is taken from the FrontPage Personal Web Server example Resource Configuration file in Listing 3-3, all backup files, autosave files, **#readme.htm** files, and access control files are ignored when the software indexes a specific subdirectory.

Alias

The next uncommented directive in the Resource Configuration subdirectory is the Alias directive.

Purpose. This directive creates a virtual document or directory on your server. Any accesses to this virtual document or directory are satisfied by redirection to a different file or directory.

Syntax.

```
Alias   virtual path
```

The variable *virtual* is the translated location of the file or directory. The variable *path* is the full path name of the file or directory which should be used to fulfill the request. Several Alias directives can appear in any given configuration file.

Examples.

```
Alias   /images   /ftp/pub/images
```

This example would cause requests for /images to be satisfied from the directory **\ftp\pubs\images**. As a result, if someone requests /images/ paul.gif, the Personal Web Server would return **\ftp\pub\images\paul.gif**.

```
Alias /icons/ c:/frontpage\ webs/server/icons/
```

In this example, which is found in the FrontPage Personal Web Server example Resource Configuration file in Listing 3-3, any request for / icons/back.gif will be served from **webs\server\icons\back.gif**.

WinScriptAlias

The next uncommented directive in the example Resource Configuration file is the WinScriptAlias directive.

Purpose. This directive creates a virtual directory on your server. All accesses to this virtual directory will be satisfied by returning the output of a Windows CGI script in that directory.

Syntax.

```
WinScriptAlias    virtual path
```

The variable *virtual* represents the translated location of the script directory. The variable *path* is the full path name of the directory where the server scripts used to fulfill the requests can be found. Several WinScriptAlias directives may appear in any given configuration file.

Examples.

```
WinScriptAlias    /cgi-win c:/httpd/cgi-win
```

In this example, requests such as /cgi-win/guest.exe will be satisfied by running the Windows program **c:\httpd\cgi-win\guest.exe**.

```
WinScriptAlias /cgi-bin/imagemap/ c:/frontpage\ webs/ ⊃
content/cgi-bin/imagemap.exe/
WinScriptAlias /cgi-bin/htimage/ c:/frontpage\ webs/ ⊃
content/cgi-bin/htimage.exe/
WinScriptAlias /_vti_bin/_vti_adm/ c:/frontpage\ webs/ ⊃
content/_vti_bin/_vti_adm/
WinScriptAlias /_vti_bin/_vti_aut/ c:/frontpage\ webs/ ⊃
content/_vti_bin/_vti_aut/
WinScriptAlias /_vti_bin/ c:/frontpage\ webs/content/ ⊃
_vti_bin/
WinScriptAlias /cgi-bin/ c:/frontpage\ webs/content/ ⊃
cgi-bin/
```

In these examples, which are taken from the FrontPage Personal Web Server example Resource Configuration file in Listing 3-3, the various imagemap and special programs have been redirected to the location to be used in the FrontPage Personal Web Server.

Optional directives used in the Resource Configuration file

The following alphabetical list of directives includes some of those that the Personal Web Server's Resource Configuration file recognizes. Again, some of these directives may have been discussed previously in the chapter but are included here so that you can examine how their use with the Resource Configuration file may differ.

AccessFileName

Purpose. When the FrontPage Personal Web Server returns a document to a client, the server looks for access control files in the document directory as well as the parent directories. AccessFileName sets the name of the file that the Personal Web Server will look for to find the access control file. The default filename begins with # so as to make it easy to hide these files from directory indexes.

Syntax.

```
AccessFileName     file
```

Here, the variable *file* is a specific file name. Only one AccessFileName directive is allowed in any given configuration file.

Default. If no AccessFileName is specified in the configuration files, the Personal Web Server will assume

```
AccessFileName     #haccess.ctl
```

Examples.

```
AccessFileName     #acc.ctl
```

In this example, all access control files are set to **#acc.ctl**.

AddDescription

Purpose. The AddDescription directive tells the FrontPage Personal Web Server how to describe a file or a file type when the server is generating a directory index. This directive also pertains to the Access Configuration file.

Syntax.

```
AddDescription     "text_field"    fileident
```

or

```
AddDescription     `text_field`    fileident
```

Here, the variable *fileident* is either a filename extension, such as **.htm** or **.txt**, a filename, or a full, real path name to a file on your computer. The variable *text_field* must be surrounded by either quotes, as in the first example, or backtics (accent grave characters) and is a short description of the file. It is generally preferred that this description be less than one line.

The backtic form is provided so that you can put hyperlinks into your descriptions if you want to. You can use as many AddDescription directives as you wish.

Default.   There are no default descriptions in the FrontPage Personal Web Server Resource Configuration files.

Examples.

```
AddDescription     "Current Clients" Construction
```

If you were to look at the Personal Web Server's index of Construction's directory, you would see that the index includes a line reading

```
Construction: Current Clients (12000 bytes)
```

AddType

Purpose.   The AddType directive allows you to add entries to the Personal Web Server's default typing information without editing the typing configuration file. This is the preferred method of adding types. The use of this directive will override any conflicting entries in the TypesConfig file. This directive is also used with the Access Configuration file.

Syntax.

```
AddType type/subtype     extension
```

Here, the variable *type/subtype* represents the MIME-like type for the document. The variable *extension* represents the filename extension to map to this particular type. This can either be a filename extension, a full path name, or a filename.

You can use as many AddType directives as you want to.

Default.   The default types for the Personal Web Server are found in the types configuration file. We'll be discussing the types configuration file later in this chapter.

Example.   Here is an example that we recommend you enter:

```
AddType x-world/x-vrml    wrl
```

Adding this to your Access Configuration file allows your server to serve Virtual Reality Modeling Language (VRML) worlds to your users over the World Wide Web.

 If you wish to know more about VRML worlds, may we shamelessly plug our book, *Creating Cool 3D Web Worlds with VRML* (IDG Books Worldwide, Inc. 1995)?

DirectoryIndex

Purpose.
If a user requests a directory, the FrontPage Personal Web Server can return a pre-written index or it can generate one from the file system. The DirectoryIndex directive tells the Personal Web Server the name of the file the software should look for as a pre-written index for a specified subdirectory.

Syntax.

```
DirectoryIndex    file
```

Here, the variable *file* represents a specific filename. Only one DirectoryIndex directive can exist in any given configuration file.

Default.
If no DirectoryIndex directive is specified in any configuration file, the Personal Web Server will assume

```
DirectoryIndex    index.htm
```

Examples.

```
DirectoryIndex    .index.htm
```

In this example, the file that the Personal Web Server would search for as a pre-written index for a specific directory is .index.htm. A request for /dir would cause the Personal Web Server to look for the file DocumentRoot/dir/.index.htm. If this file is found, the Personal Web Server sends this file back to the client. Otherwise, the Personal Web Server creates and returns an index from the file system.

FancyIndexing

Purpose. This directive designates whether you want to use more detailed directory listings with icons and file sizes, or just standard directory indexing.

Syntax.

```
FancyIndexing    setting
```

The variable *setting* is either on or off. Only one FancyIndexing directive should appear in any configuration file.

Default. If no FancyIndexing directive is present in the configuration files, the FrontPage Personal Web Server assumes

```
FancyIndexing    on
```

Example.

```
FancyIndexing    off
```

In this example, FancyIndexing is turned off. As a result no icons or file sizes are used in directory indexing.

Redirect

Purpose. The Redirect directive creates a virtual document on your server that points to a different URL. Any accesses to the virtual document are therefore redirected to the new URL.

Syntax.

```
Redirect  virtual URL
```

The variable *virtual* is the translated location that should trigger the redirect. The variable *URL* is the URL of the new document. Several Redirect directives may appear in any given configuration file.

Examples.

```
Redirect /work   http://newserver.ourcompany.com/work
```

In this example all requests for /work would be redirected to the new location as specified by http://newserver.ourcompany.com/work.

You've now looked at the various directives that are used in the Resource Configuration file with the FrontPage Personal Web Server. We'll now examine the types configuration file.

Types Configuration with the Personal Web Server

When you installed FrontPage and the Personal Web Server, a subdirectory called **\conf** was created where the various configuration files were installed.

Near the bottom of this subdirectory should be a file named **mime.typ**. You should never edit this file. Instead, use it only for reference. We've already shown you ways to add types using the AddType directive. You may also remember that the TypesConfig directive tells the FrontPage Personal Web Server where to find this file.

If you open **mime.typ** using NotePad or WordPad you will see something similar to Listing 3-4.

**Listing 3-4:   MIME.TYP - Types Resource Configuration file
                      for the FrontPage Personal Web Server**

```
application/activemessage
application/andrew-inset
application/applefile
application/atomicmail
application/dca-rft
application/dec-dx
application/mac-binhex40
application/macwriteii
application/news-message-id
application/news-transmission
application/octet-stream        bin
application/oda                 oda
application/pdf                 pdf
application/postscript          ai eps ps
application/remote-printing
application/rtf                 rtf
application/slate
application/mif                 mif
application/wita
```

(continued)

Listing 3-4 (continued)

```
application/wordperfect5.1
application/x-csh              csh
application/x-dvi                 dvi
application/x-hdf                 hdf
application/x-latex              latex ltx
application/x-netcdf            nc cdf
application/x-sh                  sh
application/x-tcl                 tcl
application/x-tex                tex
application/x-texinfo           texinfo texi txi
application/x-troff              t tr roff
application/x-troff-man         man
application/x-troff-me     me
application/x-troff-ms     ms
application/x-wais-source       src
application/zip                  zip
application/x-bcpio             bcpio
application/x-cpio               cpio
application/x-gtar              gtar
application/x-shar             shar
application/x-sv4cpio           sv4cpio
application/x-sv4crc            sv4crc
application/tar                 tar
application/x-ustar            ustar
#
# Added for PC stuff
#
application/x-lzh               lzh
application/x-gzip             gz
#
audio/basic                    au snd
audio/x-aiff                   aif aiff aifc
audio/wav                      wav
image/gif                      gif
image/ief                      ief
image/jpeg                     jpeg jpg jpe
image/tiff                     tiff tif
image/x-cmu-raster            ras
image/x-portable-anymap       pnm
image/x-portable-bitmap       pbm
```

```
image/x-portable-graymap       pgm
image/x-portable-pixmap        ppm
image/x-rgb                    rgb
image/x-xbitmap                xbm
image/x-xpixmap                xpm
image/x-xwindowdump            xwd
message/external-body
message/news
message/partial
message/rfc822
multipart/alternative
multipart/appledouble
multipart/digest
multipart/mixed
multipart/parallel
text/html                      html htm
text/plain                     txt
text/richtext                  rtx
text/tab-separated-values      tsv
text/x-setext                  etx
video/mpeg                     mpeg mpg mpe
video/quicktime                qt mov
video/msvideo                  avi
video/x-sgi-movie              movie

# Microsoft types
application/msword             doc
application/ms-excel           xls
application/ms-powerpoint      ppt
application/ms-project         mpp
application/ms-works           wdb wks wps wcm
```

If you are exceptionally adventurous (and some might suggest, exceptionally foolhardy) you might want to add types to your server for local use directly into this file. We don't recommend it and know few who do. What we do recommend is that you use the AddTypes directive. Our reason for this recommendation is that an error in this file will bring down your server while an error in the AddTypes directive will simply prevent that type from being recognized.

However, for those who must know, the format of the types configuration file is as follows:

➡ Each line contains information for one http type and only one http type. Types resemble MIME types. If you must add new ones, use subtypes beginning with x-, as in application/x-myprogram.

➡ Remember that lines beginning with the # symbol are comment lines and are therefore ignored.

➡ Each line will consist of the following syntax:

```
type/subtype     ext1 ext2 … extx
```

The variable *type/subtype* is the MIME-like type of the specific document. The variables *extx* are any number of space-separated filename extensions that will be returned to the client when the file with the given extension is referenced.

Again, we recommend you use the AddType directive rather than modify this file.

The Windows CGI Interface

FrontPage WebBots, which we discuss in detail in Chapter 6, enable you to use most of the interactive programming features that most users want to add to their webs. However, sometimes you will need custom CGI scripts. FrontPage makes it easy to call a custom CGI script.

The FrontPage Personal Web Server takes advantage of the Windows CGI interface. It does this by including a reference implementation in Visual Basic which contains a re-usable module. This module creates the CGI environment within a given Visual Basic program. This implementation of CGI support operates under Windows 3.1 and later operating systems using the CGI.BAS module. It also works under Windows 95 and Windows NT using the CGI32.BAS module. This implementation results in a native Windows back-end.

Because Windows has no native command interpreter, any back-end must be an executable program. Microsoft's goal was to keep the interface simple and minimize any back-end programming. The result was that a file-based interface was chosen; request content is therefore placed in a content file and results are written to an output file.

The way to access a given CGI script is to lay out the form in the FrontPage Editor as you would any script. You can use text input fields, scrolling text boxes, check boxes, radio buttons, drop-down pick lists, and pushbuttons in this form. After you've completed the form you'll be given the opportunity to specify what action you want taken by that form. One of the possible actions is to invoke a custom CGI script on the server. All you have to do is provide the URL to that specific CGI script.

Moving On

In this chapter we have introduced you to the FrontPage Personal Web Server. This introduction has included a detailed look at

➡ The Server Configuration file

➡ The Access Configuration file

➡ The Resource Configuration file

In addition, you've reviewed some of the directives that are recognized by these files.

We also took a look at the types configuration file and provided an overview of the Windows CGI interface used by the FrontPage Personal Web Server.

In the next chapter you'll begin to see how you can use the FrontPage Editor and Explorer in the creation, control, and maintenance of your webs.

Learning to Use FrontPage

PART II

Getting to Know FrontPage

FrontPage is a web authoring tool that has been specifically designed to be easy to use. It's familiar interface allows even the non-programmer to build web sites without having to write a line of code. FrontPage provides access to its features through three simple components of the program: FrontPage Editor, FrontPage Explorer, and the To Do List. This chapter focuses on the first two, which are the components of the program used to create and edit your actual pages and create and set permissions for who can work on or access your web site. (You run into the To Do List, which helps you manage the activities of those creating and maintaining your site, in future chapters.)

So, just what do Explorer and Editor do? In a nutshell, you can think of Explorer as the component of the program that you use to create your web site and view the structure of your site: how pages are linked to other pages, and what individual pages make up your site. Editor, on the other hand, is very like a word processor for the web. It's here that you build the actual contents of your web pages.

Overview of the FrontPage Environment

When you select the Windows Start menu and find Microsoft FrontPage in the list of Programs loaded on your computer, you see a side menu like the one shown in Figure 4-1. The two choices in this menu which allow you to enter the FrontPage environment are the FrontPage Editor or FrontPage Explorer.

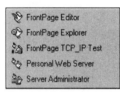

Figure 4-1: Enter FrontPage through either Explorer or Editor.

Although it doesn't matter which you choose — you can move between these two components quite easily after either one is opened — when you are just starting FrontPage for the first time, you are likely to select the Editor view so that you can begin to build your first page.

 Although earlier versions of the Vermeer FrontPage software, the FTP FrontPage software, and the Microsoft beta versions of FrontPage ran under earlier versions of Windows, FrontPage version 1.1 runs only under Windows 95 or Windows NT 3.51.

First look at FrontPage Editor

Editor is the feature you use to design and build web pages. The Editor view can be used for tasks such as

➡ Creating a new web page

➡ Entering and formatting text on your web page

➡ Establishing links between objects on your page and other web pages

➡ Inserting objects like tables, text boxes, check boxes, radio buttons, drop-down menus and push buttons on your web page

➡ Drawing objects on your page

You perform these tasks using the various tools and menu commands available to you.

Editor toolbars

When you open Editor you'll see a blank screen with menus and two rows of tool buttons across the top. Until you open a file, these tools are shaded in gray, but after a file is open in Editor, the tools will appear something like those shown in Figure 4-2. Note that some of these tools may or may not be available on your screen depending on what type of object you have selected on your page at the moment. For example, when you select an image, the drawing tools become available.

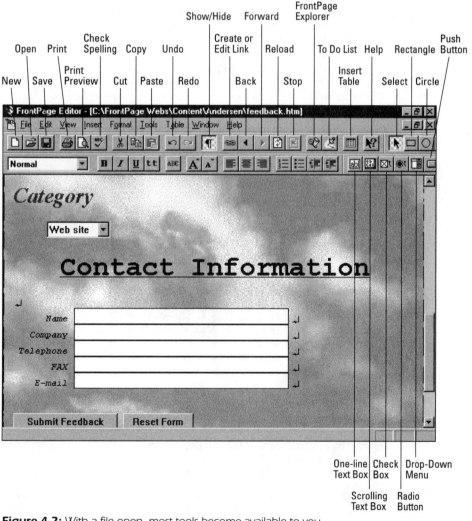

Figure 4-2: With a file open, most tools become available to you.

In the interests of readability, tools which are probably familiar to you from using word processing programs (such as text style, bold, italic, text size and alignment, as well as tools for formatting bulleted and numbered lists) are not called out in Figure 4-2. These are the majority of the tools contained on the second line of the toolbar. Many of these tool functions are self-evident from their names; others will be explained as we encounter them in performing tasks. However, note that there is a tool to switch to either the FrontPage Explorer or To Do List view, as well as tools to establish HTML links and insert various types of objects on your page.

If you open the View menu, you see that several types of toolbars are available to be displayed. By default, all the toolbars display: the two rows of tools shown in Figure 4-2 are actually several separate toolbars, such as the Standard Toolbar, Format Toolbar and Forms Toolbar. You can choose to display all of these, as in Figure 4-2, or just some of them. Just open the View menu and click on a toolbar's name to toggle between displaying and hiding a toolbar.

Editor menus

The toolbars contain shortcuts to the most commonly used functions of Editor, and of course all of these functions can also be accessed through menu commands. Menus also contain commands for less frequently used functions, such as making settings for your page setup. Briefly, these are the types of functions that are controlled by each of Editor's menus:

- **The File menu.** This menu contains commands for creating a new file, opening an existing one, closing and saving a file, setting page properties, and printing.

- **The Edit menu.** This menu contains commands for common editing functions such as cut, copy, and paste, as well as find and replace selections. You can also find commands here for adding items to your To Do List, placing bookmarks, and establishing links.

- **The View menu.** This menu controls what is displayed on your screen: which toolbars, the status bar, and formatting marks, as well as one command that allows you to view the HTML code on your page.

- **The Insert menu.** This menu is used to insert various types of objects onto your web page, including headings, drop-down lists, form fields, WebBots, and even whole files.

- **The Format menu.** Through this menu you can access dialog boxes where you can make settings for individual text characters or paragraphs of text. You can also remove any formatting you've already applied.

- **The Tools menu.** A bit of a mixed bag, this menu contains things like a spell checking function, commands to display Explorer or the To Do List, and commands to move around the pages in the open web or follow a link.

➡ **The Table menu.** This menu's commands will seem familiar to anyone who has used tables in a word-processing program. You can insert tables, add rows, columns, or cells, establish table properties, and select the various elements of a table.

The Window and Help menus have the kind of standard Windows commands you've seen before in similar menus. The Window menu controls whether multiple windows on your screen will tile or cascade. The Help menu takes you to a standard Windows-style help system.

Note that at the bottom of the Window menu is a list of the last several pages you had open in Editor. To reopen one of these pages, just go to the Window menu and click on its name in the list.

First Look at Explorer

You can move to the Explorer component of FrontPage from Editor by either choosing the Show Front Page Explorer button on the toolbar, or selecting the Tools menu and choosing Show FrontPage Explorer. The FrontPage Explorer is used to create and manage your web site, and includes tasks such as

➡ Creating a new web site (remember, you create web *pages* in Editor and web *sites* in Explorer)

➡ Viewing the structure of pages in your web

➡ Adding pages to existing webs

➡ Controlling the access authors and users have to a web

➡ Copying a web from one server to another (even when the servers are on different operating platforms)

➡ Verifying internal and external links

Explorer has its own set of tools and menus to help you perform these functions.

The Explorer toolbar

After seeing the 48 or so tools on the Editor toolbars, when you first see the tools available in Explorer (see Figure 4-3), you'll probably breathe a sigh of relief. There are only 11 little tools to learn here!

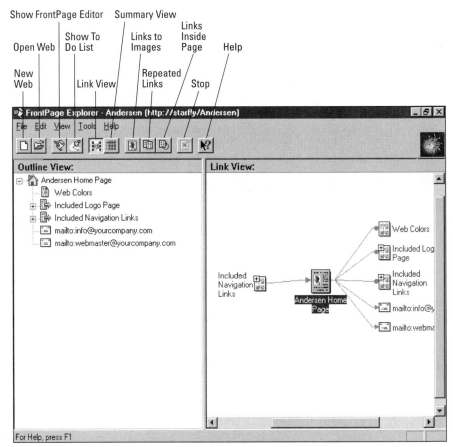

Figure 4-3: Get a view of your links or of the outline structure of the pages in your web site in Explorer.

The New Web and Open Web tools are used to create or open web sites. The next two buttons take you to the Editor or To Do List. The Link View and Summary View buttons allow you to shift between Link view and the third view in Explorer, Summary view (described later in the chapter). To the right of these are three tools that control what types of links are being displayed in the Outline or Link view. Finally, use the Stop tool if you've started to open a web site, but change your mind as it's loading.

Explorer menus

As with Editor, all the functions accessed through buttons on the toolbar in Explorer can also be invoked through menu commands — plus a few more. The Explorer menus contain the following types of commands:

➡ **The File menu.** This menu allows you open new or existing webs, copy and delete webs, close webs, and import and export web files.

➡ **The Edit menu.** You can't edit text or objects on your pages in Explorer; rather, the Edit menu allows you to delete pages from the web site, add tasks to your To Do List, and set web properties.

➡ **The View menu.** Here you can select to display the toolbar or status bar, choose between the Link or Summary views, and control how links are displayed in Explorer.

➡ **The Tools menu.** This menu contains commands for establishing and viewing web settings (such as the designated server and IP address), setting permissions and passwords, associating editors with file types (for example, Windows Notepad as the editor for ASCII text files with a .txt extension), and displaying the Editor or To Do List.

Again, there's a standard Windows-type Help menu also available.

Explorer views

As you saw in the previous section, there are three views available in Explorer: Outline, Link, and Summary. These views allow to see a wealth of information about your web site, its pages, and links from slightly different perspectives.

You can only have two of the three views on your screen at one time. You can switch back and forth between the Link and Summary views, but the Outline view always stays in place on the left side of your screen. You can also modify how much of the screen is taken up by each view. Click on the bar between the two displayed views and a double-sided arrow cursor appears. Drag this cursor to the right or left to reveal more of either the left-hand view or the right-hand view onscreen.

By clicking on any web page listed in any of the three views with your right mouse button, you have access to a shortcut menu. Using the commands on this menu (which are also available in the Edit menu) you can open, delete, or view the properties of the selected page.

The Outline View

The Outline View shows the hierarchical structure of a web site (see Figure 4-4). In this view you see a list consisting of icons and names. The icon indicates whether the item is a page or a file, with a special icon in the shape of a house to indicate your home page. The home page is listed at the top of the outline, with each succeeding connected page shown beneath it.

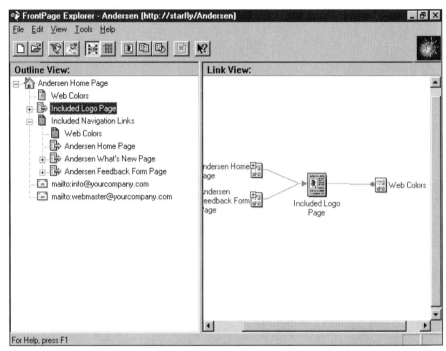

Figure 4-4: Understand the hierarchical structure of a web with the Outline View.

A plus sign to the left of an icon indicates that that item has links established. You can expand or collapse the outline to show the details of these links. Click on the plus sign and the links will be listed in the outline. The plus sign turns to a minus sign, indicating that all links have been expanded. Click on the minus sign to collapse the display again. If you see a gray arrow in front of an icon, you'll know that that page has been expanded from some other point in the Outline View list.

Other icon symbols used in the Outline View are described in Table 4-1. You'll also notice that some of these icon symbols are also used in the Link View, discussed in the next section.

Table 4-1	Outline View Icons
This Icon	**Indicates**
Broken page	A broken link
Page with red arrow	The page has links

This Icon	Indicates
Portrait	An image appears on this page
Envelope	A mailto link
Red pyramid	An error has occurred in a page
Globe	The page has a link to the World Wide Web

The Link View

By default, the Link View is displayed to the right of the Outline View when you enter Explorer for the first time. With a web site open this view shows a graphical display of the web (see Figure 4-5), with web pages shown as page icons, and the page titles listed next to these icons. When a web is first loaded the home page will be placed in the center of this Link View. You can easily see the relationship of this center page to other pages in your web.

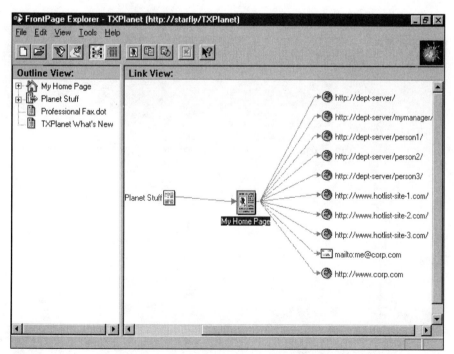

Figure 4-5: The Link View helps you visualize the relationships among pages in your web.

You can select any page in your web to be the center page in this display by clicking on its listing in the Outline view. Alternately, you can click once on any page in the Link view, then click your right mouse button. A shortcut menu offers the command Move to Center. You can only move a page to the center of your Link view if your server has control over that link.

The Summary View

To change from the Link View to the Summary View, choose the Summary View button on the toolbar. Figure 4-6 shows the Summary View slightly enlarged by dragging the center bar to the left so you can see more of its contents. By default, more of the Outline View would fill the screen. Note that whatever second view you have selected when you close a web, Link or Summary, that same second view will be showing when you next open the web.

All the pages of your web are listed here, with information such as the title, file-name, size, and the date last modified in the columns across the screen. One final column, Comments, isn't visible in Figure 4-6.

Title	File Name	Size	Type	Modified Date	Modified By	Page URL
clouds.gif	clouds.gif	122KB	gif			clouds.gif
Andersen Feedback Form...	feedback.htm	2KB	htm	7/17/96 3:55:47 PM	PaulS	feedback.h
Andersen Home Page	index.htm	2KB	htm	7/17/96 3:55:46 PM	PaulS	index.htm
Included Logo Page	logo.htm	305	htm	7/17/96 3:55:45 PM	PaulS	_private/lo
Included Navigation Links	navbar.htm	449	htm	7/17/96 3:55:46 PM	PaulS	_private/na
Andersen What's New Pa...	news.htm	2KB	htm	7/22/96 10:33:32 AM	PaulS	news.htm
Schedule Stuff Product D...	product.htm	3KB	htm	7/22/96 10:35:57 AM	PaulS	product.htn
Web Colors	style.htm	905	htm	7/17/96 3:55:45 PM	PaulS	_private/st

Figure 4-6: Review the details of your pages' properties in the Summary view.

You also can find out this same information by clicking on a page in any of the other views, selecting the Edit menu and choosing the Properties command.

Besides offering you information about all your pages' properties, you can use the Summary View in conjunction with the Outline View to locate specific pages within your web. With a large, complex web site, this can be very helpful. Select a page in the Summary View and click your right mouse button. Now the shortcut menu that appears offers a Find in Outline command. Select this, and the page you chose in Summary View is now highlighted in the Outline View.

One final function in Summary View that's most helpful is the ability to sort your pages by various criteria. Simply click on a column heading to sort by that information. For example, to sort your pages by file size, click on the column heading Size, and the pages are sorted from smallest to largest. Or, click on the Title column heading to sort the pages alphabetically by title.

Displaying links in views

One final note about Explorer views: There are three tools on the Explorer toolbar that affect how links are displayed in the Explorer views. You can select any one or any combination of these buttons to see different types of link information. These three tools are

➡ **Links to Images.** Choose this to display or hide any links to images within your web in the Outline and Link views. Note that any page with a link to an image will be displayed with the portrait icon next to it.

➡ **Repeated Links.** Display or hide multiple links that have been established from one page to another in the Link View. By default you would only see a single link for a page; when you select this button, all links are displayed.

➡ **Links Inside Page.** Choose this to display or hide the links a page has to itself. This kind of link is inserted on a page when you create it so that a reader can easily get back to the page.

You can also choose these display types by selecting their corresponding commands in the View menu.

Creating Your First Web

A quick and easy way to get started using FrontPage is to use a built-in Personal Web template to create your first web site. FrontPage offers several wizards and templates for both webs and pages that give you a head start on many of your web creation projects. Running a wizard and following its steps will create a web and several standard pages within that type of web. For example, running a Corporate Presence Web Wizard will create pages such as a product description page and feedback form. Using a template will simply create a web with a home page and links to your server, but this web will not contain any additional pages.

After you've created a site with either a wizard or template, you can create additional web pages using FrontPage Editor, and make settings to the web for who has permission to access it and how the web is set up on your server (these last settings are discussed in detail in Chapter 9).

When you first open Explorer, you see the Outline View and Link View, but both will be blank. Follow these steps to start a new web:

1.   **Select the File menu and choose the New Web command.**

2.   **The New Web dialog box shown in Figure 4-7 appears.**

Figure 4-7: *Notice that a description of each web template or wizard is included at the bottom of this dialog box when you've selected that item in the list.*

3.   **Select the Personal Web template and choose OK.**

4.   **Next, a dialog box appears where you can specify the Web Server location and Web Name.**

    Your server should be listed in the Web Server box. Type a Web Name and choose OK to proceed.

5.   **The next dialog box to appear is shown in Figure 4-8.**

    Creating a web requires that you enter your user name and password here. You will automatically be made the administrator of the <Root web>. Enter this information and choose OK.

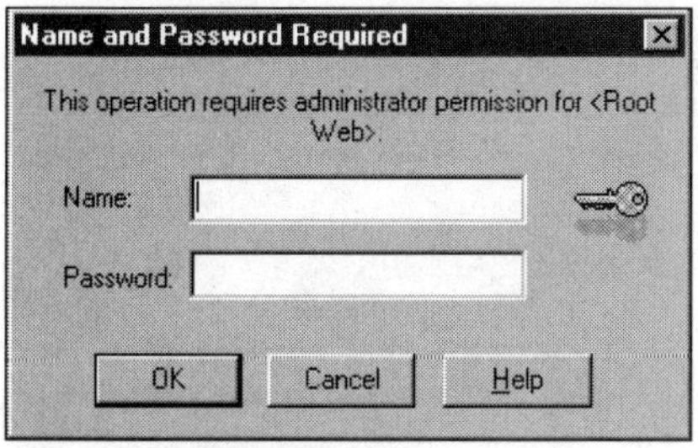

Name and Password Required ☒

This operation requires administrator permission for <Root Web>.

Name: [   ]

Password: [   ]

[OK]   [Cancel]   [Help]

Figure 4-8: Enter the user name and password you established for yourself when you installed FrontPage.

Your new personal web will now appear as in Figure 4-9, with the Outline and Link views showing the links to your server and placeholders for various World Wide Web locations. You don't have to save this web: It's saved automatically when you create it.

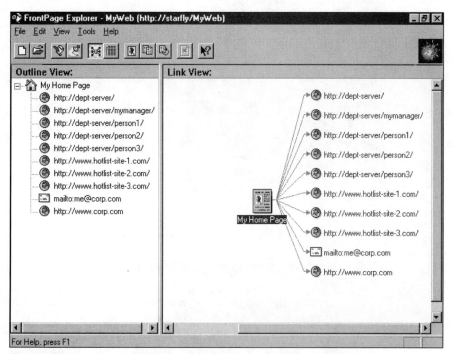

Figure 4-9: The Personal Web template gives you a basic web structure with a home page.

Adding a Web Page to Your Site

At this point you could edit the home page created when you used the template by simply selecting the Home Page icon in the Outline or Link view, opening the Edit menu and choosing Open. You can also use the keyboard shortcut Ctrl+O. This takes you to that page within the FrontPage Editor. We'll discuss editing an existing page in Chapter 5. For now, we'll look at the process of adding a new page to your web from the FrontPage Editor.

If you are in Explorer, choose the Show FrontPage Editor button on the toolbar. If you have left FrontPage, open the Editor from the Windows Start button. Editor appears with no page currently open. Follow these steps to create a new web page:

1. Select the File menu and choose New. The New Page dialog box shown in Figure 4-10 appears.

Figure 4-10: Pages have their own set of wizards and templates to help you get started.

2. Select the What's New page template from this list and choose OK.

   If you were to select a wizard it would walk you through several steps to create the design and elements of the page for you. You can learn more about using wizards in Chapter 6.

3. The template page shown in Figure 4-11 is displayed on your screen.

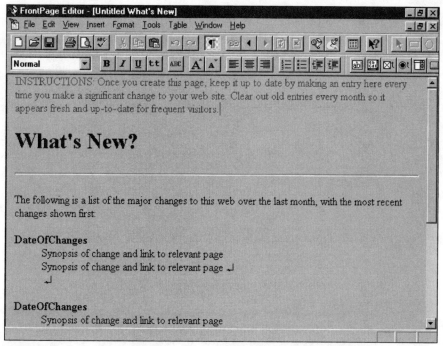

Figure 4-11: The instructions at the top of this page advise you how to keep this page current.

Taking a look at a page template

On the top of this page are instructions on how to use and maintain it. These instructions will not be visible to visitors to your page. There is a title appropriate to the topic of the template, in this case, *What's New?*. Beneath that is a standard phrase telling your visitors what's included on this page.

Under the introductory sentence are several blocks of information or text fields where you can replace text with your own information. In this case, there are a couple of fields for listing the latest changes to your web, one block that automatically shows the date your page was created, and at the bottom of the page (not shown in Figure 4-11) a block for author information, copyright, and date the page was last revised.

To change any of the text in these placeholder fields, simply highlight the text and type in new text. Repeat this procedure to replace or add text as you wish.

Part II: Learning to Use FrontPage

Saving your page

To save this page, select the File menu, then choose the Save command. The Save As dialog box shown in Figure 4-12 appears.

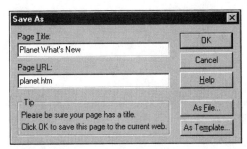

Figure 4-12: *Personalize the title of your new page when you save it.*

Type a title for the page and a URL. If the current web is on a server which is running on UNIX, Windows NT, or Windows 95, you can enter a URL of up to 64 characters. The extension should be .htm or .html. If you save a page as a file, it is saved to the current web (that is, the web you had open in the Explorer view when you created the page). You can also save a page as a template so you can use it as the basis for creating other web pages. In that case the page isn't saved as a page in the current web but will appear on the New Page list of wizards and templates from now on.

After you've saved the page, choose the Show FrontPage Explorer button on the toolbar. Notice that the new page has been added to whatever the current web was in the Outline view. In our case, as shown in Figure 4-13, the MyWeb What's New page is listed at the bottom of the Outline view on our personal web. Because there are no links yet established, this page doesn't show in the Link view.

Inserting Objects on a Page

After you've created a web site, you can edit pages that have been saved to it from the FrontPage Editor. If you have a site open in Explorer, just click on the name of the page you'd like to edit in any of the views, then select the Edit menu and choose the Open command. Alternately, you can simply open Editor from the Windows Start menu; when Editor opens, select the Open File command from the File menu.

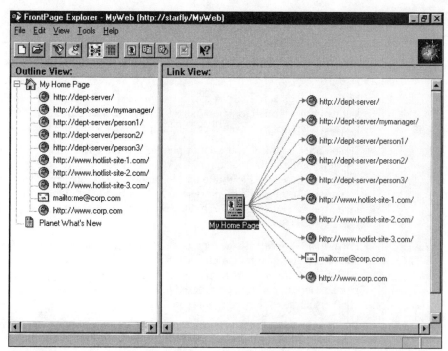

Figure 4-13: The new page appears as the first page listed under the home page.

After you've opened a page you can insert a variety of items on it using either the buttons on the Forms Toolbar or the commands in the Insert menu. Some of these items simply insert a preformatted text placeholder on your page. For example, if you insert a bulleted list, a single bullet will appear on your page. When you enter text for your first bullet point and press Enter, a second bullet will appear and so on. Other choices on the Insert menu open a dialog box so that you can enter the contents of the item to be inserted. An example of this would be the drop-down menu form field, which you'll see demonstrated in a later section. Still other Insert menu choices offer a dialog box with a list of different items of that type to insert. For example, if you wish to insert a WebBot, there are several bots to choose from.

What can you insert?

There are several items that you can insert on your page. After an item is inserted you can move it around the page as you like using cut and paste functions from the toolbar or Edit menu.

The items you can insert include

- **Heading.** Choose from a variety of preset styles for your headings. The exact format that visitors will see for each heading is determined by the web browser each is using.

- **List.** You can insert a bulleted or numbered list, a directory, or a menu (these last two are intended for short lists of items, but note that the HTML tags they use are often not interpreted correctly by browsers that are currently available).

- **Definition.** Use this if you want to place a term and its definition on your page. The term appears flush left, and the definition appears indented. You must designate three fields to make up a definition: List, Term and Definition. You insert each from a side menu reached through the Definition command in the Insert menu. Note that different web browsers may perceive the formatting of this slightly differently.

- **Form Field.** There are several types of forms you can insert, including a one-line or scrolling text box, a check box, a radio button, a drop-down menu, a push button and images. Typically you will be asked to supply a name/value pair so that the information entered by visitors to your site through a form field can be submitted to a form handler.

- **Paragraph.** This choice is for multiple lines of text which can be in normal text style, formatted, or address style.

- **Horizontal Line.** This inserts a horizontal line running across your page just where your cursor was when you inserted the line.

- **Line Break.** Because many web browsers won't display empty paragraphs, you might want to use a line break to place space between items on your page. Line breaks are displayed as white space by all browsers.

- **Image.** Use this command to insert an image from either a URL or file. If you insert from a file the image is actually added to your page when you save it. If you insert an image from a URL, the image is not saved to your page; rather, the image is inserted from the designated location on the World Wide Web when a user visits the page.

- **WebBot.** You'll learn much more about WebBots in Chapter 6. Basically, they are instructions for your web to perform a function at that point, such as substituting one thing for another, or placing a table of contents on your page. When you choose to insert a bot, you will be presented with that bot's configuration dialog box for you to make selections regarding how the bot will function.

- **Special Character.** This choice opens a character set from which you can choose to insert things like copyright symbols, symbols for foreign currency, and percentage signs.

- **File.** You can insert the contents of a file on your page by simply locating it on any drive on your computer or from a network drive.

Inserting a form field

To get an idea of just how inserting an item on your page works, we'll insert a drop-down menu on a page. Any item you select to insert on a page will offer you similarly simple and straightforward choices.

You can configure your drop-down menu to allow users multiple choices, or constrict them to only one. When a form containing a drop-down menu is submitted to your site by a web browser, both the name of the form and a list of any choices that have been selected is forwarded to the form handler for your site using the name/value pairs you designate.

With a page open in FrontPage Editor, place your cursor where you'd like the drop-down list to appear. (If there is nothing on your page yet, your cursor will only be available at the top left-hand corner of the page; that's okay, you can move the item later, once there are more objects on the page.) Follow these steps to insert a form field:

1. Select the Insert menu, then choose the Form Field command. A side menu, shown in Figure 4-14, appears.

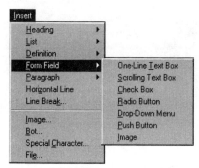

Figure 4-14: There are several types of form fields that can be added to a page.

2. Scroll down to select the Drop-Down Menu item. The Drop-Down Menu Properties dialog box appears.

3. Type a Name for your menu in the Name text box shown in the dialog box in Figure 4-15.

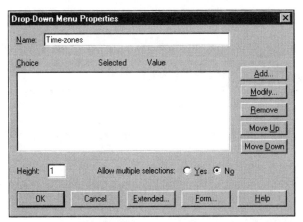

Figure 4-15: The name of your drop-down menu will be reported to your Form Handler.

4. **To add choices for your menu, choose the Add button. The Add Choice dialog box appears (see Figure 4-16).**

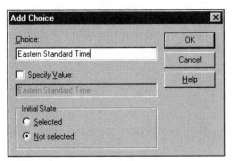

Figure 4-16: Add choices to your drop-down menu by filling out an add dialog box for each choice.

5. **In this dialog box you enter the name of your menu choice and the value.** By default, the value that's submitted for this name will be the name of the menu choice itself. However, you can associate this choice with a different value, if you like. For example, if you have a drop-down list of your products for visitors to select by name, but you want the value returned to your form handler as product model numbers, you could designate that here. If you want this choice to be the initially selected choice (for example, if this is the most popular choice and you wish to allow your visitors to choose it by default) click on the Selected radio button in the Initial State section of this dialog box.

6. **Choose OK to add the choice to the Drop-Down Menu Properties dialog box.**

At this point, you can use the other buttons in the Drop-Down Menu Properties dialog box to add more choices, modify existing choices or remove choices. You can also add extended attribute/value pairs to the HTML tag (the default is <INPUT>), or modify the form handler settings (the default here is Customer CGI script). You can choose to make more than one listing in the drop-down menu visible by making the height in this dialog box equal to the number of choices. If you want the menu field to display only one choice, letting your visitors display the other choices by clicking on the drop-down menu arrow, leave the default value of 1 here. When you accept your choices by choosing OK, your drop-down menu appears on your page. Figure 4-17 shows a drop-down menu with a height of 1.

Just so you can see how much effort you've saved by using FrontPage to insert things on your page, take a look at the HTML code which was automatically generated by FrontPage (Figure 4-18). You can display this by displaying a page in Editor, selecting the View menu and choosing HTML.

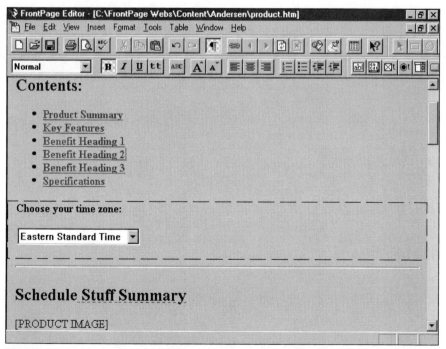

Figure 4-17: *Visitors can tell you something about themselves by making selections in this drop-down menu.*

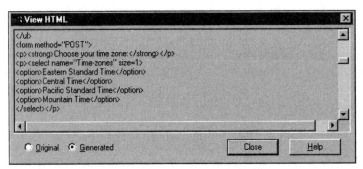

Figure 4-18: The HTML tags to begin and end fields are generated automatically when you insert a field on a page.

In this chapter you had your first glimpse of the FrontPage Explorer and Editor environments, and saw how some of their menus and tools work. You've created a web and a page within the web. In addition, you've learned about inserting various types of items on your page.

In the next chapter you begin to see how to make settings to your web, such as establishing links between pages and setting permissions for who can access your site. In addition, you explore how you can edit objects and text on your page to begin to design pages that work for you.

Formatting and Organizing Web Pages

In the last chapter you created your first web and web page. That's a start. After you've created a basic web page and inserted some elements on it, it's time to decide what else you want to do to customize and enhance the appearance of those elements to make the best page possible.

In this chapter you'll first learn how to use formatting tools to modify the appearance of text and assign properties to your page. You'll see how to use the Table menu to insert a table on a page and format it.

Next, we'll take a look at some of the ways you can manipulate pages within your web, for example by moving or deleting them.

Finally, you'll get your first glimpse at the process of linking pages, a procedure that's explored in much more detail in Chapter 10.

We'll start by taking a look at the To Do List, where you can make some notes to yourself about what tasks you want to accomplish next.

Using Your To Do List

You've seen two of the key components of FrontPage: Explorer and Editor. One final component that you will use often is the To Do List. The To Do List is helpful not only when you are first building your web, but also as an integral tool for maintaining your web. Keep in mind that a web is essentially a living thing: it must grow, change, and shift in its focus if you want to keep your visitors interested and the content current. Keeping track of the steps involved in making those changes is of key importance.

If you are the only person working on your web, a To Do List becomes a simple but valuable scratch pad where you place reminders to yourself to perform tasks associated with your web. However, if you work with others in your company or your organization to create and maintain your web, a To Do List becomes even more essential. It is a centralized listing of responsibilities which all contributors can check to avoid duplication of effort or even conflict. It can also help you to identify gaps you may have in completing the steps needed to reach your goal.

Using a To Do List is very simple. You can reach the To Do List from either Explorer or Editor. Each offers both a button in the toolbar for viewing the To Do List and a command called Show To Do List in their respective Tools menus. Either of these methods will open the To Do List window shown in Figure 5-1.

Figure 5-1: A To Do List is an invaluable tool for building and maintaining your web.

There are really only three steps involved in using your To Do List:

➡ Adding new tasks by naming the tasks and assigning them to someone

➡ Doing those tasks

➡ Indicating tasks are complete by either marking them as done or deleting them from the list

Adding new tasks

The first step is to add a task to your list. Choose the Add button in the To Do List window. An Add To Do Task dialog box appears, as shown in Figure 5-2.

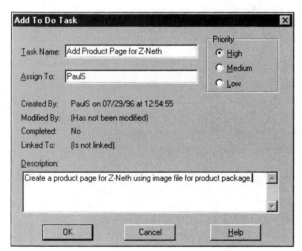

Figure 5-2: Enter a few simple pieces of information to create a To Do List item.

There are only a few items you need to enter to create a task:

➡ **Enter a task name.** Remember to make this a name that you and others in your group will recognize if they look at it on the To Do List.

➡ **Assign the task.** By default, it will be assigned to the administrator of the Root Web (this is the person who created the web). You can change this by simply clicking in this field and typing a different name. (See Chapter 9 for more about assigning authors and administrators to your web and giving them permissions to perform certain functions).

➡ **Set a priority for the task.** It's a good idea if you're working with others on a web to agree with them about what constitutes a high-, medium- or low-level priority task.

➡ **Enter a description of the task, if you like.** This may help other people in your group to understand exactly what the task involves or why it needs to be done.

Notice that certain things have been entered in this form by default. The person who created the task and when it was created and modified are entered automatically by FrontPage based on its own user settings and the computer clock. For a task to be marked as completed you would have to perform a procedure to mark it as such (which you'll see how to do shortly).

Finally, the Linked To: field is also completed by FrontPage. It works this way:

➡ If you first open the To Do List by choosing the Show To Do List button on the toolbar or selecting the Show To Do List command from the Tool menu, when you choose the Add button to add a task, there will be no link listed.

➡ On the other hand, if you move directly to the Add To Do Task window from Explorer or Editor (in effect bypassing the FrontPage To Do List window) by selecting the Edit menu and choosing the Add To Do Task command, the task shown in the Add To Do Task dialog box will be linked to one of two items: if you are in Editor and select Edit, Add To Do Task, the active page will be linked to the task; if you are in Explorer and select Edit, Add To Do Task, the selected page, image, or file will be linked to the task.

To save the new task, choose the OK button. It will now appear on the To Do List.

You can sort this list by clicking on any of the column headings in this window to sort by task name, assignment, priority, and link.

Doing the task

When you are ready to perform the task you've created, FrontPage offers you a little shortcut. Simply open the To Do List, select the task, and choose the Do Task button. FrontPage opens whatever page, file, or image this task is linked to in the Editor window, ready for you to perform whatever steps are necessary to complete the task.

Marking a task as complete

After you've completed a task it's important that you mark it as completed on the To Do List. Doing so will save you from duplicating your own efforts, if you've forgotten that you already worked on a particular task. But, more importantly, if you are working with others on your site it will let them know the status of the tasks you've been assigned to.

To mark a task as complete, simply open the To Do List window, select a task and choose the Complete button. The dialog box shown in Figure 5-3 appears. Here you have the choice of marking the item as done, or actually deleting it. Keep in mind that if you want to use this feature while working with others on a web project, it might be better to leave the task on the list marked as completed than to delete it. That way, they know you were aware of the task and it has been taken care of.

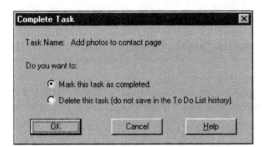

Figure 5-3: To make really effective use of the To Do List, you must mark tasks you've finished as complete in this dialog box.

In order for you or others to see these completed tasks in the To Do List, you must select the Show history check box in the To Do List window. If you wish to display only tasks that still need to be done, remove the check mark from the Show history box by clicking there again.

Formatting Your Pages

When you use the templates and wizards that FrontPage provides for creating new pages, basic formatting of the elements on your page is pretty much handled for you. However, you'll probably want to take the design of your page further and customize its appearance to your own taste. FrontPage offers many features that allow you to refine and customize the look of your page.

There are tools for formatting text in FrontPage that work just like your favorite word processor's text-formatting tools. In addition, you can modify the properties of your page to adjust the way color works for things like the page background, text, and links.

Working with text

Whether text was placed on your page by a template or wizard, or you inserted a text box on the page yourself, you will find that you may want to reformat that text in some way. You do this in the FrontPage Editor.

You have two options for formatting text: use the buttons on the Format Toolbar, or go through the Format menu.

Using the Format Toolbar

You can use the tools on the Editor Format Toolbar, shown in Figure 5-4, to format text that you have selected on your page.

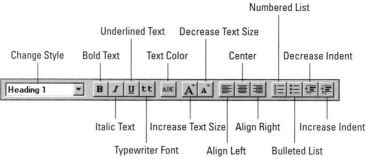

Figure 5-4: The Format Toolbar offers standard formatting options.

Most common formatting functions are represented by a tool, but not all. The most comprehensive set of formatting functions are accessed through the Format menu.

Here's a rundown of what these tools allow you to do to selected text:

➡ **Change Style.** Apply preset heading styles to paragraphs. You can also change paragraph heading styles from a dialog box by selecting the Format menu and choosing the Paragraph command.

➡ **Bold Text, Italic Text, Underlined Text.** Apply bold, italic, or underlined styles to your text in any combination.

➡ **Typewriter Font.** Change the selected text font to a typewriter style. Note that some web browsers don't recognize this style when displaying a page.

➡ **Text Color.** When you select this button you get a color palette of 48 preset colors, and the opportunity to define up to 16 custom colors.

➡ **Increase/Decrease Text Size.** These two buttons increase or decrease the size of your text in preset increments.

➡ **Align Left/Center/Align Right.** Choose any of these three buttons to change how selected text is aligned on the page.

➡ **Numbered List/Bulleted List.** Turn selected text into one of these list forms. New numbers/bullets will be inserted at every carriage return in the text.

 You can use the List command in the Insert menu to insert text pre-formatted as a numbered or bulleted list to save yourself this formatting step.

➡ **Decrease/Increase Indent.** These buttons will move your text in or out by preset indent increments.

Using the Characters Format command

The tools on the Format Toolbar offer you the most common text formatting options, however, they don't offer you all text formatting options. To see those, you select the Format menu, and choose the Characters command. The Character Styles dialog box shown in Figure 5-5 appears.

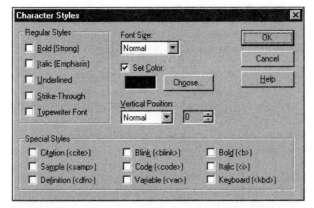

Figure 5-5: Note the Special Styles section of this dialog box, which offers you some coding shortcuts.

Most of the settings in this dialog box are identical to those invoked through the toolbar buttons already described. However, the section titled Special Styles in this dialog box deserves further explanation. These special styles won't all show on your page from within FrontPage. They may not be read correctly by all browsers to your site. For that reason, FrontPage documentation advises you to stick to regular FrontPage styles when working with text. However, Microsoft has included these options here since you may find them in pages that you open and be curious about their functionality. Here's a brief rundown of what formatting style each applies, along with the HTML code behind them:

- **Citation** (<cite>). A manual, section, or book.
- **Sample** (<sample>). A sequence of literal characters. This is close to the typewriter font in appearance.
- **Definition** (<dfn>). A definition, sometimes using italicized text.
- **Blink** (<blink>). Blinking text. This is one many browsers can't display accurately.
- **Code** (<code>). Code sample, also similar to the typewriter font.
- **Variable** (<var>). A variable name, often using italicized text.
- **Bold.** Bold text. To ensure that your text is perceived as bold by all browsers, you are better off using the Bold (Strong) setting under the regular styles.
- **Italic** (<i>). Italic text. To ensure that this is perceived accurately, it's preferable to use the Italic (Emphasis) regular style.
- **Keyboard** (<kbd>). Indicates text the user should enter. This is usually formatted in typewriter font.

Finally, notice that there is a drop-down list in the Character Styles dialog box to select subscript or superscript styles. These adjust the vertical position of the text above or below the normal style position on a line.

After you've made any combination of settings you like in this dialog box, choose OK to put them into effect on selected text.

Modifying page properties

You can customize the background pattern and colors used for various elements of your page. Experimenting with these colors can give you a unique look to your pages. With a page open in Editor, select the File menu, then choose the Page Properties command. The Page Properties dialog box appears (see Figure 5-6).

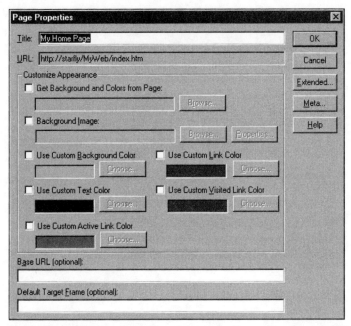

Figure 5-6: The Page Properties dialog box offers options for modifying colors on your page.

You can make several settings affecting the background image and color scheme on your page through this dialog box:

➥ Get Background and Colors from Page and its associated Browse button allow you to copy a background and color scheme from another page on your site that you happen to like.

➥ Background Image is where you can choose an image you'd like to use in the background of your page. You can either type in the name of a file to use, or use the Browse button to get an image from either a file or URL. You can edit text that appears on the image you select using the Properties button.

➥ Use Custom Background Color is the selection you use to modify the color of the page background. When you choose the Choose button at this selection, a color palette opens so you can make your choices.

The last four settings allow you to customize the color of text on the page, link text, link text for links that have already been visited, and active links.

You can also use the Extended or Meta buttons. The first allows you to add an attribute to your page using an HTML value/name pair. The second button takes you to a dialog box where you can associate meta tags, which provide special instructions for a browser, such as an expiration date, to your page.

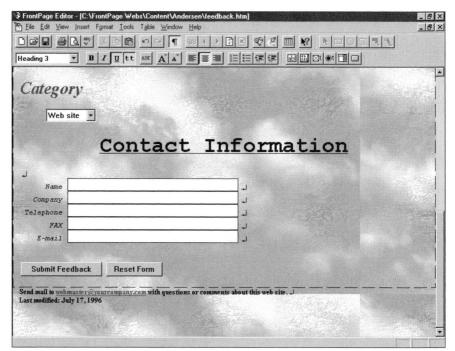

Figure 5-7: The heading "Category" has been italicized, while the heading "Contact Information" has been centered, enlarged, and changed to the Typewriter style font.

Feel free to experiment with colors on your page, but do be careful. Busy background images and pale colored text can make for an unreadable page. If possible, test your choices by viewing that page with several different browsers to see what effect you've created.

Figure 5-7 shows a web page where the Windows cloud bitmap was used for the page background image. In addition, some of the text styles have been modified.

Customizing Your Page

In addition to customizing text formats and page colors and background, you may find that you need to reorganize the elements on your page from time to time, delete elements, or insert new elements. This section looks at the mechanics of editing your page and the process of using the Table menu to insert a table on an existing page.

Editing and organizing content

Logically enough, you edit your page from the Editor component of FrontPage. Microsoft has made the functions in Editor which you use to work with the elements on your page very similar to the same features in its popular Word for Windows word-processing program. If you're familiar with that or any other common word processor, you already know how to edit your web pages.

Table 5-1 provides a description of common editing procedures using FrontPage Editor.

Table 5-1	FrontPage Editing Functions
Function	**Procedure**
Insert Text	Place your cursor at the point where you want to add text and begin typing.
Select Text	Click in the selection bar to the left of a line of text to select the entire line. Click and drag your mouse over as much text as you like to highlight it. Use the Select All command in the Edit menu to select all text on your page.
Select Objects	Click on an image or click to the left of it in the selection bar; handles appear around its edges indicating it's selected.
Delete Text or Objects	After selecting the text or object, press the Delete key or the Backspace key on your keyboard.
Cut Text or Objects	Select the text or object, then use the Cut button on the toolbar, Cut command in the Edit menu, or Ctrl+X on your keyboard to cut it to the Windows clipboard.
Copy Text or Objects	Select the text, then use the Copy button on the toolbar, Copy command in the Edit menu, or Ctrl+C on your keyboard to copy it to the Windows clipboard.
Paste Text or Objects	Place your cursor where you want to insert the text or object and use the Paste button on the toolbar, the Paste command in the Edit menu, or Ctrl+V on your keyboard.

Don't forget that you also have the common Undo/Redo functions in FrontPage Editor. These allow you to undo your last task or redo your last task by using the buttons on the toolbar, or the Undo/Redo commands at the top of the Edit menu.

 It's worth noting that although you can have more than one page open in Editor at one time, the OLE technology that permeates other Microsoft products doesn't work here. You can't click and drag objects or text from one web page to another. Rather, you must use the cut, copy, and paste tools to move an image from one page to another.

Adding a table to a page

Just as editing features in FrontPage resemble those in Word for Windows, so do the tools and procedures you use to insert and format a table on your page. Tables are useful for showing a great deal of information in a compact and easily-readable format. That makes them a perfect tool for the web designer who wants to save his visitors from having to search around several pages to find this quantity of information.

Inserting a table

To insert a table you can either choose the Insert Table button on the toolbar, or select the Table menu and choose the Insert Table command. The Insert Table dialog box shown in Figure 5-8 is displayed on your screen.

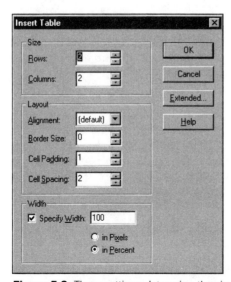

Figure 5-8: *These settings determine the size and layout of your table.*

The settings to make using this dialog box are very straightforward:

➡ How many rows and columns you'd like in your table

➡ The alignment of the table on your page

➡ Whether you'd like a border and if so, what width the border line should be

➡ How much space you'd like around the text in your cells and between cells

➡ The width of your table as a percentage of your page

You can choose the Extended button to add non-standard HTML attributes that aren't supported within FrontPage.

Once you've made your choices, choose the OK button to place the table on the page.

Formatting a table

You now see a blank table, similar to the one shown in Figure 5-9. Obviously, depending on how you set the number of rows and columns, use of a border, and the table width, your table may differ slightly in appearance.

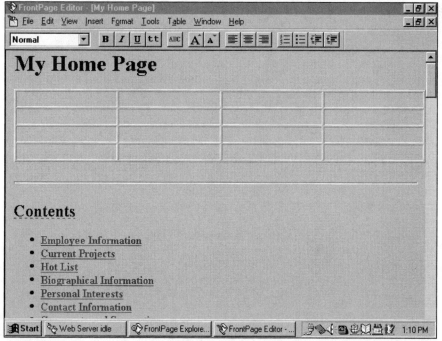

Figure 5-9: This table uses the 100% width and a 1-point border; it has four rows and four columns.

You can click with your mouse button in any cell to place your cursor there, ready to enter text. You can also move from cell to cell using the up, down, left and right arrow keys on your keyboard.

The Table menu offers you several commands to modify your table:

➡ Insert Rows or Columns allows you to add to the number of cells in your table and choose whether the new rows or columns will appear above or below the cell your cursor is resting in when you open this command.

➡ Insert Cell inserts a single cell to the right of the cell your cursor is resting in.

➡ Insert Caption inserts a text box above the table where you can type a title or caption for the table. You can only have one caption, so once you've selected this command, it becomes unavailable.

➡ Merge Cells allows you to merge selected columns or rows of cells into one single cell which can span several columns of a table. You can select two or more whole columns by placing your cursor at the top of a column until you see a bold black arrow, then clicking on the column and dragging your cursor to the right or left to select as many columns as you want. When you then merge the selected cells, they become one cell. Figure 5-10, for example, shows a table where all cells in the first two columns were merged, forming one large cell. Also notice that this table has a caption added at the top.

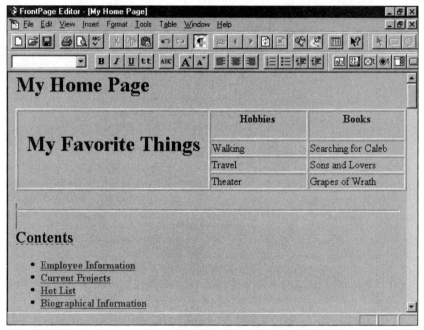

Figure 5-10: Two merged columns produce a single block on the left side of your table.

➥ Split Cells lets you split a single cell into two or more columns or rows.

The next four commands in the Table menu enable you to select a cell, row, column, or the entire table. Finally, the Table Properties command at the bottom of the Table menu offers the same layout and width options you set when you created the table so you can make changes to these at any time.

You can format the text that you enter in your table cells just as you format text anywhere else on your page using the Format Toolbar, or commands in the Format menu. In Figure 5-10, for example, the text in the merged cell has been enlarged and set in italic, and the text that represents headings in the second two columns has been made bold.

Managing Web Pages

After you've created and begun to format several pages in your web, you may find that you want to manipulate those pages in some way. Perhaps you need to move a page from one folder in the web to another. Maybe you'll want to import a file into your web to create a page without having to reenter information that already exists. And at some point, you'll probably need to delete some pages from your web. These are all simple operations to perform in FrontPage.

Moving pages

You can move a page in a web to a different folder that already exists within the web, or you can move a page to a new folder which FrontPage will add to your web. Either procedure involves just a few simple steps:

1. Open Explorer and from any of its three views click on the name of the page to select it.
2. Select the Edit menu and choose the Properties command.
3. From the General tab of the Page Properties dialog box (see Figure 5-11) simply edit the folder portion of the page URL in the Page URL field.
4. Choose OK to accept the new URL.

If you have edited the folder name to the name of an existing folder, FrontPage will move the page to that folder. If you've added a folder name that doesn't exist, FrontPage will create that folder, then place the file in it. Any links to this page will also be updated automatically.

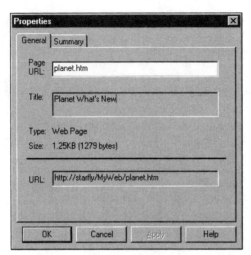

Figure 5-11: Just type a folder name in the Page URL field to move the page.

Importing files to your web pages

Occasionally you may want to import a file into a web. You can do so to either include the file on an existing page, or set up a direct link to that file from your web pages.

Import a file to a web by following these steps:

1. **Open FrontPage Explorer, and open the web you'd like to import a file to.**

2. **From the File menu, select the Import command.**

3. **When the Import File to Web dialog box appears, choose the Add File button to see the Add File to Import List dialog box (see Figure 5-12).**

4. **Use the various settings in this box to locate and open the file you want; choose Open to return to the Import File to Web dialog box.**

5. **Choose the Import Now button.**

    The button changes to a Stop button so you have a method of stopping the Import while it's in progress.

    After a few moments the Stop button becomes grayed out and unavailable to you, and the new page appears at the bottom of your web outline in Explorer Outline view.

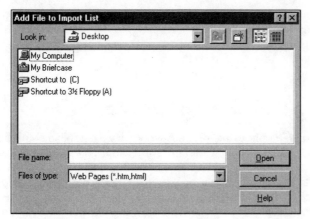

Figure 5-12: You can click on one file and use the shift key to select multiple files to open, if you like.

Deleting pages from a web

While looking at the pages on your web in the FrontPage Explorer view, you'll occasionally see pages that you want to delete, perhaps because they've become obsolete or duplicate another page's content. From any Explorer view, click on the name of the page you want to delete to select it. Select the Edit menu and choose the Delete command. The page is deleted; however there are two important things you should know about this procedure:

➦ A page, once deleted, can't be retrieved.

➦ Any links to the page are broken.

Setting Up Links

Later in this book (in Chapter 10) we go into more detail about how to establish links. However, because this is a key concept in understanding how FrontPage is used, we'll give you a brief overview of how to establish links and view them using FrontPage Explorer.

Links are what make the World Wide Web go round. A link simply provides the URL of a location on the Web. When a user clicks on a linked object, he or she is taken to that URL. In the past, people have used HTML to code links into their web pages. FrontPage allows you to easily set up links so your visitors can move from one page to a related page either within the same web, or in any other location on the World Wide Web. Links can be made from text or images on your page. The beauty of FrontPage is that you don't have to know a thing about HTML to establish a link: it's all taken care of for you. All you need to know is the target page URL.

Understanding the linking process

To give you an idea of how this process works, we'll establish a link between a single cell in a table to a page within the same web. To establish a link you first need to designate the text or object on a page that you want to be the target of the link. You do this by creating a *bookmark*. A bookmark is a named character set in a paragraph which will be the target of the link. Once you've placed a bookmark on the target page, you establish a link from the linked page to the bookmark on the target page. When that's done, your visitors can simply click on the linked object and be taken to the target page.

For example, if a visitor sees the table in Figure 5-10 listing your company's products, it might be very useful to provide a link from each product name listed in the table to a separate page that gives more detail about that product. You would simply create a link from the text in a cell to a bookmark at the top of the product specification page.

Creating a bookmark

Creating a bookmark is simplicity itself. Open the page where you want to place the bookmark (the target page). Select the text or object you want to associate with the bookmark. Typically just taking the user to the heading at the top of the linked page is the most logical thing to do. From the Edit menu, choose Bookmark, or use the keyboard shortcut Ctrl+G. In the Bookmark dialog box shown in Figure 5-13, type the bookmark name and choose OK.

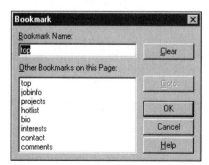

Figure 5-13: Accept the default name of the bookmark or name it something different here.

After a bookmark has been placed on text, the text appears with a dotted blue line underneath it.

Establishing the link

Go to the page where you want the visitor to be able to initiate the link. In the table example, you'd go to the page that contains the table and select one product name from a table cell. You can make this process of moving between the first page and the target page easier by simply tiling your two page windows onscreen, as shown in Figure 5-13. After you select the text or object to link, choose the Link button on the toolbar to display the Create Link dialog box shown in Figure 5-14.

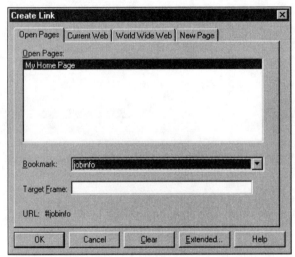

Figure 5-14: *Another way to get to this dialog box is to select the Edit menu and choose the Link command, or use the keyboard shortcut Ctrl+K.*

Notice that the various tabs in this dialog box allow you to create a link to open pages, any page in the currently active web, any page on the World Wide Web, or even a new page FrontPage can create on the fly as you establish the link. Once you select the page to link to, just select the bookmark name on that page from the Bookmark drop-down list. When you've made your selections, choose OK. The linked text now appears in blue.

Save both files. Now if you switch to Explorer and click on either page you'll see its links in the Link view. Figure 5-15 shows this relationship in Explorer for a link between a What's New page and a Product Description page.

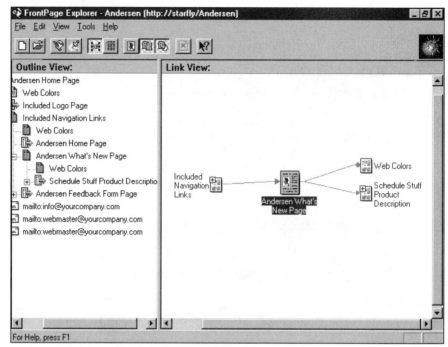

Figure 5-15: The product name in the table on the What's New page has been linked to the Product Description page.

You can view the HTML code created by these steps by going to the linked page, selecting the View menu and choosing the HTML command.

Managing links

After links have been created you can manage them in slightly different ways from the Editor or Explorer views.

From the Editor you can get rid of existing links by selecting the text you've attached the link to, then choosing the Link button on the toolbar. In the same dialog box you used to create the link, you can choose the Clear button to get rid of it.

In Explorer, you can select the linked page, then use one of two commands in the Tools menu to manage links:

➡ **Verify Links.** This command will make a Verify Links dialog box available (see Figure 5-16). Here you can verify whether links are intact or broken. When you open this dialog box, all internal links are verified. If you want to check external links, choose the Verify button in the dialog box. The Edit Link button takes you to a dialog box where you can repair a broken link. The Edit Page button opens the page that contains the selected link so you can edit the link right on the page.

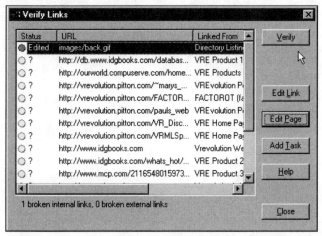

Figure 5-16: Links, whether intact or broken, are shown in this dialog box.

➡ **Recalculate Links.** This command updates the Explorer display of links for the active web. This is especially helpful if other authors are working on the same web and you want to be sure you're seeing their most recent changes.

Moving On

In this chapter you worked with adding tasks to and editing your To Do List. You also used formatting options for the text on your page in the FrontPage Editor. You customized a page by learning how to reorganize objects on the page and add a table. We demonstrated the simple processes of moving, importing, and deleting pages on your web. Finally, you got your first glimpse of the process of establishing and managing links using FrontPage.

In the next chapter you learn more about using FrontPage templates, wizards and WebBots: handy shortcuts for designing webs, pages, and functions.

FrontPage Web Templates, Wizards, and WebBots

In This Chapter

Using wizards to create a web

Using templates to create pages

Using WebBots

Creating your own templates that incorporate bots

In the previous two chapters you were introduced to the FrontPage Explorer and the FrontPage Editor. You were shown how to use templates and wizards from the New Page dialog box, and saw the command to insert WebBots in the Insert menu. In this chapter, we will show you how to use those templates, wizards, and WebBots.

What Are FrontPage Web Templates, Wizards, and WebBots?

Of course, the first thing that we should do in a chapter about these three features is to define them:

➡ *Templates* are sets of pre-designed formats for text and images on which pages and webs can be based.

➡ *Wizards* create pages and webs by asking you questions about the features you want to include on the page or on the web you are constructing.

➡ *WebBots* (usually called *bots)* are used to include dynamic features that are evaluated and executed when an author saves a page to a server, or when a user links to a specified page.

We're going to start examining templates, Wizards, and WebBots by looking at the part of FrontPage where you were first exposed to them. That first exposure was in Chapter 4 where we discussed the New Web command on the File Menu.

Creating a New Web Using Templates and Wizards

You can display the New Web dialog box, as shown in Figure 6-1, either by selecting the File menu and choosing the New Web command, or by choosing the New Web button on the toolbar.

Figure 6-1: Select the New Web button on the toolbar and bring up the New Web dialog box.

There are eight templates and Wizards listed in the New Web dialog box:

➡ Normal Web is a template that creates a new web with a single blank page.

➡ Corporate Presence Wizard creates a professional-looking Internet presence for your organization.

➡ Customer Support Web is a template that creates a web to improve customer support services. This web is particularly useful for software companies.

➡ Discussion Web Wizard creates a discussion group with threads, a table of contents, and full-text site searching.

➡ Empty Web is a template that creates an empty web with nothing in it.

➡ Learning FrontPage is a template that helps you learn FrontPage by using the Learning FrontPage tutorial available in FrontPage Help.

➡ Personal Web is a template that creates a simple web with a personal home page.

➡ Project Web is a template that creates a web for a project. The web will contain a list of project members, status pages, schedule pages, archives, and discussion areas.

We begin by walking you through the creation of webs using these templates and wizards. Keep in mind that after creating a web from templates and wizards, you still probably need to make modifications to the individual pages and add content to customize and individualize them for your particular needs.

The Normal Web

To create a web using this template, select Normal Web in the Template or Wizard list and then choose OK. The New Web From Template dialog box shown in Figure 6-2 will appear.

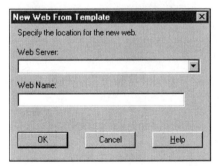

Figure 6-2: You must enter certain information in the New Web From Template dialog box before you can continue.

First you must specify the location of this new web. Type the name of the web server on which your new web will be stored or select a server from the drop-down list, which includes all those servers that you have either administrative or author access to. There will be at least one server in this list.

Next, you need to provide a name for the new web. This web name will correspond to a folder name on the web server. As a result, the web name is subject to the length, character restrictions, and case sensitivity of that particular web server. For example, if you have installed FrontPage under Windows 3.1, your web name can not be more than eight characters in length. Under Windows 95, you have no such restriction.

After you've chosen the server and named the web, choose OK. You have now created not only a subdirectory on the server where this new web is located, but also the web's default home page. The home page has been given the name index.htm. You are still looking at the FrontPage Explorer, but you now have a diagram of this new web in the Link view and a list of the files displayed in the Outline view. If you were to double-click on the page image at the center of the Link view which represents the file index.htm, you would retrieve it into the FrontPage Editor. From there you could edit this page as you wished.

We return to this page later to build on what we have started here. Select the File menu and choose Close Web. For now, we turn our attention to the Corporate Presence Wizard.

Corporate Presence Wizard

Corporations today have looked around and discovered that their competition is on the Web. This seems to give them enough justification to get on the Web themselves. As a result, many companies, both large and small, have created webs to communicate with customers, provide technical or customer support, or to provide product information. Many of these corporate webs have similar elements which frequent visitors look for, such as press releases, new product information, and information on how to contact the corporation itself. Microsoft has taken these most common corporate web elements and worked them into the Corporate Presence Wizard that is included in FrontPage.

To create a web using this template, select Corporate Presence Wizard in the Template or Wizard list in the New Web dialog box and choose OK. The New Web From Template dialog box will appear.

Type the name of your company's server and your company name in the dialog box and choose OK. The Corporate Presence Wizard appears on your screen.

Choosing what pages to include in your web

The first dialog box of the Wizard simply requires that you choose Next to proceed. The second dialog box gives you the opportunity to choose the main pages that will be included on your corporate web from among six choices:

➡ Home Page (this one is required)

➡ What's New

➡ Products and Services

➡ Table of Contents

➡ Feedback Form

➡ Search Form

You select a page and form by using the check box next to it. Check the pages and forms that you want to include in your corporate web site. (We'll review each of the choices in what follows.)

After you've made your selection, choose the Next button. We suggest you choose all at this point in time. If you decide that you don't want to include something later, you can choose the Back button, come back to this page, and remove it.

What topics should you include on your corporate home page?

In the dialog box that follows you have four choices of topics to include on your corporate home page:

➡ Introduction

➡ Mission Statement

➡ Company Profile

➡ Contact Information

A home page is where all of your visitors will first come to your web site. As you learned in the discussion of the Normal Web, the home page in FrontPage is the file index.htm. Your corporate home page should tell your visitors, as succinctly as possible, what your company does and what can be found on your web site.

Mission Statement and Contact Information are default choices in this list. These are both extremely important topics for a corporate page as they tell your visitors what your company's goals are and how to contact you. The Company Profile tells your visitors some detail about what your company does. This is a good idea if you are trying to make your company more personable. The Introduction can be used to give your visitors a general introduction to your company. Select those topics you wish to include on your web by using the check boxes and choose the Next button again.

What should you include in a What's New page?

The next thing the Wizard displays is the What's New page dialog box shown in Figure 6-3. Here you are offered three possible items you can include on your What's New page with associated check boxes to select them:

➡ Web Changes

➡ Press Releases

➡ Articles and Reviews

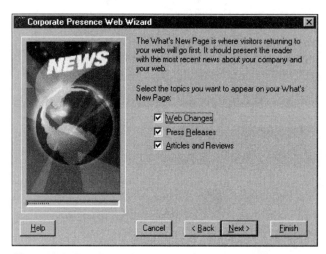

Figure 6-3: The What's New page of this Wizard offers three standard options.

The What's New page is where visitors returning to your site will go first to find out what has changed since their last visit. You should include the most recent news about your company and your web here. If you frequently generate press releases to announce new products or services and you use Microsoft Word to create those press releases, you can copy those documents onto your server and create a hyperlink from your Press Releases web page. Some companies also create articles, customer newsletters, annual reports, or professional publications which they can post on their web and create hyperlinks to from their Articles and Reviews web page (We show you how you can do this in Chapter 10.)

Only the Web Changes option is checked by default. We recommend that you choose all of these selections at this point and, should you decide that you don't need them at a later date, remove them. Including them all will allow you the greatest flexibility in creating your corporate presence. Make your selection and choose Next again.

What should you include on
Products and Services page?

The next dialog box displayed by the
modify the Products and Services pag
containing hyperlinks to individual pa
services your company offers. You ar
many services you want listed. Simp
Products text box and the number of
in the dialog box in Figure 6-4.

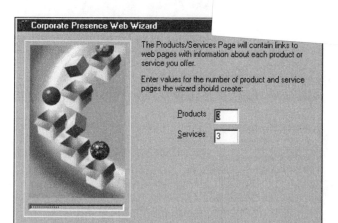

Figure 6-4: Designate the number of products and services you want to provide information about here.

A page will be created for each of the number of products and number of services that you have entered. Choose the Next button.

The next dialog box of the Wizard asks what kind of information you wish to include on the individual pages for the products and services you have specified in the previous dialog box. Your choices for products are

➠ Product image

➠ Pricing information

➠ Information request form

choices are made via check boxes as shown in Figure 6-5. Including the product image option on your product page will provide a spot for you to insert a graphic of the product. A standard template for product pricing information will be included on the page if you select the Pricing information option. Finally, if you select the Information request form, a form allowing your customers to request more information about the product will be automatically created and added to the bottom of the page.

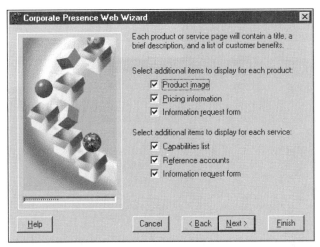

Figure 6-5: Information from pricing to an image of a product can be selected here.

An example of a page containing all three of these options is included on the CD-ROM in the form of the FACTOROT product.

Your choices for services are

➡ Capabilities list

➡ Reference accounts

➡ Information request form

On the services page, choosing to include the Capabilities list will provide a template for you to describe the capabilities of a particular service your company provides. You can include comments from reference accounts by checking the Reference accounts option. Finally, as with the product, you can include a form at the bottom of the page that will allow your customers to request more information concerning your services by choosing to include the Information request form. Select those options you wish to include on your products and services pages and choose Next.

What should you include on a Feedback Form?

You're now presented with choices concerning what types of information you would like your visitors to provide to you in their responses by using the feedback form. This allows you to gather demographic data about your visitors and potential customers when they submit comments about your site, your products, and your services to you. These options include

➥ Full Name

➥ Job Title

➥ Company Affiliation

➥ Mailing Address

➥ Telephone Number

➥ FAX Number

➥ E-mail Address

The default checks all of the options above except for Job Title and Mailing Address. Every bit of information you can gather about your potential customers and clients is valuable. Make your choices and choose the Next button.

What format should you use for user data?

When your visitors submit comments, suggestions, or questions via these forms, the information returned to you has to come in some readable format. This dialog box is where you decide what type of format you want your web feedback form to use in returning data to you. Your two choices are tab delimited format and web page format.

The default is to use the tab-delimited format. Keep in mind that all user input is collected and stored in a file on your server. You might want to load that information into a spreadsheet or database program later. If so, you'll want to leave the tab-delimited format specified. With this option the data is stored in a file called input.txt. When you're ready to gather the data you can open this file in a web browser and then save it to your local disk or copy and paste it into a spreadsheet or database program.

If you decide you want to view or print the information in a web browser, specify the web-page format here. The results of the user input are then stored in a file called input.htm. You might use this format if you don't think you'll need to copy the information into another program to manipulate it, but simply wish to read it online. Choose whichever format you want to use and choose Next.

Presenting your table of contents

Next, the Wizard asks you to make choices concerning the table of contents in the dialog box shown in Figure 6-6. The table of contents page displays a set of links to every page on your web. This format is very similar to the Outline view in the FrontPage Explorer. This helps your visitors get an overview of what pages are available on your web. You are offered three presentation options:

➡ Keep page list up-to-date automatically

➡ Show pages not linked into web

➡ Use bullets for top-level pages

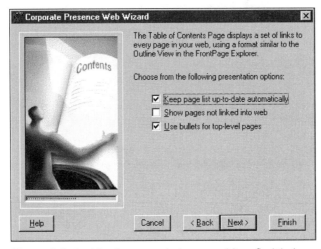

Figure 6-6: A table of contents helps your visitors find their way around your site easily.

The default checks only the Use bullets for top-level pages option. If you choose to keep the list up-to-date automatically, this would allow you to add pages to your web and not have to worry about adding them to the table of contents.

The other option, Show pages not linked into web, provides a different type of access. Occasionally, you will have pages contained in your web's subdirectory that will not be linked into the web itself. The files input.htm and input.txt discussed previously are examples of these types of pages. If you want these pages listed in the table of contents, and therefore accessible to customers visiting your web, choose this option.

Select those options you desire for your web and choose the Next button to proceed.

What information should you include in headers and footers?

The Wizard next asks you what kind of information you wish to include at the top and bottom of each page in your web in your page headers and footers. At the top of your pages you can include

➡ Your company's logo

➡ Page title

➡ Links to your main web pages

At the bottom of your pages you can include

➡ Links to your main web pages

➡ The e-mail address of your webmaster

➡ A copyright notice

➡ The date the page was last modified

Notice that the Links to your main web pages option is available for inclusion both at the top and the bottom of the page. It's up to you if you want to include it in both places, or choose one or the other. On extremely long pages, it is now considered good web design to include it at both locations.

These headers and footers will be added to every page within this specific web that has been created by using this Wizard. You can, however, go back later and designate that certain pages should use different headers and footers. That, however, is not part of this Wizard's function. Select the options you want to include and choose the Next button.

How will your page look?

Your next option in the Wizard concerns the appearance of your standard web page graphics. You have four options here:

➡ Plain

➡ Conservative

➡ Flashy

➡ Cool

Your choice is made by selecting the radio button for the style you want to use. The view on the left of the dialog box (see Figure 6-7) shows you what each of these styles looks like. The Plain option includes no graphics but simply text. This might be your choice if you are planning to include custom graphics on your web. The other three choices vary the level of graphics. Choose a look based on the Corporate image you wish to project: a stock brokerage might wish to use the Conservative option while a computer company might use either the Flashy or the Cool options. Make your selection and choose the Next button.

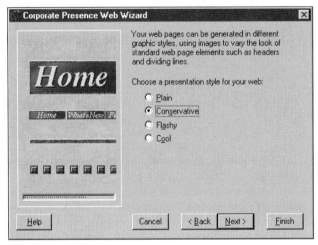

Figure 6-7: The looks available to you are most distinctive when viewed in color on your screen.

What color will your pages be?

Next the Wizard allows you to select the colors for your pages (see Figure 6-8). All the pages will present a consistent color background, consistent text colors, and consistent link colors. The Wizard creates a page called style.htm inside your web. Every page within your web draws its background, colors, and type styles from this page.

This page can be seen as a forerunner of the cascading style sheet specification that will allow you more control over how your web pages are seen, no matter what browser your visitor may be using. This consistency is advantageous to you as a web designer because it gives your visitors a feeling of familiarity and consistency within your site. If visitors are familiar and comfortable with your site, they will be able to move around it more easily and will return more often. Make your choices and choose the Next button.

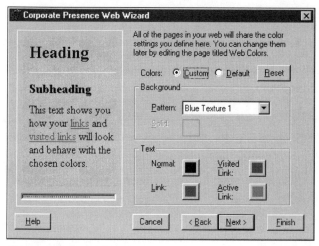

Figure 6-8: The right colors can make your site a more pleasant place to visit.

Should you use an under construction icon?

You now have the opportunity to identify those pages that are under construction with a construction icon. There are many varieties of these under construction icons. FrontPage provides you with one that you can use if you wish. Many webmasters consider the inclusion of these icons as a sign of amateurs. Others like to identify those pages that are under construction so that people are aware that the site is not finished.

You're likely to see these icons on pages on the Web telling you that the author hasn't had time to finish the site and to please return when the site is completed.

Most people in-the-know concerning the Web suggest that a web page be changed often if you want to keep visitors returning to your site. Your web would therefore never be truly finished. The inclusion of this construction icon is redundant and we don't suggest using it. Features such as a "coming soon billboard" for upcoming additions — as well as the New icon for items that have recently been added to a web and a "this page last updated" statement at the bottom of the page are much more professional and keep your visitors aware of how often you work with your site. Make your choice and choose the Next button.

NOTE Keeping your site current is more than good housekeeping. We know of one company whose president was fired over six months prior to the writing of this book, yet the company's web page still contains information about the former company president and what he is doing to improve the company. This is poor web site maintenance and poor public relations.

Including company and contact information

The next two requests from the Wizard concern the name and contact information for your company. The first dialog box provides three text boxes for company name and address information. Fill in the full name of your company, a one-word version of the company name, and the company address. Choose Next to move on to the next dialog box.

The next dialog box requests company contact information. This information includes your phone and fax numbers, webmaster e-mail address, and general help e-mail address. This dialog box allows the entry of one phone number, one fax number, and two e-mail addresses. If you need more, you can enter them manually on pages at a later time. This information will appear in various places in your web and will be available to any page within your web. Fill in the information and choose the Next button.

Finishing up the Corporate Presence Wizard

After you have completed this Wizard, you have the basics of your corporate presence web site. However, you will probably want to add much more specific content to these pages in order to make them truly your own. This will mean customizing them to add links and graphics concerning your company that will be of interest to your visitors. The last page of this Wizard offers you the opportunity to create a To Do List to help you plan the tasks involved in the completion of your web contents. If you want to create this To Do List, leave this option checked. Choose the Finish button. Your corporate web will now be created.

If you leave the To Do List option checked in the last page of the Wizard, a To Do List, such as the one shown in Figure 6-9, will appear on your screen.

A typical Corporate Presence site

Now you've created a corporate web presence using a Wizard. At this point it might be helpful to look at a site that used the FrontPage Corporate Presence Wizard to create their web site. The company we've chosen as the example here is PMP Computer Solutions located in Womelsdorf, PA.

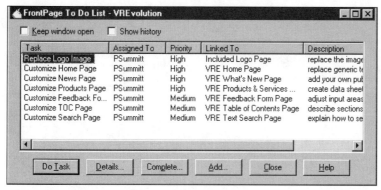

Figure 6-9: There are typically several things you'll want to do to finalize your web site after you complete a wizard.

This site was created by company owner, Peter Perchansky, in three days using FrontPage (he was also working on other things at the same time). Peter used the FrontPage Publishing Wizard to post his pages to his web site, which is located at

```
http://home.sprynet.com/interserv/pmpcs/
```

Notice in Figure 6-10 how Peter used his own custom graphics within the page templates set up by the FrontPage Corporate Presence Wizard. This is an excellent example of customizing and personalizing the page templates provided by FrontPage.

This home page contains many of the options we discussed earlier in this section. Scolling down the page you will find sections concerning the company introduction, the company mission, a company profile, and, as shown in Figure 6-11, company contact information.

Another thing you might notice about Peter's home page in the preceding figures is that the navigation bar is located both at the top and the bottom of his company home page. This allows visitors to move on to the next page in his web without having to return to the top of the page.

We asked Peter why he chose to use FrontPage for his web site. His reply was threefold. He cited ease of use of the FrontPage Explorer and Editor, web consistency as demonstrated in the comparison of the sample pages shown in Figure 6-10 and 6-12, and ease of maintaining the web after it was constructed.

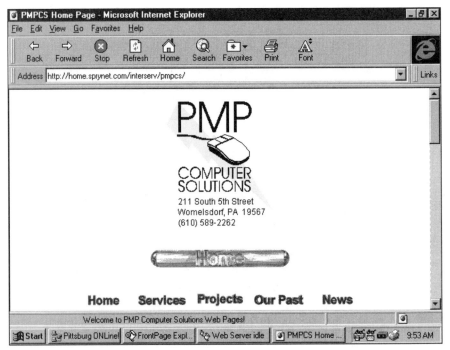

Figure 6-10: PMP Computer Solutions' web site was created using FrontPage's Corporate Presence Wizard.

The consistency among the pages in Peter's company web provides a sense of familiarity to his visitors. This web is an excellent example of how FrontPage can be used even when using a service provider who does not use the FrontPage Server Extensions. We'll return to this web later in this book to examine Peter's use of Java with FrontPage.

Creating a Customer Support web

The next template in the New Web dialog box is the Customer Support Web template. A Customer Support web can be a very useful site to both you and your customers. You can provide a frequently-asked-questions list to the web that will provide answers to some of your customers' questions. Discussion pages can be added allowing customers to interact with your technical support staff.

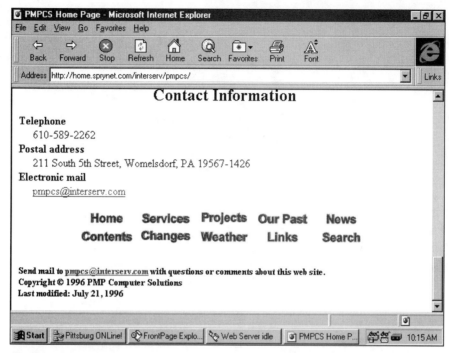

Figure 6-11: Contact information entered in the Corporate Presence Wizard can appear in many places on your web.

The methods used to create a Customer Support web are similar to those used in the previously described template and Wizard. First, from the New Web dialog box, select Customer Support Web in the Template or Wizard list and choose OK. The New Web From Template dialog box will appear again. Type in the name of your organization's server and the name of the web. Make this web name reflective of the product or service you are supporting with this web. In VREvolution's case we named the web FACTOROT_Support to indicate that this web supports our software product FACTOROT.

This template will automatically create the web. The web will consist of several pages, forms, and a discussion section as shown in Figure 6-13.

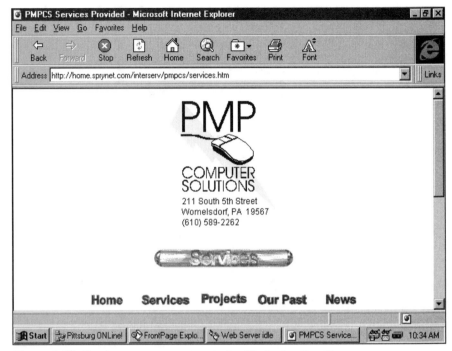

Figure 6-12: Consistency among pages is simplified using FrontPage. Compare this page with the PMPCS Home page in Figure 6-10.

We've included our FACTOROT_Support web on the CD-ROM so that you can see how to use the FrontPage Editor to enter the individual pages and make modifications, such as replacing the word CompanyName with your own company's name. Remember, the pages created with this template are generic pages; you can make as many modifications to them as you wish to enhance their visual impact. We'll discuss exactly how to make those changes in later chapters.

Creating a Discussion web

Discussion webs are an exciting form of interactivity that you can add to your web site. These webs are similar to the forums on CompuServe or message boards present on other online services. They are asynchronous; users do not need to be present at the same time to carry on conversations.

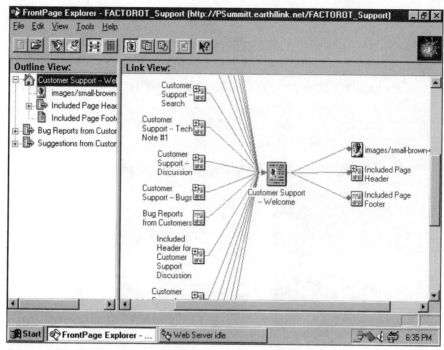

Figure 6-13: Web templates can create several pages for you.

FrontPage allows for the creation of fully threaded Discussion webs. This means that message threads concerning different topics can exist in the same Discussion web. It is also possible to have multiple Discussion webs concerning different topics. For instance, our VRE Q-Sort Project web (described later in the chapter) currently has three different Discussion webs: a requirements discussion, a programming discussion, and a knowledge base discussion. The three Discussion webs deal with different issues.

A Discussion web is a feature that allows you insight into the needs of your users as well as giving users access to each other. This can be valuable, in that users can sometimes answer each other's questions.

From the New Web dialog box, select Discussion Web Wizard in the Template or Wizard list and choose OK. The New Web From Template dialog box will again appear. As with other Wizards and templates, type in the name of your organization's server. This time name the web something reflecting the topic of discussion you are providing with this web. For example, in another VREvolution's example web we named the web VR⇨Discussion to indicate that this web is primarily for the discussion of virtual reality. We've placed these webs on the CD-ROM included with this book for your examination.

After entering the server and name of the web, choose the OK button. As with other Wizards, a screen will appear and begin your walk-through of the creation of your Discussion web. Choose the Next button to proceed.

Choosing the main features of your Discussion web

Your first option will be to select the pages you want to include in your Discussion web in the dialog box shown in Figure 6-14.

Figure 6-14: The pages you choose to include in your Discussion web may be determined somewhat by your discussion topic.

A submission form, which is the form your users will use to submit comments, is required. Other pages you might want to place in your web include

➠ A Table of Contents page will include hyperlinks to all posted articles in the discussion. We strongly recommend you include a table of contents.

➠ A Search Form will allow visitors to find messages that contain certain words or phrases inside the web.

➠ Threaded Replies will allow users to post a reply to a specific message.

➠ A Confirmation page will tell the person posting a message that the message has been posted and what it contained.

Check those features you wish included on your Discussion web and then choose the Next button.

Naming your discussion

Each page in a Discussion web includes a title describing the Discussion web topic. This next section of the Wizard allows you to enter that title, which will appear at the top of every article page and supporting page in the Discussion web.

The title you give to the Discussion web is also the name of the subdirectory where messages will be saved. When you've named the web, choose the Next button to proceed.

Modifying submission form input fields

In this area of the Wizard you select the input fields in your submission form. You have three choices:

➥ Subject and Comments

➥ Subject, Category, and Comments

➥ Subject, Product, and Comments

In the case of a company having multiple products served by only one Discussion web, it is a good idea to include the product field so that people reading the messages will know what product is being discussed. You might also set up categories for this Discussion web; for example, if you have software products that are available on different platforms such as Windows 3.1, Windows 95, or Windows NT. If you don't know exactly what you want at this point, don't worry. You can add more fields later using the FrontPage Editor. For now, select one and then choose the Next button.

Who can post to a Discussion web?

The next area of the Wizard, shown in Figure 6-15, allows you to decide if you want the Discussion web to be protected or not. Your two choices are

➥ Yes, only registered users can post articles.

➥ No, anyone can post articles.

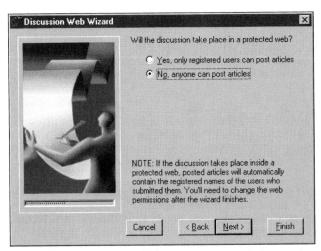

Figure 6-15: Limiting the ability to post to your web to registered users can help you keep control of the discussion.

If you decide to use the first option and have the discussion take place inside a protected web, you'll need to change the web permissions after the Wizard is finished. We discuss changing web permissions in Chapter 9. One advantage of a protected web, however, is that posted articles will automatically contain the registered names of the users who submitted the articles. Keep in mind that these messages are not being e-mailed to the individuals involved; rather, the messages are posted on your server for all to read. In a Discussion web that is open to all for posting messages there is no requirement for identifying oneself. Make your selection by checking the option you want in effect for your Discussion web, and choose the Next button.

How user registration works

You can register users to your site by using the User Registration template (one of the new page templates found in Editor, discussed later in this chapter). Users fill out this form to become registered users. This is only useful in the <Root Web>. Keep in mind that some web servers won't accept self-registration. You'll know if there's a problem when you save a user registration page to a web. FrontPage Explorer will test for this capability at that point. If there's a problem, Explorer will flag your page with a red triangle in the Outline view.

This page has to be saved into the <Root Web> in order to function properly. You'll need to edit the form's properties to set the name of the target web. The target web is the protected web to which your users want to gain access. Replace all instances of the text [Other Web] with the target web name.

After your users fill out and submit the form on this page, they'll be registered users of the web on the server you specified on the form. This target web must already exist on your server before you save the user registration page. Once you've performed this operation, the option of selecting registered users as being the only ones with access to your Discussion web becomes viable.

Creating a Registration web

If you decide to create a Registration web, you must set up your registration form in the <Root Web> and create a protected web. This registration form can only be set up in the <Root Web>; it will not work from any other web. The <Root Web> acts as a gatekeeper to the protected web; it forces your visitors to register before they can have access. Then follow these steps:

1. **From within the FrontPage Explorer, choose the Open Web command in the File menu.**

2. **Select the web server where you want to locate the Registration web and choose the List Webs button.**

3. **Choose the <Root Web> from the webs box and choose OK. Now, type your user name and password and choose OK again.** The FrontPage Explorer will open the <Root Web>.

4. **Select the page that you want to use to restrict access to your web and choose Open in the Edit menu to start the FrontPage Editor.**

5. **Place the cursor where you want the first registration form field on the web page. From the Insert menu, choose the Form Field and then select One-Line Text Box.**

6. **Name the box and choose the OK button.** This name is required. You'll use it to define properties for the form later.

7. **Place the cursor within the dashed boundary of the form and insert a form field for the password. Choose the Form Field in the Insert menu and select One-Line Text Box.**

8. **Type a name into this Name field and select Yes next to the Password field option. Choose OK again.** Keep in mind that the name you've typed in this box must be different from the name you gave in the earlier name box. Again, this information is required; you will use it when you fill in the form properties.

9. **Place two push button fields inside the dashed boundary of the form.** One button will allow your users to submit the form and the other will allow them to reset or clear the form.

The properties for the first button should be a name of your choice that you enter in the name field; type a label such as submit in the Value/Label field. Select Submit for the Button Type and choose OK.

The properties for the second button should be a name of your choice that you enter in the name field; type a label such as Reset or Clear in the Value/Label field. Select Reset for the Button Type and choose OK.

Now is the time to define the properties of the form.

1. **Using the right button of your mouse, click within the dashed boundary of the form and select Properties from the shortcut menu. In the Text Box Properties dialog box, choose the Form Button.** The Form Properties dialog box is now displayed.

2. **In the Form Handler List choose Registration bot and then Settings. Select the registration tab and type the name of the protected web in the Web Name field.** This can be an existing web or a new web.

3. **In the User Name Fields field, type the user name you specified earlier.** Make sure that you enter this name exactly as you entered it earlier in the Text Box Properties dialog box.

4. **In the Password Field box, enter the word you specified earlier for the Password.**

5. **Select the Results tab. In the File for results field, type the name of the file that will contain the authorized user list for the protected web.**

6. **Select a file format and choose OK. This returns you to the Form Properties dialog box. Choose OK to return to the Text Box Properties dialog box, then OK again to return to the page.**

Add labels to identify your form fields and add any other information you feel is needed before saving and closing your page. Now switch to the FrontPage Explorer to set permissions for the web.

1. **If you called for a new web in the Web Name box in the preceding steps, choose New Web in the File menu. In the New Web dialog box, select the template you want to use and choose OK.**

2. **If you specified an existing web in the Web Name box in the preceding steps, choose Open Web from the File menu.**

3. **Select the web server you selected earlier, then choose OK.**

4. **In the Tools Menu, choose Permissions, then choose the settings tab.**

5. Choose the Use Unique Permissions for this web option and then choose the Apply button.

6. Select the End Users tab and choose the "Yes, Registered Users Only" option.

7. Choose the Apply button. If this option is already selected, you still must select it again. Choose OK.

Congratulations, you've just created a Registration web.

Sorting your messages

Next you have to decide how you want your table of contents page to sort the messages posted to your discussion list. You have two choices:

➥ Oldest to Newest (this is the default)

➥ Newest to Oldest

Choose the way you want the messages to be sorted and choose the Next button.

Making your table of contents the web's home page

Your next decision to make is whether you want the table of contents for the Discussion web to also be the home page for the web. Your choices are simple: yes or no. If this web only contains the Discussion web, then the table of contents would be a good choice as the home page. Keep in mind, however, if you choose yes, the Wizard will overwrite the current home page, if there is one, for this web. If you are adding the Discussion web to an already existing web, you should not make the Discussion web table of contents the home page for the entire web. Choose one or the other and choose Next again.

What kind of information can be searched for?

The search form will report different types of information about the documents it finds using the search criteria. You have four choices as to what you want reported:

➥ Subject

➥ Subject and Size

➥ Subject, Size, and Date

➥ Subject, Size, Date, and Score

The size will be reported in kilobytes. While size might not be indicative of the quality of the response, it can be useful in ascertaining the extent of the response. Date is also useful as a basis for a search because out-of date materials can be identified and ignored. The date reported is the date the article was submitted. The score is a measure of the relevance of the query term to the specific article. As before, make your selection and choose the Next button.

What color will your web pages be?

The Wizard next asks you to select the colors for your web pages. All the pages will present a consistent color background, consistent text colors, and consistent link colors. Make your choices and choose the Next button.

To use frames or not?

Frames were an extension to the HTML standard offered by Netscape. Frames are used to divide the users' screen into multiple, scrollable regions. You are actually including different web pages in the different regions or frames on your page. Some feel that this provides for a more flexible and useful presentation of information. Others feel that even Netscape has been unable to get frames to provide a consistent and user-friendly interface for the Web. Whichever way you feel about this, one thing is for certain: the more frames you place on a page screen at one time, the more cluttered and hard to read this page becomes.

Only those people using browsers capable of viewing frames can see them. As most people are currently using either a Netscape browser or one of the newer Microsoft browsers, most people will be able to view your pages if you use frames. Keep in mind, however, that not everyone will be capable of viewing frames.

You can configure your Discussion web documents to use frames as shown in Figure 6-16. If you use frames, both the table of contents and articles will be viewed in individual frames.

You have four choices of how you want the Discussion web constructed:

➡ No frames

➡ Dual interface (this option will cause the page to use frames if the user's browser is capable of displaying frames)

➡ Contents above current article (this option creates a page using frames where the Discussion web contents are seen above the article currently being displayed)

➡ Contents beside current article (this option creates a page using frames where the Discussion web contents are seen to the left of the article currently being displayed)

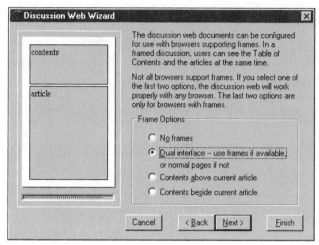

Figure 6-16: Your visitor must be using a browser that can view frames or he won't see them.

Remember that not all browsers support frames. If you choose one of the first two options above, your Discussion web will work properly with all browsers. The last two options, while providing some layout options, will work only with browsers that support frames. Those visitors with browsers that do not support frames will see nothing.

Make your selection and then choose the Next button.

Finishing the Discussion web

Next you'll see a screen telling you what the names of the main pages in your Discussion web are. Choose Finish and FrontPage will begin uploading the pages for your Discussion web to your server. As discussed earlier, we've included examples of Discussion webs we've created at our site on the CD-ROM included with this book. Figure 6-17 shows what one of our Discussion webs looks like from the Outline and Link views in Explorer.

Maintaining a Discussion web (see the example in Figure 6-18) is easy using the FrontPage Explorer. Any message you do not wish to allow to remain in the web can be deleted simply by selecting it and choosing the Delete command from the Edit menu.

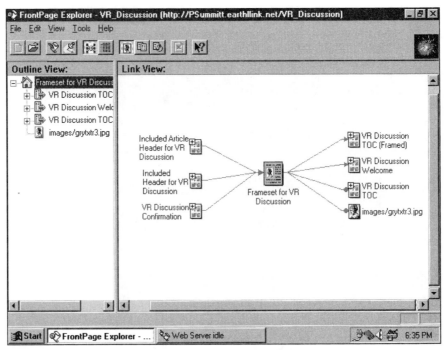

Figure 6-17: You get a good sense of the organization of a Discussion web through Explorer's views.

Creating an Empty web

Using this template creates a web that has nothing in it. The procedure for doing so requires only that you choose the template in the New Page dialog box, and then enter the server and web name.

Choose OK and a web with absolutely nothing in it will be created. Remember, in the FrontPage Explorer, the act of creating means that the web is automatically saved. One use of this template is to allow you to use pages created in another web in FrontPage: copy a web into a new subdirectory, create an Empty web on this new subdirectory, and FrontPage will automatically convert the pages in this web for use by FrontPage. We'll show an example of this later.

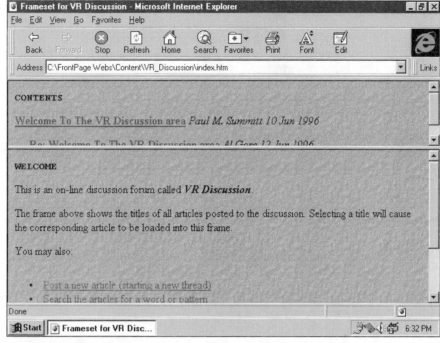

Figure 6-18: Here's our VR Discussion web.

Creating the Learning FrontPage Tutorial web

Another template available in the New Web dialog box is the Learning FrontPage Tutorial web. You won't use this as a template for a web which you publish; rather you yourself use this tutorial to practice building a web to learn more about how to use the FrontPage software.

You can also use the FrontPage Help system to access and use the Learning FrontPage Tutorial. You'll find Learning FrontPage listed under the Help Contents. The tutorial has five lessons. You don't have to do all five lessons at once, but you must do them in order.

Keep in mind that the FrontPage tutorial describes how to access, manage, and use files while using Windows 95. If you're using an operating system other than Windows 95, the process you will use to access and manage files will be different. However, the names of the files and folders, or directories, will be the same.

Creating a Personal web

A Personal web is simply a web where you can talk about yourself. The FrontPage Personal Web template provides a place where, for example, individual employees can create web pages for themselves. As with some of the other templates, the template will automatically create the web. This web will consist of one page, although you can add more. You'll want to use the FrontPage Editor to enter the contents of this page and make modifications to and personalize it. Remember, with most of these pages created using these template webs, these are generic pages; you really should make many modifications to them to enhance their visual impact and make them yours, as Mary has done on her home page shown in Figure 6-19.

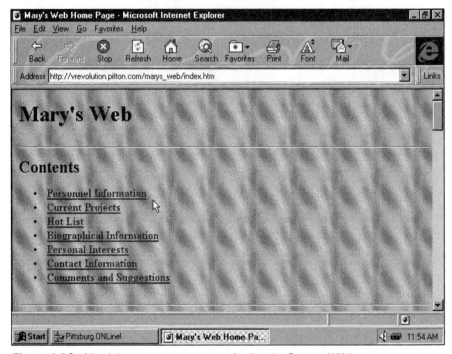

Figure 6-19: Mary's home page was created using the Personal Web template.

Creating a Project web

The last template in the list of templates or Wizards is the Project Web template. A Project web allows you to create an area in cyberspace where a new project can be created and completed. This web consists of pages that include

➡ A list of individual members of the project

➡ The project schedule

➡ The current status of the project

➡ An archive area where background information and example files can be maintained

➡ A search engine used to search the project web site

➡ Two discussion areas dealing with project requirements and information necessary for an understanding of the project

When you type in the name of your web give it a name that reflects the kind of web project it is.

In our case, we've named the web VRE_Q-Sort_Web_Project (see Figure 6-20) to reflect an Internet project we're involved in. The objective of this project is to create an online web-based Q-sort mechanism whereby Q-method researchers will be able to gather data for their studies of subjectivity via the World Wide Web. We've included this web on the CD-ROM as an example of a project web created with this template. This project web allows for individuals from around the world to participate in the creation of this project.

Creating a New Page Using Templates and Wizards

Some of the web templates and Wizards accessed in the New Web dialog box created webs containing a single page, some multiple pages, and one, no pages at all. Although you use the FrontPage Explorer to create new webs, you use the FrontPage Editor to create new pages. Editor has its own set of templates and Wizards used to generate pages.

Open the FrontPage Editor. Choose the New Page command in the File menu to bring up the New Page dialog box shown in Figure 6-21. Note that choosing the New button on the toolbar will not take you to this list of templates and Wizards; it will simply create a new normal page.

Figure 6-20: This is our Q-method related project web.

Figure 6-21: Choose File/New to bring up the New Page dialog box.

There are a total of 28 templates and Wizards available from inside the New Page dialog box. These are listed, along with a brief description of how you would use each, in Table 6-1. The functioning of these web page Wizards and templates is very similar to the detailed examples given earlier in this chapter for web Wizards and templates, and you should have no trouble providing the responses to create these pages as you did with webs.

Table 6-1	Page Templates and Wizards
Template or Wizard Name	**Description**
Normal Page	Creates a single blank page.
Bibliography	Creates a generic page used to refer to related or source printed or electronic works.
Confirmation Form	Creates an acknowledgment receipt that will be sent to a user from either a discussion, a form result, or a registration form.
Directory of Press Releases	Creates a generic page with a directory of hyperlinks to all of your company's press releases, sorted by dates.
Employee Directory	Creates an alphabetized listing you can fill in with the names of your employees. Using a hot-linked table of contents, you can place this employee information on the web site.
Employment Opportunities	Creates a listing of employment opportunities, including an online form for requesting more information.
Feedback Form	Creates the form user can fill in to submit feedback about your site, products, or organization. Consider sending a confirmation form (mentioned above) to acknowledge receipt of such a feedback form.
Form Page Wizard	Creates a form page for gathering various types of information.
Frames Wizard	Creates a page divided into tiled areas called frames, each of which can contain a page or image.
Frequently Asked Questions	Creates a FAQ page to answer commonly asked questions of visitors.
Glossary of Terms	Creates a page with term definitions divided into alphabetized sections.

(continued)

Table 6-1	Page Templates and Wizards
Template or Wizard Name	**Description**
Guest Book	Creates a page where visitors can leave their comments in a public log. You need to specify where the output of this page is to be saved.
Hot List	Creates a page with hyperlinks to your favorite sites. You can divide these sites into categories.
HyperDocument Page	Creates a page that will be one section of a larger hyperlinked manual or report. Link this page to the hyperdocument's home page and table of contents.
Lecture Abstract	Creates a page describing an upcoming lecture or event. This is often used in conjunction with the seminar schedule template.
Meeting Agenda	Creates an agenda for a scheduled meeting, including date, time, location, purpose, major topics, and who should attend.
Office Directory	Creates a page on which you can enter a list of all locations of your company offices.
Personal Home Page Wizard	Creates a personal home page.
Press Release	Creates a generic press release template. Link this to the press release directory template.
Product Description	Creates a page with sections for you to describe a product's features, benefits and specifications.
Product or Event Registration	Creates a page where users can register for product support or to attend an upcoming event. You may edit the properties of the Save Results bot that handles form input, described later in this chapter, to change how user input is stored.
Search Page	Creates a page visitors use to search for keywords or phrases across all the documents in your web, including the default text index created when new pages are saved.

Table 6-1	Page Templates and Wizards
Template or Wizard Name	Description
Seminar Schedule	Creates the main page in a hierarchical web that describes seminar events. Each title on this page would be linked to a separate page describing the seminar (such as Lecture Abstract).
Software Data Sheet	Creates a data sheet page describing features and benefits of your software product.
Survey Form	Creates a page containing a survey form to gather information from your visitors and store it on your web server. Form Page Wizard may help you design a survey.
Table of Contents	Creates a page with hyperlinks to every page in your web displayed in outline form. Use the Table of Contents bot to show what pages can be reached from a given starting page by following links.
User Registration	Creates a page where users can self-register for access to a protected web (only used in the <Root Web>).
What's New	Creates a page, which you should update frequently, telling users about recent changes on your web site, sorted by date.

Keep in mind that after creating these pages from these templates and Wizards, you'll still need to make modifications to the individual pages in order to customize and individualize them to fit your particular needs.

Using WebBots

WebBots are usually referred to as just *bots*. Bots are used to include dynamic features that are evaluated and executed either when you save your page to the server or when one of your visitors loads your page into their browser, depending on the bot.

The Bot command is accessed through the FrontPage Editor Insert menu. Selecting this option brings up the Insert Bot dialog box shown in Figure 6-22.

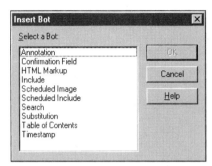

Figure 6-22: The Insert Bot dialog box.

The bots currently available in the Insert Bot dialog box are

➡ Annotation

➡ Confirmation Field

➡ HTML Markup

➡ Include

➡ Scheduled Image

➡ Scheduled Include

➡ Search

➡ Substitution

➡ Table of Contents

➡ Timestamp

We will now discuss each of these bots. To use any bot, you select it from the list in the Insert Bot dialog box. You will then be presented with a dialog box which you fill in with the appropriate information, as described below, for that particular bot.

Annotation bot

The Annotation bot inserts text onto a page that can be seen from the FrontPage Editor, but not seen by a visitor to your site using a web browser. This would be useful for inserting placeholder text or making notes to yourself concerning the construction of the web page.

In the Annotation Bot Properties dialog box, enter the information you want to place on your web, but that you do not want seen by others, as in Figure 6-23.

Choosing OK places the information you've typed into the Annotation Bot Properties dialog box on your web page, but only someone viewing the page using the FrontPage Editor will be able to see this information.

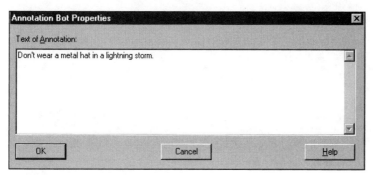

Figure 6-23: The Annotation Bot Properties dialog box.

Confirmation Field bot

The Confirmation Field bot is replaced with the contents of a form field. Basically, the bot inserts the user input from a form into an HTML page. This is useful on a form configuration page where the Confirmation Field bot will echo back the data that a user enters into a field or fields for confirmation.

Place the cursor of your mouse where you wish the bot to be placed on a page and click the right mouse button. Then, select the Confirmation Field bot from the shortcut menu that appears, which will bring up the Confirmation Field Bot Properties dialog box shown in Figure 6-24.

Figure 6-24: The Confirmation Field Bot Properties dialog box.

HTML Markup bot

The HTML Markup bot is replaced with any text that you might want to enter when you create the bot. You can use this, for example, to add HTML code that FrontPage might not recognize but that a specific web browser would.

In the HTML Markup dialog box shown in Figure 6-25 we've entered an example of this type of code.

Enter the name of the form field you want confirmed and choose the OK button. The bot will be placed on your web page in the desired location, ready to confirm the requested information.

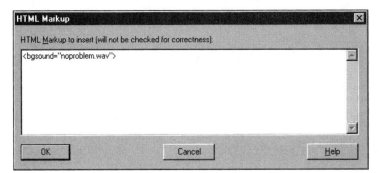

Figure 6-25: The bgsound command is Microsoft Exclusive and not recognized by the FrontPage software yet.

In order to use the Microsoft HTML extensions, you'll need to use this HTML Markup bot. In the case of the code shown in Figure 6-25, the audio is placed on the page and will be played by the web browser. Currently this is only a capability of Microsoft Internet Explorer.

Include bot

The Include bot is replaced with the contents of another page. You identify that page when creating the bot.

The Include Bot Properties dialog box is shown in Figure 6-26.

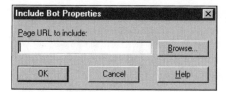

Figure 6-26: The Include Bot Properties dialog box.

Enter the name of the HTML file you wish to be included and choose OK. This bot can be used to create a standard header and footer file that would be included on a web page. You would need to place the Include bot containing these header and footer files on each page on which you wanted them included.

Scheduled Image bot

This bot is replaced with a pre-selected image for a specified period of time. When the specified time period expires the pre-selected image will no longer be visible on the web.

The Scheduled Image Bot Properties dialog box is shown in Figure 6-27.

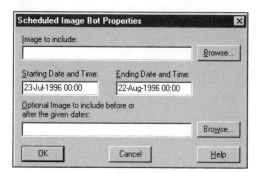

Figure 6-27: The Scheduled Image Bot Properties dialog box.

Enter the name of the image you want displayed. Next, enter the starting date and time and the ending date and time. Finally, if you wish, enter the name of a graphics file you want to use both before the starting date and time, and after the ending date and time. Finally, choose OK.

Scheduled Include bot

This bot is replaced with the contents of the file that you specify for the period of time that you specify. As with the Scheduled Image bot, when this time period is over, the contents will no longer be displayed.

The Scheduled Include Bot Properties dialog box is shown in Figure 6-28.

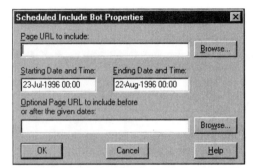

Figure 6-28: The Scheduled Include Bot Properties dialog box.

Enter the name of the file you want displayed. Next, enter the starting date and time and the ending date and time. Finally, if you wish, enter the name of a file you want to use both before the starting date and time, and after the ending date and time. Choose OK.

Search bot

The Search bot will search through the pages of your web for words or phrases and display links to those pages that match the specified criteria.

Enter any criteria you wish for the search in the Search Bot Properties dialog box, as shown in Figure 6-29.

Choose OK and the search form will be placed on your web page. Remember, this bot will create a form that will allow the visitors to your site to type in the word or phrase that they want to use to search on your web.

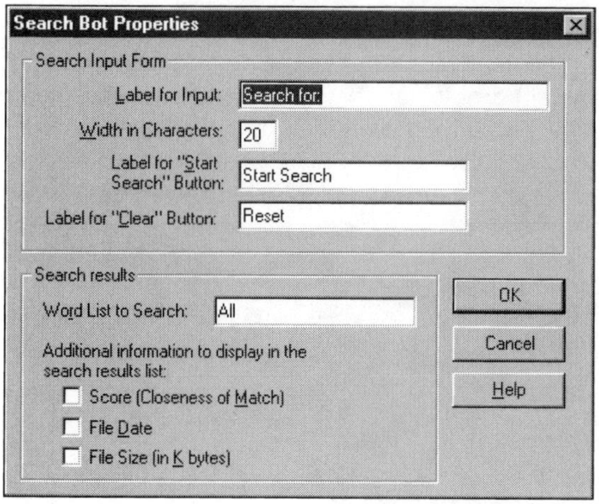

Figure 6-29: The Search Bot Properties dialog box.

Substitution bot

The Substitution bot is replaced with the value of a selected page configuration, or a selected web configuration variable. The Substitution Bot Properties dialog box is shown in Figure 6-30.

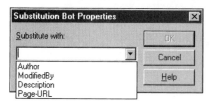

Figure 6-30: The Substitution Bot Properties dialog box.

Select the words you wish to substitute with alternate text. Next, enter the name of the variable you want to use as a substitute. These variables were assigned using the Parameters tab of the Web Settings dialog box. The variables you assign will then be available for your use in the drop-down list present in the Substitution Bot Properties dialog box.

Make your choice by selecting the variable from the drop-down list. Choose OK and your selected substitution will be placed on your web page in the spot you've designated.

Table of Contents bot

The Table of Contents bot creates a table of contents page for your web. This page includes hyperlinks to all pages within your web.

The Table of Contents Bot Properties dialog box is shown in Figure 6-31.

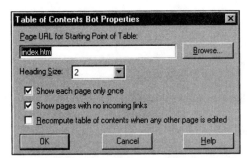

Figure 6-31: The Table of Contents Bot Properties dialog box.

Enter the URL of the page you wish to be the starting point of the table of contents. This should probably be the home page in most cases, but you can select any page you wish. You are given the opportunity to set the heading style. You can use anything from Heading 1, the largest text, through Heading 6, the smallest, or you can choose none. Choosing none leaves the table of contents in the normal font.

There are also three choices in regard to presentation:

➡ Show each page only once (default)

➡ Show pages with no incoming links (default)

➡ Recompute table of contents when any other page is edited

It would probably confuse most users to show the same page more than once in the table of contents, so leaving each page only shown once, the default, is a good idea. Showing pages that are not linked into the web (pages with no incoming links) is also a good idea in most cases. The only time when this might not be so is when there are files being created by your users form responses that only you should be looking at. Finally, we feel that recomputing the table of contents when any page is edited or added is a good idea; this allows the table of contents to be kept up to date automatically.

When you've made your choices, choose OK. A Table of Contents page will be automatically created for your web.

Timestamp bot

The last of the WebBots is the Timestamp bot. This bot is automatically re-placed with the date and time that the page in question was last modified.

The Timestamp Bot Properties dialog box is shown in Figure 6-32.

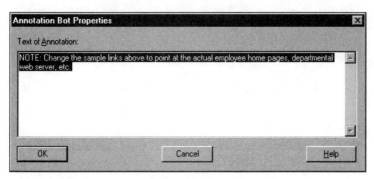

Figure 6-32: The Annotation Bot Properties dialog box.

Select what information you want to display:

➡ Date this page was last edited (default)

➡ Date this page was last automatically updated

You can also select the date and time formats that you wish to have used. When you've made your changes, choose OK. Your Timestamp bot will auto-matically create a notation of the time and date that this web page was last modified.

Creating Your Own Page Template Using Bots

In addition to using the templates that are built in to FrontPage, you can create and save your own templates. Once created, you can use those templates just as you do FrontPage templates to save yourself time in creating new pages.

In the example we'll provide here, we build a template for our specification pages. An examples page generally is used on our web to demonstrate a programming language capability, provide the proper syntax procedure, pro-vide examples of how the keyword is used and what it is used for, and provide other topics that are related to the keyword for additional information.

Creating your own page templates is easy to do using the FrontPage Editor. You basically create a page and save it as a template. Follow along as we build our examples page, then save it as a template. If you follow these steps, you'll have your own copy of the examples page template when you finish. To create the page, follow these steps:

1.   While in the FrontPage Editor, select the New Page command in the File menu.

2.   In the New Page dialog box, choose Normal Page and choose the OK button.

To place an image on the page and center it, simply perform these steps:

1.   Press the Center Text button on the toolbar.

2.   Select the Image command in the Insert menu. The Insert Image dialog box appears.

3.   Choose the From File... button in the Insert Image dialog box.

4.   Change to the /IMAGES/ subdirectory of the *Creating Cool FrontPage Web Sites* CD-ROM.

5.   Choose the EXAMPLES.GIF graphic and choose Open.

6.   The image will be inserted onto your page.

The next thing we wanted to add to our example page was an Annotation WebBot where we would remind ourselves to enter information about our examples. We did this with these steps:

1.   Press Enter to go to the next line. Choose the Bot command from the Insert menu. The Insert Bot dialog box appears.

2.   From the list of bots provided in the Insert Bot dialog box choose the Annotation Bot and choose OK. The Annotation Bot Properties dialog box appears.

3.   In the Annotation Bot Properties dialog box type Enter information as to what kinds of examples are provided on this example page and choose the OK button.

The text you just typed will appear in purple. This means that you can see it from within the FrontPage Editor, but no one accessing this page with a web browser will be able to see the text. The next part of creating our examples page was to begin to enter example headings and annotations to remind us to enter specific information for each example. This was a matter of typing and formatting the text for the heading and adding Annotation WebBots, as demonstrated in the following steps:

1. Press the down arrow on your keyboard to move down to the next line.

2. Change the style for this new line to Heading 1 using the style drop-down list on the toolbar.

3. Type Example 1: and press Enter.

4. Change the style on this new line to Normal.

5. Press the Increase Indent button on the toolbar.

6. Press the Typewriter font button on the toolbar.

7. Select the Bot command from the Insert menu to display the Insert Bot dialog box.

8. Choose the Annotation bot and choose OK.

9. In the Annotation Bot Properties dialog box that appears type Place the first example code here and choose the OK button in the dialog box. Again, the text you just typed will appear in purple and no one accessing this page with a web browser will be able to see this text.

10. To enter another example heading, press the down arrow on your keyboard and move to the next line.

You can now simply repeat the preceding Steps 2-9 to add as many example headings and Annotation bots as you like.

We next added a graphic on our page, which we've included on the CD-ROM in this book so you can follow along:

1. Select the Image command in the Insert menu.

2. Choose the From File... button to get a browse dialog box where you can select the location to get the image from.

3. In your computer's directory change to the /IMAGES/ subdirectory of the *Creating Cool FrontPage Web Sites* CD-ROM.

4. Choose the LINE06.GIF graphic and choose OK. This graphic is now placed on your specification page.

Finally, to format and place a copyright notice and date stamp on the bottom of this page, follow these steps:

1. Press Enter to move to the next line on your page.

2. Change the text style to Heading 5.

3. Press the Center Text button on the toolbar.

4. **Type** Place Copyright Information here **and press Enter.**

5. **Type** This page last updated. **(Make sure you add a space after the word updated).**

6. **Select the Bot command in the Insert menu.**

7. **Choose the Timestamp bot and choose the OK button.** The Timestamp Bot Properties dialog box appears.

8. **Make sure the Date this page was last edited option is chosen and the date format is the one you want. We accepted the default properties. Choose the OK button and place a period at the end of the sentence.**

Now comes the part where you actually save this page as a template so you can use it again any time you like. Follow these steps:

1. **Select the Save As... command in the File menu and the Save as... dialog box appears.**

2. **Change the Page title to** Examples Page **and the Page URL to EXAMPLES.HTM and press the As Template... button.**

3. **In the Save as Template dialog box, change the name to** Examples **and the description to** Create an examples web page.

4. **Press the OK button.**

That's all there is to it. You've created your own examples page template which you can use for presenting your code examples. When you open a New Page dialog box, this template will be listed right along with built-in FrontPage templates, and you just select it from that list. Figure 6-33 shows what the template page looks like when completed.

Keep in mind that when you create a page template, you are creating something designed for a specific purpose. A résumé template, for example, allows you to quickly place and update the important information about your professional experience on the Web. Templates can be real time savers. When you create many pages with similar content, it's much easier to call a template than to create the page over and over.

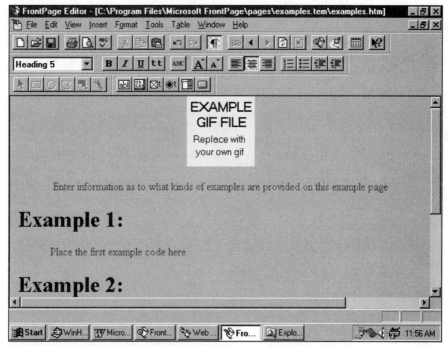

Figure 6-33: The Examples Page template allows you to post your programming examples in a standard form.

Moving On

In this chapter we have looked at the FrontPage templates, Wizards, and WebBots. Specifically, we have looked at:

➡ How to access and use web templates and Wizards to create webs for specific purposes, such as customer support or Discussion webs.

➡ How to access and use web page templates and Wizards to create pages on your web that help you do things such as getting feedback from your users, announcing meetings and lectures, building forms, and describing products.

➡ How to use WebBots to perform tasks such as confirming user entries, providing links to other files, building a table of contents, or helping users perform searches on your web.

➡ How to create your own templates which incorporate bots and save them.

In the next chapter you take your first steps toward creating cool pages with FrontPage.

Putting FrontPage in Action

Defining Your Site's Purpose

In This Chapter

Determining your needs

Customizing your site

Placing your page on the Web

In this chapter we discuss the creation of your web site and, by default, the creation of your web and the individual web pages. You'll take what you've learned in previous chapters about the FrontPage Explorer, the FrontPage Editor, and the FrontPage templates, wizards, and WebBots and use them to create your web content.

You should begin by deciding what you want to create and why.

What Do You Want Your Web Site to Achieve?

While using Microsoft FrontPage is considerably easier than working with straight HTML in the creation of a web site, it still takes effort and time on your part. If you know what you want to say, to whom you want to say it, and why, the design and implementation of your web site will be a great deal easier. To begin designing a web, you should start by answering these questions:

➡ What is the purpose of your site?

➡ What do you want to say?

➡ Who do you want to visit your site?

➡ How do you want your visitors to use your site?

If you begin to create a web site without a clear idea of what you want that site to achieve, you'll waste time designing elements that you might later discard. You also may build illogical and confusing links. Not only does a lack of focus in building your site waste your time, but you may end up with a site that presents a confused and scattered presentation to your visitors.

What is the purpose of your site?

This is quite possibly one of the most important questions you should ask before you begin creating your site. In most cases, the purpose for addressing a message to a specific audience is to call them to action, whether that action is to become informed, to respond to the message, or to do something specific, such as becoming a member or buying a product.

The question in your mind as you prepare to create your site should be "What is it that I want someone to do after he has visited my web?"

You may want your audience to

➥ Vote for a specific political candidate

➥ Use your particular brand of plug-in applications for their web browser

➥ Accept your justification for why and how the West was conquered

➥ Not drive while intoxicated

Each of the messages above represents a call for action on the part of the audience. Each of them also is a legitimate use of the Web.

In effect, you are trying to convince people that you're a nice person with your personal web page, that your company is the best in its business with your corporate pages, or that your issue is just.

It's not as easy as you might think to determine what your site's purpose is. There are often at least two levels of purpose involved. These two purposes can be looked at as the site's ostensible purpose and the site's true purpose.

Ostensible purposes might include

➥ Performing a community educational service

➥ Providing customers with a convenient way to get information about your products

➥ Public relations

Your true purposes for the site can sometimes be more difficult to find and acknowledge. True purposes generally are ego related and might include

➥ Establishing yourself as an expert on a topic

➥ Saving yourself the cost of the middle-man in selling products

➥ Wanting to put a more positive spin on negative news coverage

A true purpose for a site might be to create an outlet for your programming skills. However, while pursuing your own interests you have to design the site so that it interests your visitors, as well. Then, they'll enjoy your work and visit again. When you can admit to your true purpose honestly, meeting the purposes of your web site is much easier.

What do you want to say?

Knowing the purposes behind the creation of your web allows you to determine exactly what you want to say. Your web site is a form of communication and, as such, it will have a topic and an image to present.

What's the topic?

Generally, the topic of your web is easy to determine. The trick here is to stay focused on that topic. Don't start a web about antique model trains, then stray into model ships and Amtrak train schedules. Don't build a web page that says at the outset that it is about one thing, then by its end strays to another agenda. To be effective, a web, or at the very least a specific web page, should have only one topic. We'll use a page from our VREvolution web site, shown in Figure 7-1, as an example.

Despite the fact that each of the webs hyperlinked from this page might have different topics, this page has only one topic: what webs are available at this site.

The question of what is the topic of the web, or web page then, is easy to answer. The question of what image you want to present might not be so easy.

What image do you want to project?

The image you give your page reflects your attitude towards the topic of your web or web page. Ask yourself what it is about the topic that you want to say. What flavor or feel do you want to convey to visitors? Then incorporate that feel into the design of your site.

Figure 7-1: The topic of this page is "What webs are available at this site?"

For instance, the background you use for your page or web can say a great deal about how you want visitors to feel about your site. The background for VREvolution's business pages, as seen in Figure 7-2, is a textured gray. This background is used for the entire web, giving the web a consistent, business-like and professional appearance.

While using this background reflects a good image for a business site, you might want to use something completely different for a personal web site, as shown in the personal web in Figure 7-3.

The use of a particular background is just one example of how design can impact the image of your web. Other components such as type, graphics, sound, and text styles can also impact on this image.

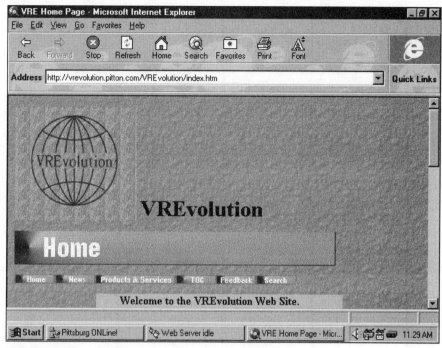

Figure 7-2: The background can help give a web a more professional appearance.

Who do you want to visit your site?

The next question you need to ask yourself concerns the audience that you're aiming for in designing your web's content. Implicitly or explicitly, every web and every web page, just like every other form of communication, has a target audience. This is especially true when you are trying to inform, influence, or inspire.

There are two very important pieces to this question:

➡ Who is your audience?

➡ What does your audience know?

To say that a web is aimed at everyone on the Web is to admit that you don't have a clear idea of what your message is. People accessing the Web possess multiple and divergent layers of experience. Is your computer graphics web, for example, aimed at a computer beginner or at a programming expert? They're both out there. The programming expert will probably leave your site with snorts of disgust if you present your site as an advanced graphics discussion, but your message is not worthy of his or her attention.

Figure 7-3: The image for a personal web site is much different than that for a business site.

In general, as with any method of communication, the broader the audience, the harder it is to provide anything meaningful via a web page or web. The more focused your audience is, the greater your chance of getting your message across. By tailoring your web presentation to the tastes, interests, attitudes, and feelings of your intended audience, you can maximize the appeal and impact of your web.

What does your audience know?

If your audience has at least some knowledge of your site's topic you can assume that they have come to your site because they want to hear your message. The more they know about the topic, the less background and explanation you need to offer.

If you are aiming your pages at experts in a topic who you know would be interested in the cutting-edge information you're presenting, your web pages do not need to sell visitors on the value of the site with lots of graphics and special effects. If a visitor is interested in hard data, too many graphics and special effects on a web might cause him to go elsewhere for the information.

The point is that how the visitor wants to use the site should be considered when you're designing it. If you're trying to appeal to hard-core researchers looking for data, fancy graphics and sounds only get in their way. If, on the other hand, you want to provide an overview of a topic to get newcomers to it intrigued enough to learn more, you might want to provide graphics, games, and other goodies so they visit, browse around, and enjoy the content.

Beginners, who know little or nothing about your topic, require a hook to maintain their interest in your site. This hook might be the use of special effects such as a marquee effect or background audio files that play music during a visit to your web page. A hook could be Java or CGI applications that spruce up an otherwise dull page.

Learn everything you can about your audience

A recent study suggested that the profile of the average web surfer is changing. Previous versions of the study indicated that the average web surfer was a financially stable, young white male. The 1996 study from the Georgia Institute of Technology suggested that the Web is diversifying, with larger numbers of women and minorities.

Don't assume that you know who is on the Web, and therefore part of your potential audience. Get out on the Web. Surf around and look at the various sites. Visit forums that are visited by the type of person you want to speak to. Don't take it for granted that you know what your audience's tastes and level of knowledge are. Never assume that their tastes and levels of knowledge are the same as yours. Use every means at your disposal, such as guest books and visitor registration online forms on one of your web pages, to gather information about your visitors (see Figure 7-4).

Finally, don't be tempted to stray from your original purpose simply for the sake of greater numbers of visitors to your site. Keep your site's focus, and the kind of visitor you want will find you.

Creating Your Web's Content

Now that you understand the purpose of your web, what you want to say, and who you want to say it to, you can turn your attention to creating your web. Of course, every web is different depending on what you decide to include and how you'd like your visitors to use it. In the following example we're going to walk you through the creation of our company's web so you can begin to see the typical activities involved in building a web site.

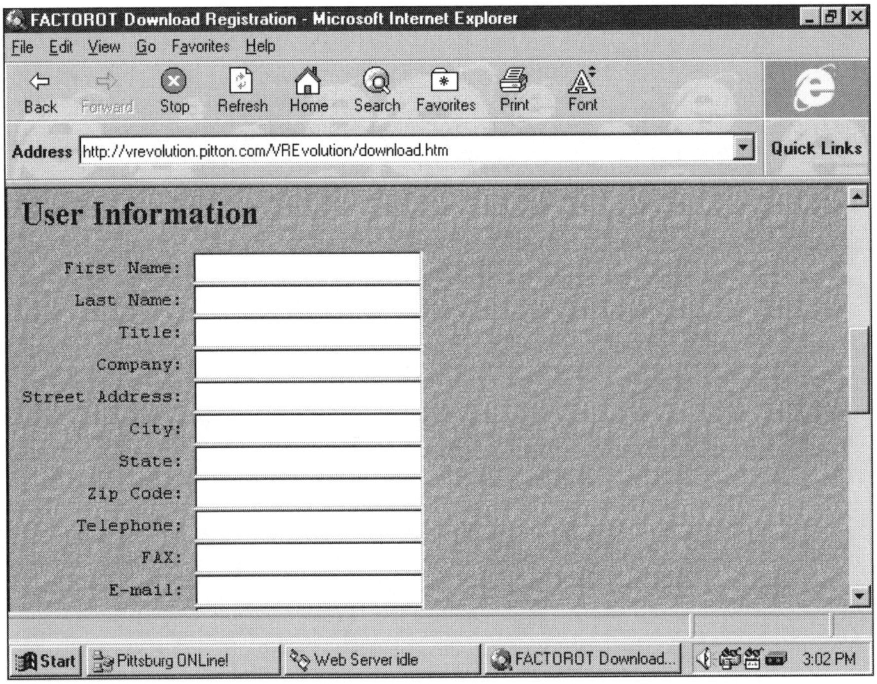

Figure 7-4: Gather information about your audience from every source.

Creating the Corporate Presence web

You can probably use one of the wizards or templates discussed in Chapter 6 as the basis for most webs. In that chapter we walk you through the creation of a corporate web using the Corporate Presence Wizard. The web created by that wizard formed the skeleton for our company site. After we had the wizard completed, we began to build on it by making changes to customize the content.

Making changes to the Corporate Presence web

When we created a Corporate Presence web we entered several To Do List items. Clicking on the To Do List button on the toolbar we could see what needed to be done to finish this web. Figure 7-5 shows the To Do List for the VREvolution web.

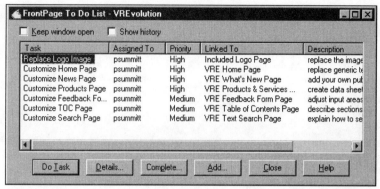

Figure 7-5: The FrontPage Corporate Presence Wizard created a To Do List for us for the VREvolution company web.

What's on our To Do List?

This list is sorted by its links and by priority. The first item on this list is for us to replace the generic Logo Image on the Included Logo Page with our own company logo. This was assigned to Paul Summitt as the webmaster for our site.

 Remember that you can see and even modify the details in the To Do List by clicking on the Details button in the To Do List dialog box.

By highlighting the task and clicking on the Do Task button in the To Do List dialog box the Included Logo Page was loaded into the FrontPage Editor, as shown in Figure 7-6.

Replacing a logo

The first step in replacing the generic logo with our own was to click on the words "Company Logo" on our page to select them. In the Insert menu we chose the Image option and the Insert Image dialog box appeared.

There are three different methods you can use at this point to insert a logo graphic, depending on where the logo file is located. The three possible locations for such a file would be within the current web, on the World Wide Web, or from a file located on a local system.

➡ **From within the current web.** If you choose this option, the display box contains all the image files contained in the current web. If a logo is already in the web, select it from this location, then click on the OK button.

➡ **From the World Wide Web**. If you want to get a logo graphic from somewhere on the World Wide Web, click on the From URL button to display the Open Location dialog box. Type in the URL where the graphic is located in the Location field, then click on the OK button.

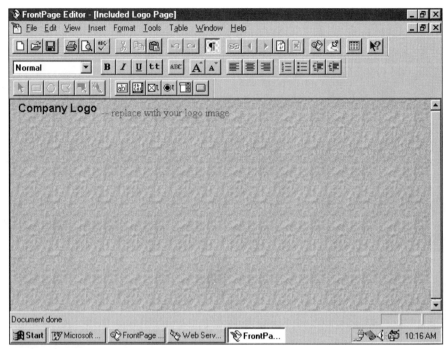

Figure 7-6: We needed to replace the image with our company logo.

➦ **From a file.** In our case, our logo was in a subdirectory on our local system, so we clicked on the From File button. We then selected the drive and subdirectory where our logo file was located and opened our logo file. Clicking on the Open button caused our logo file to replace the generic file that was located on the Included Logo Page, as shown in Figure 7-7.

 It doesn't matter what format your logo file is in. If you select a file that is not a .GIF or .JPG file, FrontPage will convert your logo file to a .GIF file.

Notice the text (" – replace with your logo image") to the right of our logo in Figure 7-6. This text was inserted with the Annotation WebBot discussed in Chapter 6. Once you place a logo you can delete this WebBot. This is done by clicking on this text to select it. When you do, your cursor will take on the shape of a little robot. You can click on the Cut button from the toolbar to remove the WebBot.

One final step in creating our web was to put our company name beside the logo. We accomplished this by choosing the Style drop-down menu on the Format toolbar and selecting the Heading 1 style.

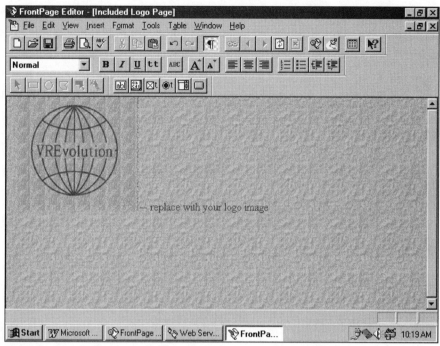

Figure 7-7: The Logo has been replaced, but we're still not finished.

An alternative method you can use to change the style is to choose the Paragraph option in the Format menu and then select Heading 1 from the drop-down Style list in the Paragraph dialog box.

We then entered the name of our company, as shown in Figure 7-8.

To save the changes, we chose the Save option from the File menu.

Clearing the task from the To Do List

After a task is completed, it's a good idea to mark it as complete on the To Do List. We clicked on the To Do List button to bring up the To Do List on our screen, highlighted the Replace Logo Image task, and clicked on the Complete button in the To Do List dialog box. When you click on the Complete button, the Complete Task dialog box, as seen in Figure 7-9, is displayed.

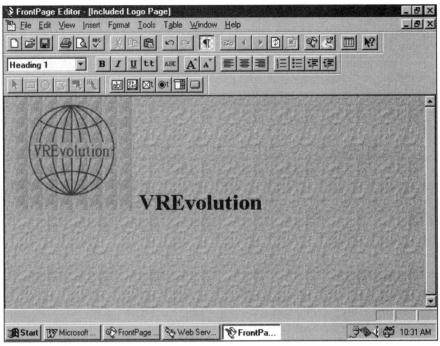

Figure 7-8: Our Included Logo Page is finished.

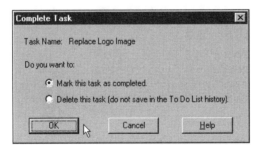

Figure 7-9: Don't forget to let the To Do List know that you've completed the task.

This dialog box offers the options of marking the task as completed and deleting the task. If we had chosen to delete the task, the task would not have been saved to the To Do List history. We chose to mark the task as completed but not delete it. Doing this allows us to keep track of the changes that have been made to our site over time and serves to keep members of our web team informed of the progress of each other's assignments. Because we had chosen to view just tasks still to be done, the Replace Logo Image task disappeared and we were left with the six tasks listed in Figure 7-10.

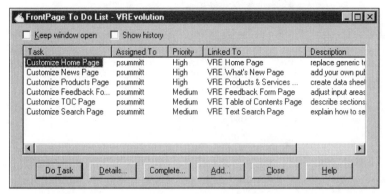

Figure 7-10: The six tasks we have left to do are shown on the To Do List.

Customizing the home page

The next thing we wanted to do was to customize our home page. We highlighted the Customize Home Page task and clicked on the Do Task button. Our corporate home page was loaded into the FrontPage Editor. We scrolled down the page until we saw instructions which we had placed on the page using the Annotation WebBot. These instructions (see Figure 7-11) told us what information we needed to place on the page and where on the page to place it.

Figure 7-11: Much of our work was identified for us by FrontPage.

We replaced the generic text with something specifically related to our company, as shown in Figure 7-12.

After we completed this task and replaced all of the generic material with material specific to our company, we returned to the To Do List and clicked on the Complete button. We then repeated this entire procedure to add other content by performing the Customize News Page, the Customize Products Page, the Customize Feedback Form, the Customize TOC Page, and the Customize Search Page tasks.

Placing Your Page on the Web

After you've completed these tasks, you'll have a well-constructed, consistent, and professional looking web. You're now ready to place it on the Web.

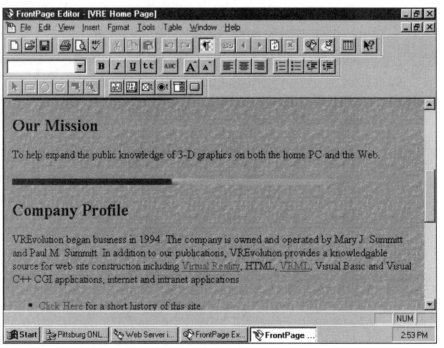

Figure 7-12: The VREvolution Company home page, after the generic material was replaced with material specific to our company.

Running FrontPage on the server machine

If you are running FrontPage on the same machine as your server software, all you have to do now is place a hyperlink from your server's home page to your corporate home page. This is simple to do using FrontPage. Refer back to Figure 7-1 near the beginning of this chapter. Each of the webs available on our server are identified and hyperlinked in the server's home page. We've provided the HTML code for this page in Listing 7-1.

**Listing 7-1 The HTML Code for the index.htm. file at
http://vrevolution.pitton.com**

```
<!DOCTYPE HTML PUBLIC "-//W3O/DTD HTML//EN">


<html>
<head>
<title>VREvolution Web Site Main Index</title>
<meta name="GENERATOR" content="Microsoft FrontPage 1.1">
<meta name="FORMATTER" content="Microsoft FrontPage 1.1">
</head>
<body background="images/starmap.gif">
<p align="left"><img src="images/vre_logo.gif" align="bottom"
width="180" height="162"> </p>
<h1>Welcome to http://vrevolution.pitton.com</h1>
<p>You will find the following webs at this site:</p>
<ul>
    <li><a href="http://vrevolution.pitton.com/VREvolution/
index.htm">VREvolution Company Site</a></li>

    <li><a href="http://vrevolution.pitton.com/VR_Discussion/
index.htm">Virtual Reality Discussion</a></li>

    <li><ahref="http://vrevolution.pitton.com/VRE_Q-
Sort_Web_Project/index.htm">VRE Q-Sort Web Project</a></li>

    <li><ahref="http://vrevolution.pitton.com/VRMLSpec1
index.htm">VRML Examples and Version 1.0 Specification</a></li>
    <li><ahref="http://vrevolution.pitton.com/FACTOROT_Support

index.htm">FACTOROT Customer Support web</a></li>

    <li><ahref="http://vrevolution.pitton.com/marys_web
index.htm">Mary's web</a></li>
```

(continued)

Listing 7-1 *(continued)*

```
    <li><ahref="http://vrevolution.pitton.com/Pauls_web
index.htm">Paul's web</a></li>
</ul>
<h6 align="center">These pages Copyright &#169;1996,
VREvolution.</h6>
<h6 align="center">This page last updated June 14, 1996 10:58
AM.</h6>
</body>
</html>
```

You can learn more about the ins and outs of adding such links to your page in Chapter 10.

Running FrontPage on a machine other than your server

If you are running FrontPage on a different machine than your server and creating the web using the Personal Web Server on your local machine, you have to transfer the web to your server. There are a couple of things you need to make sure of before you can copy the web between the machines, however:

➡ Does your service provider's server have FrontPage Server Extensions installed?

➡ Are you recognized as an administrator, or as an author, by your service provider's server?

If you answered no to the first question, all is not lost. First, you can call your service provider and request that it install the FrontPage extensions on its server so that you can install your web. Second, if your provider can't install the extensions, you can still install your web to its server. Save the web using the Export Selected option in the File menu of the FrontPage Explorer. Then, using the FrontPage Publishing Wizard, save your web pages to the server.

If you've worked with your provider to ensure the extensions and your authorization are in place, you're ready to copy the web across. Connect to your service provider as you usually do. Next, open the FrontPage Explorer and click on the Copy option in the File menu. Simply fill in the name of the Destination Web Server and the name you want the web to have on that server.

Remember to check the appropriate boxes if you want to add this web to an existing web, or if you are copying child webs. Click on OK and your web will be copied from your local machine to the server. You'll be notified when the transfer is complete.

Moving On

In this chapter we stressed the importance of knowing what the purpose of your web pages and web site are, who you are aiming the site at, and what you want to say on your site.

To demonstrate these topics, we used a corporate presence web created from the Corporate Presence Wizard and completed the tasks present in the To Do List. You were walked through the completion of some of these tasks as we performed them in context with our VREvolution company web.

Finally, we showed you how to copy your corporate web to the Internet or intranet server that would be its home.

In Chapter 8, we show you how to incorporate forms and CGI applications into your web pages.

Creating Forms Using FrontPage

Understanding the role of forms on a web

Creating forms for a Corporate Presence web

Using forms with a Personal web

Creating forms that are useful for business and educational webs

In this chapter, you see how you can use the various form creation wizards to create pages that raise the level of interactivity at your web site. Forms are a basic but important level of interactivity between you and your visitors. They allow you to find out who your visitors are, what they think and how your page has impressed them. Forms can be an excellent method of ensuring that you are offering material on your web that is useful and interesting to your visitors.

Introduction to Forms

One of the extensions to the original HTML specification allows for the inclusion of forms in your web pages. Forms were included in an extension that was added to HTML Specification 2.0, so most browsers today are capable of reading forms.

Basically, a form represents two-way communication on your web. You've placed a message on the Web and the form allows people visiting your web site to respond to your message. This two-way communication can be as simple as a single text box that allows your visitors to leave their e-mail addresses, or more complex, such as a large, multi-capacity database that allows for search and submission via the Web.

Communication such as this can be accomplished in a variety of ways. The two most basic types of the HTML form methods are the GET and POST commands. With FrontPage you don't need to know HTML commands to create forms: you simply build on elements provided by wizards and in templates to create the forms for your site. This form creation is a simple matter of selecting the type of information you want from a list of options. Then FrontPage puts these options on your page for you. FrontPage takes care of most of the details of creating forms for you; this allows you to concentrate on what kind of information you want to gather, and not about the inner workings of the form.

There were several forms created in the pages and webs generated earlier in this book. We'll take a moment to look a little more closely at the forms you've already learned to create before moving on to other forms.

The Forms of the Corporate Presence Web

There are two basic types of forms that you can include in your Corporate Presence web: Feedback Forms and Information Request forms. Feedback forms allow your visitors to express their opinion on a topic of discussion, tell you whether they like your site, or vote on an issue you've brought up. Information request forms allow your visitors to ask you to supply specific information, such as new product specs or details about ordering your product.

Feedback forms

There are a variety of options available to you in constructing your feedback form, as discussed in Chapter 6. These options will depend on what type of information you wish to be gathered from the people providing feedback to you. The items of information you can request from your users in a feedback form are

- Full Name
- Job Title
- Company Affiliation
- Mailing Address
- Telephone Number
- FAX Number
- E-mail Address

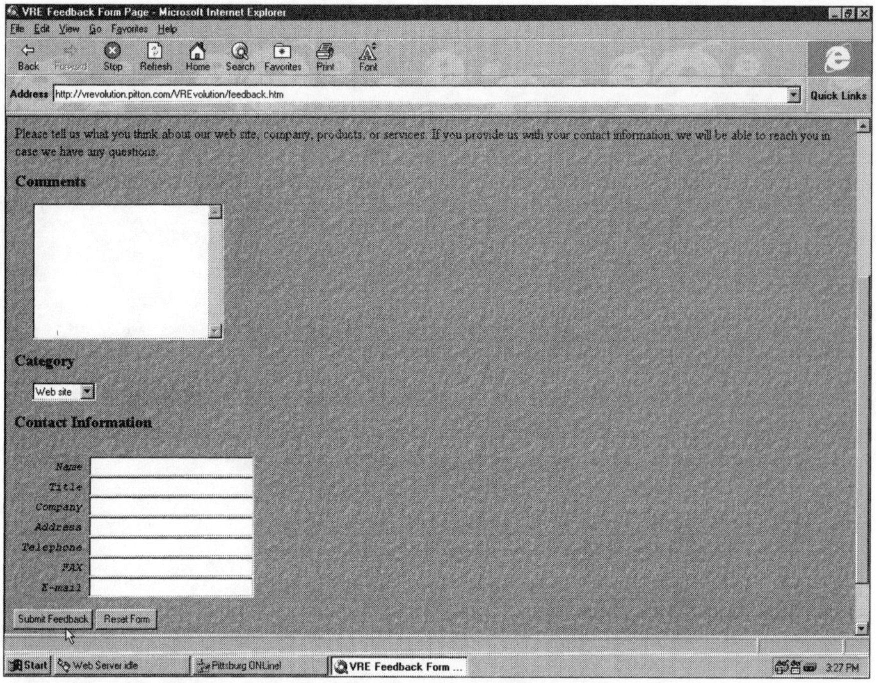

Figure 8-1: The feedback form for VREvolution's company web.

While the default choices for the feedback form present in the Corporate Presence web are the Job Title and Mailing Address options, Figure 8-1 demonstrates the use of other options. We used all of the options to create this feedback form for the VREvolution company web.

Requesting all of the information available through options gives you the opportunity to gather as much information as possible about your visitors. Knowing more about your visitors might help you to place things on your web that will get them to return to your site.

Information request forms

Visitors to your site can use an information request form (see Figure 8-2) to tell you what kinds of information they would like to receive. You can find several examples of this kind of information request form dealing with products and services at our own site.

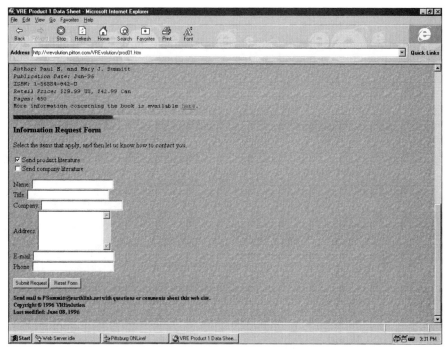

Figure 8-2: The information request form on our own site allows users to request product literature.

The creation of information request forms is an integral part of the Corporate Presence web and doesn't require a great amount of effort on your part. You can, however, make modifications to these forms. In our case, we did not want to include the option of our users asking us to call them. We simply deleted this option from the Information Request form by selecting that text and pressing the Delete key on our keyboard.

The Forms of a Customer Support Web

After you create a customer support web using the appropriate wizard, as shown in the Link View in Figure 8-3, there are several possible forms you may consider adding. We'll briefly examine some of these forms and their possibilities.

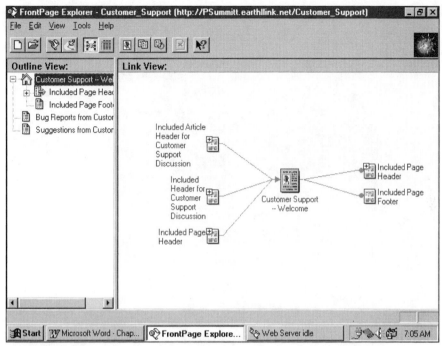

Figure 8-3: The structure of a Customer Support web ready for you to add forms.

The bug report form

The bug report form, as seen in Figure 8-4, is a simple form that allows your software users to report problems with the software.

A bug report form consists of a series of questions and requests that, once answered, should provide you with enough information to find the bug and fix it. These questions include

➡ What version of the software does the user have?

➡ What platform has the user installed?

➡ Can the user provide a description of the problem or bug?

➡ What are the steps that will reproduce this problem or bug?

➡ What are the circumstances surrounding how the problem or bug was discovered?

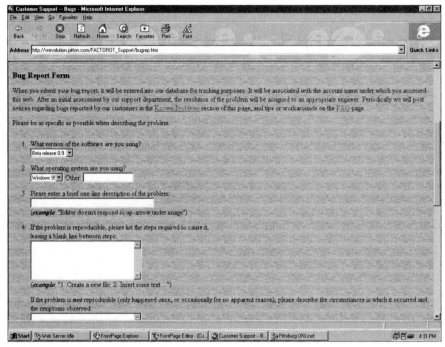

Figure 8-4: This page shows a simple bug report form.

➤ Were there any error messages that occurred when the problem or bug was discovered?

➤ What is the name, e-mail address, and phone number of the person submitting the bug report?

After the user submits this form, he or she will receive a form submission confirmation listing the information just provided. The submission will be saved in a file named buglist.htm in your Customer Support web directory. This file is not part of the web proper (that is, a page that is linked into the web from another page), but is stored in your web's directory on the server and can be reached via the Web by anyone who knows the name and location of the file. If you wish, you can change the name of this file using the settings in the Form Properties dialog box by following these steps:

1.   **Right-click the Submit button on the form.**

2.   **Select the Form Properties option.**

3.   **In the Form Properties dialog box, choose the Settings button, which displays the Settings for Saving Results of Form dialog box.**

4. In the Settings for Saving Results of Form dialog box, select the Results tab.

5. Change the name of the File for Results field by typing in a new file name.

After you change the name of this file no one will know how to find this bug report file except you and the people to whom you give the file name.

You can transfer these bug reports to a page where you list all known bugs. You can do this by using the Include Bot option of the Bot command in the Insert menu. Place your cursor in the page where you want to transfer this information, execute the Insert, Include Bot command and identify the name of the file containing the bug report. It will now be loaded into the page at this location.

Customer suggestion form

A customer suggestion form (shown in Figure 8-5) is a simple form that allows your visitors to make suggestions regarding topics such as:

➥ Web design

➥ Product features

➥ Customer support

➥ Your company

➥ Your marketing methods

The suggestion form consists of a series of questions. By answering these questions your visitors make recommendations for change. These questions are

➥ What is the category of comment?

➥ What is the subject of the comment?

➥ What is the suggestion?

When the user submits this form he or she will receive a form submission confirmation listing the recommendations and comments that were just provided. The submission will be saved in a file named feedback.htm in your Customer Support web directory. Again, this file is not linked into any other page in the web, but rather is stored in the same directory as the web on the server. As a result, this file can be reached via the Web by anyone knowing the name and location of the file. If you wish, you can change the name of this file by changing the settings in the Form Properties dialog box.

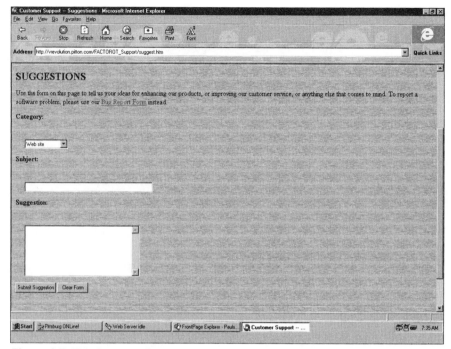

Figure 8-5: The Customer Support web suggestion form.

No one will know the name of this bug report file except you and the people to whom you tell the name. This will help you maintain control over the contents of these suggestions.

The Forms of the Personal Web

You created a personal web in Chapter 6. Including a comments and suggestions form in your Personal web (see Figure 8-6) allows you to receive comments about your site from people visiting your web so you can maintain and improve its content.

The comments and suggestions will be held in a file called, by default, homeresp.txt. Keep in mind that anyone knowing the name of this file can call it up over the Web and view it. If you wish, you can change the name of this file by changing the settings in the Form Properties dialog box. As with previous examples, changing the name of this file allows you to maintain control over who sees the comments made about your site.

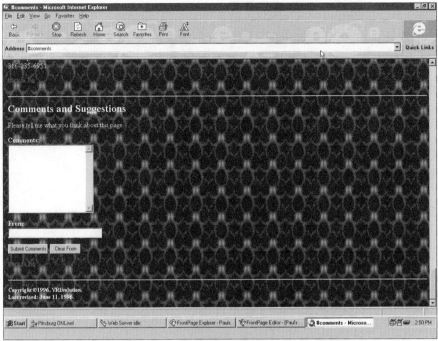

Figure 8-6: The look of a suggestion form on a Personal web may be a bit more informal than one on a Customer Support web.

Creating Useful Business and Educational Forms

Two of the most useful forms available in FrontPage, for both business and education, are the user registration and survey forms. The user registration form can be used to register software, register for events, or register visitors to your web site. Survey forms can be used to gather information about your users or to gather information about how visitors use your site. In the next few paragraphs we will show you how we have created two such forms. The first is the FACTOROT user registration form that must be filled out before visitors to our web can download the FACTOROT program. The second form is a survey form we have used to gather information about the hardware and software used by people accessing our VRE Q-sort Web Project.

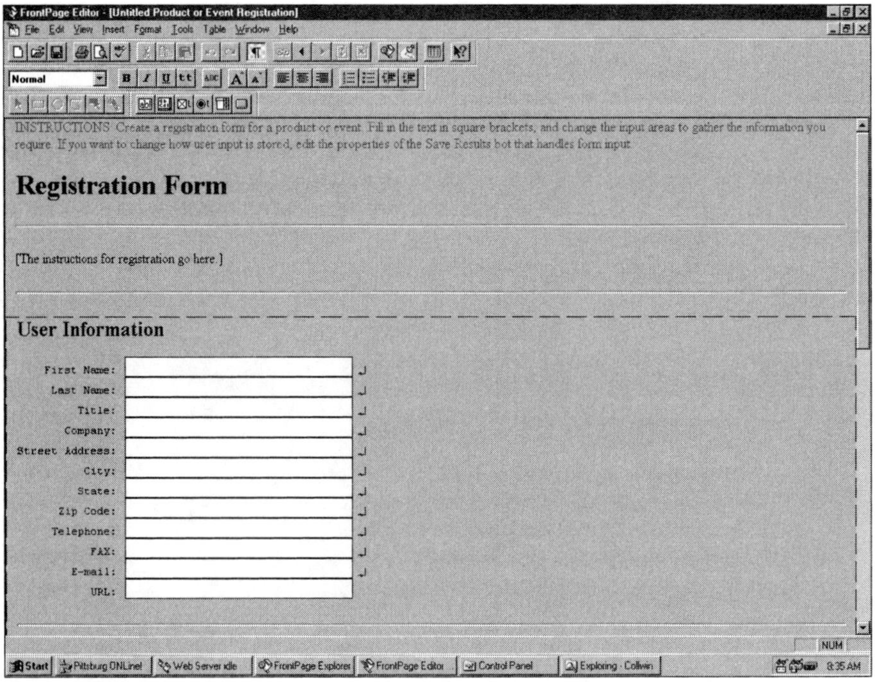

Figure 8-7: The generic Product or Event Registration form.

The user registration form

Creating a software user registration form is easy. In Chapter 6 we discussed creating the Product or Event Registration page. This page contains the user registration form seen in Figure 8-7.

For our web we decided that the beta of our FACTOROT program would be a free download, but we still wanted to know who was using it and what users would like to see in future versions of the program. We therefore placed a user registration form in the web so that the users would have to complete the registration before they could access the download page. In other words, in order to download FACTOROT, a user would first have to fill out this form.

We used the Product or Event Registration template and modified the requested information to match our needs. We also added our included logo page and included footer page and changed the background to match the rest of this web using methods that were discussed in Chapters 4, 5 and 6. A portion of the resulting form is shown in Figure 8-8.

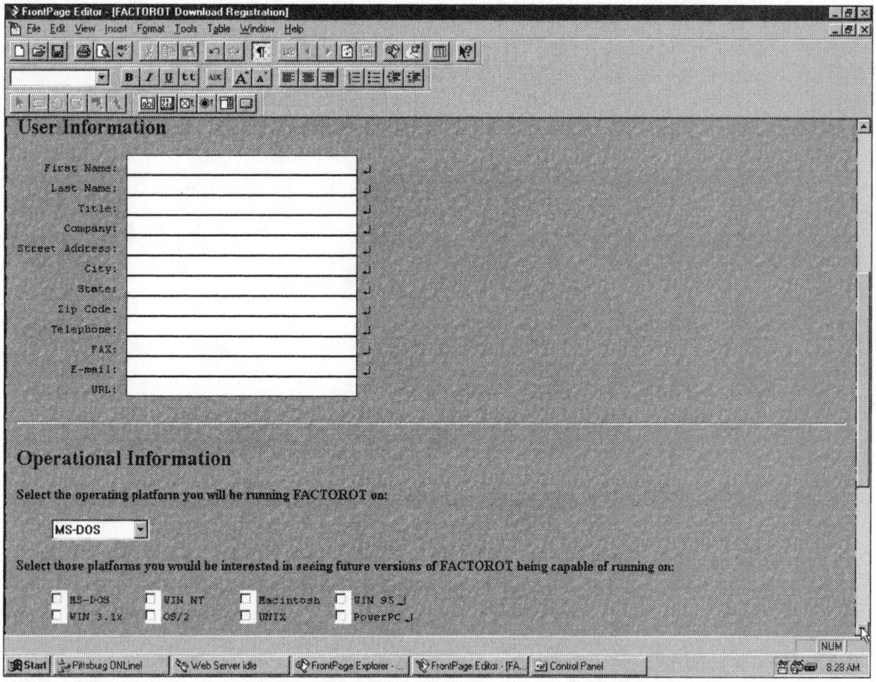

Figure 8-8: VREvolution's FACTOROT Download registration page.

The entire process of creating the page and form took less than half an hour from start to finish.

The survey form

Whether you work in business or education, surveys are an important research tool. Placing a survey form on your web site to gather information can lower the cost of such research tremendously.

We created a survey, as shown in Figure 8-9, for our VRE Q-Sort Web Project. This survey was used to gather preliminary information on the computer skill levels and other demographic data for those interested in the possibilities of performing Q-Sorts via the Web.

The information gathered using this survey form is saved by default into a file called **survresp.txt**. Again, keep in mind that anyone knowing the name of this file can call it up over the Web and view it. If you wish, you can change the name of this file by changing the settings in the Form Properties dialog box.

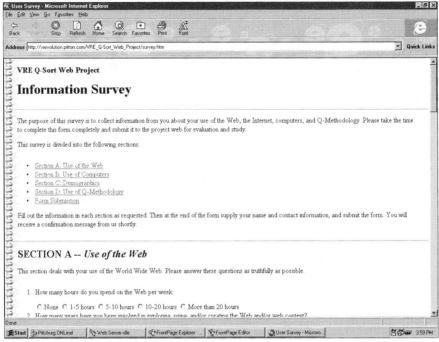

Figure 8-9: The VRE Q-Sort Web Project Information survey form.

Moving On

In this chapter you've seen how easy and quick it is to create forms using the various tools available to you in FrontPage.

In the next chapter we look at how collaboration is made possible in the creation of webs with FrontPage. We also look at the forms found in discussion webs, as well as the discussion webs themselves.

Your Page and Beyond

PART IV

Using FrontPage to Collaborate

Webster's defines collaboration as working jointly with others. An example of this is the creation of this book. Mary and Paul worked together in writing the book. Nancy and David worked hard editing it. Ellen made sure the right people were pulled together to make this book possible. People at Microsoft such as George Wang and Tracy Van Hoof helped to provide the software and the technical expertise concerning the software. All books are a collaboration. In fact, many, if not all, projects are collaborations.

Whereas a letter or an essay is quite often written by one individual, a book requires the collaboration of many. By the same token, while a small web might be easily maintained by a single individual, the larger the web, the more likely it is that more than one individual needs to be involved. Good design, implementation, ongoing maintenance, and upgrading of software are all necessary. People have to respond to visitor queries, create new pages containing requested information, and upload technical articles about the topic of the web to help to make a cohesive online presence. That kind of effort often requires several people working together.

This chapter is intended to provide you with the vision and the know-how to use FrontPage in creating and facilitating collaborative efforts. There are two types of collaboration that are made possible by FrontPage: the collaboration made possible with those who help you create and maintain webs with FrontPage and the collaboration you can enjoy with users of your web through discussions webs.

Collaboration in Web Creation and Maintenance

Web development is best accomplished via a team effort. The project can be broken down into smaller goals and each of these goals can be assigned to individual team members. One person could possibly do all the work, but it would be a full time job on a larger web. FrontPage supports either a team or an individual effort through the use of the web permissions. Using these permissions FrontPage controls who is able to administer, author, and use a web site.

Administrators are allowed to create, edit, and delete web sites; create, edit, and delete pages; and add and remove authors and users. You can have from one to as many administrators as you wish. It's probably best, however, that you have only as many administrators as are absolutely necessary. As with the old adage, "too many cooks spoil the broth."

Authors are permitted to add, edit, and delete pages in a given web site. You can have no authors, or as many authors as you wish. Having authors working on individual web pages can be of great assistance in creating large webs.

End users are allowed only to browse the pages and webs that the administrators and authors have created. You want to have as many of these as possible.

These administrators and authors can be as close to one another as the next desk, or as far away as the other side of the earth. In order to take advantage of this collaborative opportunity provided by FrontPage, however, the type and level of access being granted to team members must be designated.

Types of access

In order for us to demonstrate how these types and levels of access are controlled using FrontPage, we'll be using our VRE Q-Sort Web Project web as the example for collaborating in the creation and maintenance of a web.

We'll take a look now at how we set the access levels for administrators, authors and users in our VRE Q-Sort Web Project example. To understand this, we examine the permissions that we set when we installed the Personal Web Server in Chapter 3.

Permissions settings

You can look at permissions settings by starting the FrontPage Explorer, opening the Tools menu and selecting the Permissions command as shown in Figure 9-1.

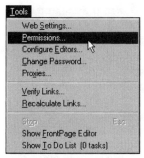

Figure 9-1: Accessing the Web Permissions dialog box.

The Web Permissions dialog box appears. The Web Permissions dialog box has four tabs as shown in Figure 9-2: Settings, Administrators, Authors, and End Users. There are two choices concerning the settings: to use root web permissions or set unique permissions.

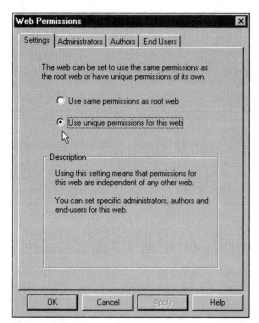

Figure 9-2: We chose to have unique permission settings for this web.

When FrontPage is installed, a set of default permissions is set up for the root web containing one administrator (usually the person doing the installation) and open access to end users. If we left the permissions the same as our root web permissions, then our web's permissions would be inherited from the root web. The permissions for this project web are then maintained using the root web: administrators, authors, and end users for the root web have the same permissions in this web.

If you prefer to use unique permissions for your project web, you would set the project web as independent of any other web and must set specific administrators, authors, and end users for the web. Because of the type and nature of the Q-Sort project, we decided to use unique permissions. This means that anyone having access to the root web will not necessarily have access to the Q-Sort project web. It is a good idea to have different settings for the different webs that are located within the site for security reasons. Our settings for those permissions can be seen in Figure 9-2.

These settings give us the ability to allow specific individuals, with chosen abilities, to make modifications and help maintain this web.

Naming administrators

Administrators can create webs and pages; delete webs and pages; designate administrators and authors; and restrict end users from accessing a web. If you leave this web's settings so that it inherits its administrators, authors, and end users from your root web, when you select the Administrators tab in the Web Permissions dialog box, the Add and Remove buttons on the left of the dialog box are unavailable.

However, since we chose to set up this web with its own unique permissions, when we select the Administrators tab in the Web Permissions dialog box these two buttons are activated and ready for us to modify the administrator settings, as in Figure 9-3.

Paul was the original administrator of the web server when it was installed and currently his user name is the sole administrator listed for the project web. Adding a new administrator is simple:

1. Select the Add button in the Web Permissions dialog box.

2. The New Administrator dialog box appears. Enter the new administrator's user name and password in the appropriate fields.

3. Confirm the password by typing it into the Confirm Password field.

4. Choose OK in the New Administrator dialog box.

Removing an administrator is also easy. Simply select the administrator to be removed in the Web Permissions dialog box and choose the Remove button. It is best if you keep the total number of administrators to a minimum. A web's

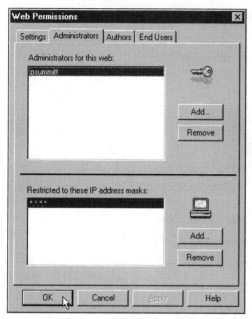

Figure 9-3: At this point, Paul is the only administrator listed for this web.

vision can get lost when more people become involved in the decision making. You can't, however, remove yourself as administrator of a web while that web is active. Another administrator must remove you. Also, your web must have at least one administrator so the last person on the list cannot be removed.

You can also restrict your administrators' access to the web through the use of specific IP addresses. If, for instance, you had a group of people at your office working on a web and you didn't want them to be able to access this web from their homes, you could allow web access only via the workplace IP address.

Choosing your authors

Authors can create and delete pages in a web. They cannot create and delete webs, nor can they designate administrators or authors, or restrict end users from accessing a specific web.

To add an author for this project web you would choose the Authors tab in the Web Permissions dialog box. Next to the Authors For This Web field, choose the Add button. The New Author dialog box appears on screen. To add an author, follow three simple steps:

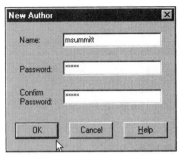

Figure 9-4: Mary's user name and password have been entered into this New Author dialog box.

1. Type the user name in the Name field.

2. Type in a password in the Password field.

3. Confirm the password by typing it in the Confirm Password field, as shown in Figure 9-4.

At this point, you can choose OK to add the name to the author's list. Again, you can restrict your authors' access to the web using specific IP addresses, as you were able to do with the administrators.

Keep in mind that when you've made a modification to the web permissions using any of the tabs inside the Web Permissions dialog box, you can use the Apply button at the bottom of the dialog box (see Figure 9-5). The Apply button makes whatever changes you've made to the various tabs in the Web Permissions dialog box take effect immediately.

Qualifying your end users

There are two options you can choose as to how you want your users to access your webs. Those two options are allowing everyone access or allowing only registered users access. How you set this up may be a personal or business-related choice. You might want to limit your users to those who have paid a fee to access your information. On the other hand, when you first set up your site you may want open access to encourage all comers.

In order to change end user access you need to choose the Permissions command from the Tools menu in the FrontPage Explorer. Choose the End Users tab in the Web Permissions dialog box. Choosing between open access and restricted access is as simple as changing which radio button is selected in the dialog box. If you do choose to restrict the use of the web to registered users, you need to set up a procedure for registering for the web. There is a template discussed in Chapter 6 that can assist in setting up this registration page. You should have a good reason for restricting access. You lose many potential users just by letting it be known that you are contemplating such a decision.

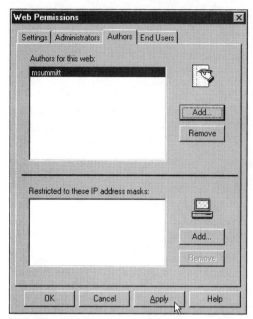

Figure 9-5: Choosing the Apply button makes the changes effective immediately.

There is one situation where you may want to consider restricting access, despite the potential losses in users you may endure. If you have a project web where the project is proprietary or where non-project participants are disrupting the use of the project web with unwelcome and unneeded comments, you may have to consider restricting this web to only registered users. Currently, the VRE Q-Sort Web Project web is open to all visitors. This, however, could change in the future should the site become more active with disruptive visitors. Figure 9-6 demonstrates how changing from open use to registered users is accomplished.

Web control via the To Do List

Every web you create has its own To Do List. You learned about creating and maintaining a To Do List in Chapter 4. This list can be extremely helpful in controlling the creation and maintenance of a web. However, it is only useful if you create good procedures and inculcate consistent habits for your team members in using it. Keep these guidelines in mind when using a To Do List in a web collaboration:

➡ It can be helpful to create standards for naming tasks. For example, if everyone begins his linking tasks with the word "Link," you can sort your To Do List by task name to find all such tasks easily.

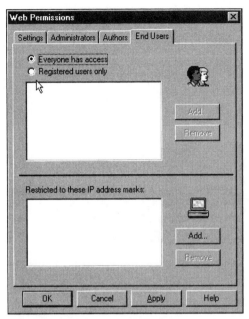

Figure 9-6: Change the radio button to change from open access to registered users only on this web.

➥ Let your team members know the importance of adding tasks to the list and marking tasks completed when they're done. That way everyone on the team can check for the latest status of a task and no two people will try to do the same task by mistake.

➥ Decide ahead of time what types of tasks are substantial enough to merit a to do item, and which are too minor to waste your time in tracking. Building a new page should definitely be on the list; changing the font on a particular heading may not be. Let all team members know these parameters for what to include in the list.

FrontPage's Limitations for Collaboration

Two defects exist in the current version (1.1) of FrontPage relative to its use for the collaborative construction of a web. These two problems can be overcome to a certain level of satisfaction with careful planning.

First, the FrontPage Explorer does allow several authors to be assigned the same user name at the same time, which could cause confusion among your team members. As administrator, make sure that you assign the users unique names and passwords. Stress to your authors that they should maintain the secrecy of their passwords.

Second, there is no file-locking capability which would prevent two or more authors from working on the same page at the same time. The first author to save the file will see a message box containing a warning stating that the most recent changes will be overwritten if a different author, at a later time, tries to save the file. This is obviously less than ideal. A work-around is for you, as the administrator, to assign pages to specific individuals, telling them to work only on their assigned pages and no other pages.

Collaborating on a Web

Collaboration in the creation of a web is not the only form of collaboration that is possible using FrontPage. You can create webs using FrontPage that enable, support, and sustain collaboration among those using the pages of the web.

Discussion webs are virtual places where people can discuss the merits of a topic, project, or approach to a problem. These discussion webs can be either open or closed, registered or anonymous. One of the possible advantages of open, anonymous discussion groups is that no one knows who the other individuals participating in the discussion are. This provides for open discussion without intimidation due to gender, rank, age, or position. In this manner, ideas that might not be presented in a registered web due to fear of embarrassment, retaliation, or ridicule, are presented before the group for open discussion.

In Chapter 6 we discuss how these webs are created using the various web and page templates and wizards. Discussion pages can be part of a larger web or webs all to themselves. Each message placed in the discussion is done by submitting a form page in your web. The messages are submitted in much the same way comments are submitted in comment forms discussed earlier.

Depending on what decisions you make concerning the discussion web, the discussion can range far and wide or can be tightly restricted to a single topic. You also have the ability to delete those messages you don't wish to be included in the discussion. This is accomplished simply by deleting the file of the message on the server.

An example of a collaborative web

Our VRE Q-Sort Web Project web is an example of a web site that is collaborative in nature. A Q-sort is a research method in which a person will sort through a stack of cards containing statements, and arrange those cards according to their own level of agreement or disagreement with those statements.

When a number of these sorts have been performed, the results are factor analyzed and the results from each person will factor into groups. Each person who performed the Q-sort is a subject. These subjects' responses can then be displayed in a 3-D manner, using programs such as FACTOROT.

During early 1996, during an online e-mail discussion with others interested in the possibilities of performing Q-sorts via the Web, we decided to create the VRE Q-Sort Web Project web and sponsor it on our web site. What we did not want, however, was for this to be thought of as a private project. This Q-Sort Web Project was intended to be a project in which several people, bringing many talents and abilities, would be working to make Web Q-Sorts happen. In other words, it was to be a collaboration.

How could we make a location that doesn't really exist real enough for collaboration between project members? The answer was easy. Collaboration is made possible through communication. Discussion groups are one of the Web's tools for fostering communication among users. FrontPage allows us to create discussion groups with ease.

Using templates to create discussion groups

One way to create discussion groups is with FrontPage templates. Two discussion groups are automatically created with the FrontPage project web template, for example. These two discussion groups are the Requirements and the Knowledge Base discussions.

The Requirements discussion as we've used it provides a place where participants can record suggestions about the features that should or shouldn't be included in the VRE Q-Sort Web Project software. This location also allows participants to engage in a public dialog regarding the merits of various requests for enhancements. Everyone is welcome to submit suggestions.

The Knowledge Base discussion area is provided as a place where participants can record common questions and answers that may crop up in the course of working on the VRE Q-Sort Web Project. Some of the topics that may be appropriate in this discussion area include software or hardware configuration or good sources of tools.

Figure 9-7 shows what the discussion areas of this web look like in the Outline and Link views of the FrontPage Explorer.

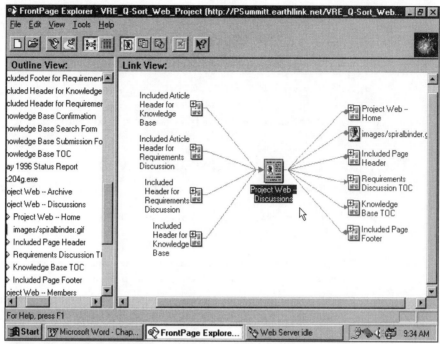

Figure 9-7: Both the Requirements discussion and the Knowledge Base discussion are accessible from the Discussions page on the web.

When we created this project web using the FrontPage Project Web template these two discussion webs were created automatically as part of the web. We were not given any choice in how these discussions were set up. We can, however, edit the pages to personalize them using the FrontPage Editor.

Adding a new discussion web

You aren't limited to using a template to automatically create discussion webs. It's just as simple to add more discussions to any web. To do this you can use the Discussion Web Wizard. You begin this process with a few simple steps:

1.   While in the FrontPage Explorer, select the New Web command in the File menu.

2.   In the New Web dialog box select Discussion Web Wizard in the Template or Wizard list and choose OK.

3.   The New Web From Template dialog box will appear.

     Type in the name of your server and what you want this discussion web to be called.

In our case, we called the new discussion web *Programming* to cover the discussions of the actual programming of the web-based user interface.

Starting the Discussion Web Wizard

After entering the name of your server and the name of this discussion web, choose the OK button. A wizard screen appears to begin to walk you through the creation of this discussion web. Choose the Next button to proceed.

The main features of a discussion web

The second wizard screen provides options for what features you wish to include on your discussion web. A submission form is required on a discussion web. Any other pages you want to place in your discussion web are completely optional. For example, you also can include

➡ **Table of Contents.** We highly recommend that this be included. The Table of Contents page will include hyperlinks to all posted articles in the discussion.

➡ **Search Form.** This page can be a valuable asset to a discussion web in that it allows visitors to find messages that contain certain words or phrases inside the web.

➡ **Threaded Replies.** This allows users to post a reply to a specific message. This is a must for a well-organized discussion web.

➡ **Confirmation Page.** This page tells the person submitting a message that the message has been posted and what information was posted. For new and old users alike, it is reassuring to have the web confirm that your message was received.

In our case we checked all of these features to be included on our discussion web, and then chose the Next button to proceed.

Naming a discussion web

Each page will contain a title describing the topic of the discussion web. The Discussion Web Wizard allows you to choose the title you want to use. This title will appear at the top of every page of the discussion web.

When you've named your web, choose the Next button and move on to the next option for your discussion web.

The input fields in the submission form

In this area of the wizard you are able to select the number and names for the input fields for your submission form. There are three choices:

➥ Subject and Comments

➥ Subject, Category, and Comments

➥ Subject, Product, and Comments

We chose Subject and Comments for our web in order to keep things simple. If you don't know which you want at this point in time, just choose the same. You can add more fields later if you want, using the FrontPage Editor. Choose the Next button to proceed to the next option.

Who can use this discussion web?

The wizard allows you to decide if you want the discussion web to be protected or not. What this means is that you can choose to make the discussion web open to all users or restricted to specific users. The two choices are

➥ Yes, only registered users can post articles.

➥ No, anyone can post articles.

We decided to have an open web and selected the second choice. If, however, you decide to use the first option and have the discussion take place inside a protected web, you'll need to change the web permissions after the wizard is finished. An advantage of this approach is that posted articles will automatically contain the registered names of the users who submitted the articles. When you've made your selection here choose the Next button to proceed.

Sorting messages

The next step is to decide how you want your Table of Contents page to sort the messages posted to your discussion list. The two choices are

➥ Oldest to Newest (this is the default)

➥ Newest to Oldest

This choice is a personal one. If you wish people to read through older messages before getting to the new messages so as to get a feel for the discussion topic of the web, leaving the default choice would be a good idea. If, however, you wish people to be able to go to the most recent messages immediately, change to the second choice. For our web we left this in the default position and chose the Next button to proceed.

Where's home?

On the next screen you have the choice of making the Table of Contents page your home page for the discussion web. If you choose Yes, the Discussion Web Wizard will overwrite the current home page for your web, if there is one.

NOTE

We chose to not make the table of contents for the discussion web our home page, but rather included it in the project web. This entailed going back later and editing the discussion page in order to add this new discussion web's table of contents to the discussion web page.

Searches

When you choose Next to move forward, you are offered four options as to what kinds of information the search form will report. These four choices are

➥ Subject

➥ Subject and Size

➥ Subject, Size, and Date

➥ Subject, Size, Date, and Score

The size will be reported in kilobytes. The date is reported as the date the article was submitted. The score is a measure of the relevance of the query term to the specific article. We chose the last option, giving our web's participants as much information as possible. When you've made your choice, choose the Next button to proceed.

Selecting colors

The wizard allows you to select the colors of your web pages. We, however, wanted our pages to be consistent with the rest of our project web. This required us to later go to the Web Colors dialog box that is part of this discussion web and edit the properties to match those of the rest of the project web. Whether you make color settings here or not, when you're ready, simply choose the Next button again to move on.

Using frames

The next step is to configure how the discussion web will use frames. You have four choices:

➥ No frames

➥ Dual interface (this option will cause the page to use frames if frames are available)

➥ Contents above current article

➥ Contents beside current article

Although not all browsers support frames, we have aimed our content at the higher-end browsers and chose to use the Dual interface option.

After we completed the few modifications discussed above, we copied the new discussion web into our project web.

A discussion web example

Before we leave the topic of discussion webs, we want to show you what is possible when you take the capabilities of FrontPage and add in other tools. One of the most interesting examples of a discussion web we know of that was partially created using FrontPage can be found at

```
http://www.riverbend.net/tower/
```

This web, seen in Figure 9-8 is known as The Tower: A Medieval Talker.

Figure 9-8: The sun sets to the west as you enter the Medieval Talker known as the Tower.

Exploring the web begins when you move down the page and choose to take the tour of the tower. There, you can examine the outside of the tower (Figure 9-9), the main hall (Figure 9-10), and the stairs (Figure 9-11).

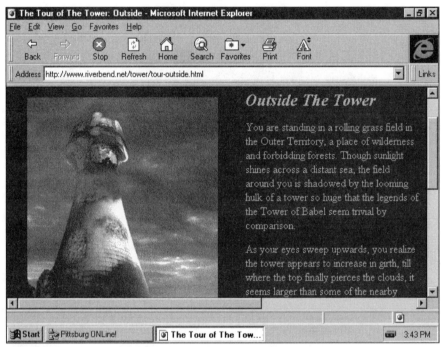

Figure 9-9: The dark and foreboding tower may be the only shelter from the angry skies.

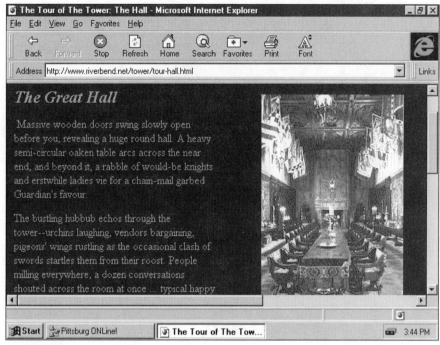

Figure 9-10: Good fellowship with lords and ladies of your own ilk is possible in the main hall.

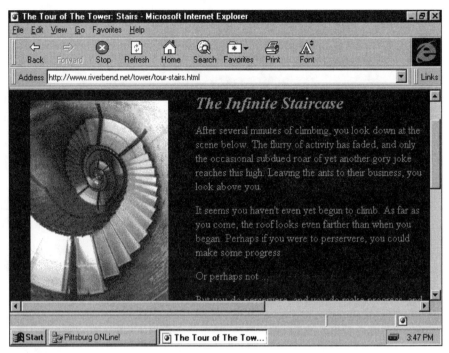

Figure 9-11: Long spiral staircases take you deeper into the Tower.

This discussion web takes the somewhat limited discussion capabilities of FrontPage and expands on a FrontPage-created web to include the capability to carry on synchronous discussions. This synchronous capability is made possible through the use of a mixture of a chat engine written in C, an interface written in Java (Figure 9-12), CGI scripts written in Perl, and HTML pages written with FrontPage.

Another interesting aspect of the Tower's operation is that the web is split between two different servers. Half of the web runs from an Apache server running on a UNIX platform, while the other half runs from a WebSite Pro server running on a Windows NT platform.

The Tower is an example of what can be done by mixing the capabilities of FrontPage with other web design tools. Michael Terretta is the webmaster of the Tower. Michael works for Vivid.Net in Atlanta, Georgia. You find a discussion of Vivid.Net in Appendix A as an ISP that can host your FrontPage webs. You also find a hyperlink to Vivid.Net's pages on the CD-ROM included with this book.

Figure 9-12: While the chat engine itself was written in C, the Tower's chat mirror interface was written in Java.

Moving On

In this chapter we've looked at how you should organize a web site team and how access levels and permissions for a web are set using FrontPage.

We looked at two deficiencies that exist in FrontPage in regard to using it as a tool to create collaborative webs.

We walked through the creation of a discussion web which allows you to interact with your visitors.

Finally, we examined a discussion web that expands on the capabilities of FrontPage to create a real-time chat room.

In the next chapter we examine the links between pages in a web and how they are created.

Linking and Importing with FrontPage

In This Chapter

Linking your pages to pages within your own web

Linking your pages to pages on the World Wide Web

Linking your pages to pages not yet created

Importing pages and webs created with other tools

Using Internet Assistants

What is a link? *Webster's* says it's a connecting structure, a bond, a tie. *The Computer Professional's Dictionary* calls it a logical connection between two differing objects. In other words, a link could represent a connection between two distinct but topically related things.

In HTML, a link points to another part of the same, or a different, document. It may, or may not, have any logical topical connection. Here, you can actually think of it just as a cause and effect relationship. Clicking on one point, the link, transports you to another point.

This chapter looks at how you can make use of material outside of FrontPage to enhance your web. You learn how to create links to other webs using FrontPage. Also, you'll see how, if you've used other tools to create your pages and webs, you can import these pages into FrontPage.

Linking Your Pages

At this point in the book, you've seen that one of the major features of any web is its ability to include active links to other pages. When a user clicks on one of these links, whatever browser he is using loads, reads, and renders the page at the new location. This new location can be on the same web, on a different web, or even on the same page.

Using FrontPage, pages you link to can include content created with other programs. Text files can be used. Word, Excel, Access, and PowerPoint documents can also be used. This linking can be done using HTML code. We've provided a brief description of this process; however, FrontPage offers a process that makes it simple to link to pages without having to enter any HTML code at all.

Linking pages with HTML

In order to understand this process, you need to understand what is happening when the user hits a web page and begins exploring using the hyperlinks available on the web pages. The user's browser software, in conjunction with a web's server software, uses the information contained in the hyperlink to connect to that site, read the information located there using the proper viewer, and display the information on the user's monitor. If the information is located on the local server, a *relative* path will allow the user's browser to find, load, read, and display the new page. A *relative* path refers to the the new path using part of the path of the current page containing the hyperlink. Because of this, you only need to specify a relative path to the new page, as in the example below:

```
HREF="Pauls_Web/summittb.htm"
```

If the link is to a page that is located on another server, you have to identify the full URL in the link, as in the next example:

```
<A HREF="http://vrevolution.pitton.com/VREvolution/index.htm">The
VREvolution Company Web Page</A>
```

These are the two ways that HTML allows us to link to other pages. FrontPage, however, allows us not only these two methods of linking, but also two additional ways to link to a page.

Linking pages using FrontPage

As you learned in previous chapters, there are four main methods of linking your pages together. These four methods are

- Linking to new pages
- Linking to open pages

➥ Linking to pages within the current web

➥ Linking to pages in the World Wide Web

We'll show you how you can link your pages using all four of these methods. We'll start with the two types of links that we discussed using HTML and show how FrontPage makes this process even easier.

Linking to pages within the current web

In Chapter 5 we discussed the use of the Link command that is available in the Edit menu. You must select a section of text before you can choose the Link command.

When you select the Link command, a dialog box with four tab selections appears on your screen. To link to another page within the current web, you choose the Open Pages tab shown in Figure 10-1.

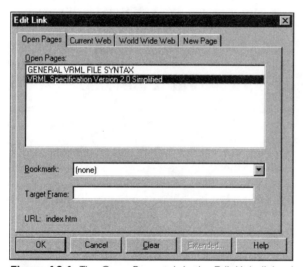

Figure 10-1: The Open Pages tab in the Edit Link dialog box.

The Open Pages tab allows you to select a page within the current web to link to. Our example shows how we added a hyperlink from the VRMLSpec2 web's **INDEX.HTM** to our General VRML 2.0 File Syntax and Structure page within our web. Clicking on the Browse button on the Open Pages tab produces a listing of the files that appear in the currently active web as shown in Figure 10-2.

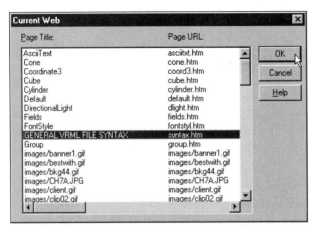

Figure 10-2: Here we see a listing of the files in our VRMLSpec2 web.

Select the file you want the hyperlink to be connected to, and choose the OK button. In our example the file is the **SYNTAX.HTM** file. When you choose the OK button again, you are returned to the file you've been editing (the **INDEX.HTM** file in our example).

Linking to pages in the World Wide Web

Another option available in FrontPage is hyperlinking to a page outside of your current web. This page could be located anywhere on the World Wide Web. In our example, we want to place a hyperlink on our VRMLSpec2 web **INDEX.HTM** page, connecting it to the VRMLSpec1 web as a reference. In order to do this, we select the words we want to use as the hyperlink, "VRML Version 1.0 Specification," and choose the Create or Edit Link button on the toolbar. To link to pages on the World Wide Web, use the World Wide Web tab as displayed in Figure 10-3.

You have the opportunity to select which type of addressing scheme you wish to use for a link. The choices are

➡ (other)

➡ file:

➡ ftp:

➡ gopher:

➡ http:

➡ mailto:

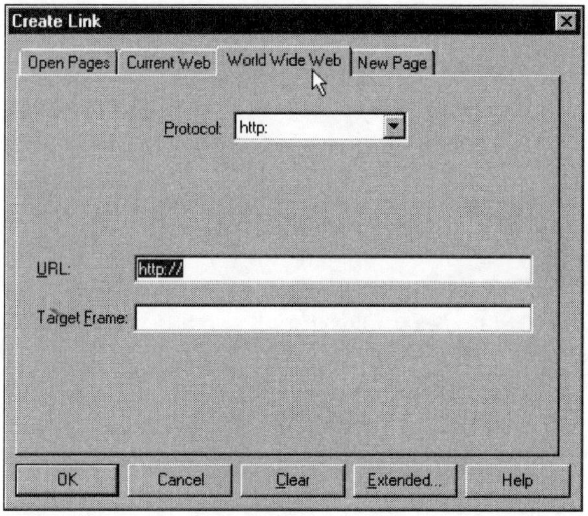

Create Link

Open Pages | Current Web | World Wide Web | New Page |

Protocol: [http: ▼]

URL: [http://]

Target Frame: [ ]

OK   Cancel   Clear   Extended...   Help

Figure 10-3: Select the World Wide Web tab in the Create Link dialog box.

➡ news:

➡ telnet:

➡ wais:

The default address scheme is http: and that, of course, is what we need in our example. At this point you would enter the URL according to the syntax required by the addressing scheme you select. In this case, we would type

```
vrevolution.pitton.com/VRMLSpec1/index.htm
```

This creates a link from the VRMLSpec2 web's **INDEX.HTM** to the VRMLSpec1 web's **INDEX.HTM**. Remember, in creating your pages and links for your web, you can choose any of the addressing schemes above and enter the link as required for that addressing scheme.

For instance, if you choose the mailto: addressing scheme for the URL you would enter the following text after the mailto: statement in the textbox, where *yourname @ address* represents your e-mail address:

```
yourname@address
```

When we place this mailto: protocol on our pages we generally enter the following e-mail address:

```
76270.551@CompuServe.com
```

We also can designate a target frame as the target for our hyperlink. You do this by simply typing in the identifier for the target frame in the specified text box.

Notice how, in these first two examples, FrontPage has made establishing a link much simpler than using HTML code. FrontPage also offers additional linking possibilities: you can also link to pages that are currently open in the FrontPage Editor, or to pages that don't even exist yet.

Linking to open pages

One way FrontPage makes your web construction job easier is through its ability to link to other pages you have open in the FrontPage Editor, no matter where those pages are located. In our web, for example, we have a graphic that we wish to use as an image map at the bottom of our pages, in the VRMLSpec2 web. The image consists of the cube/sphere/cone used in the VRML logo, with the word "Previous" under the cube, the word "Home" under the sphere, and the word "Next" under the cone. This image map will be a navigation aid allowing users the graphical choice of going back to the previous page within the web, the home page of the web, or moving forward to the next page in the web.

We must first insert the entire image into the web in the location that we want it to appear. This is accomplished by placing the cursor in the location where we want the image to appear and selecting the Insert menu. From this menu we choose the Image command, then choose the image we want to use (the VRML logo) from the dialog box that appears. Clicking on OK in this dialog box then inserts the image.

Our next task is to select that section of the image that we want to link to another page. In our example, we select the center sphere/Home area.

Next, we click on the entire graphic image, which activates the Image toolbar that you first saw in Chapter 4. Clicking on the Rectangle button on the Image toolbar causes the cursor to turn into the image of a pencil. With this pencil we can draw to create a rectangle around the center, or Home, portion of the image by holding down the left mouse button beginning in the upper left-hand corner of the area and letting go of the button in the lower right-hand corner.

When we let go of the mouse button, the Create Link dialog box will open automatically. This dialog box displays the Open Pages tab, as shown in Figure 10-4.

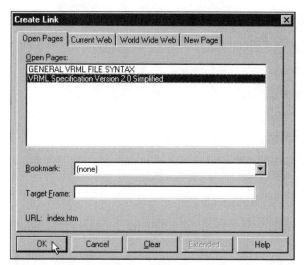

Figure 10-4: The Open Pages tab in the Create Link dialog box.

In our example, we want to link this part of the graphic to the **INDEX.HTM** page in our VRMLSpec2 web. To create the link we select the VRML Specification Version 2.0 Simplified page, **INDEX.HTM** and choose the OK button. This links the center sphere/Home portion of the image to the home page of the web.

Keep in mind that using this option, Open Pages, is only available when you already have another page open in the FrontPage Editor. If we had not had other pages open in other windows in the FrontPage Editor, there would have been no open pages to link to. In this case we would have to use the Link to Pages within the Current Web tab to achieve the same goal.

Options are also available on this tab to select a bookmark or a target frame within the currently opened page, to attach your hyperlink to.

Linking to new pages

You also have the option of creating a link to a page that doesn't yet exist. To do this you use the New Page tab of the Create Link dialog box. In our case, we will link the cone/Next portion of the image, used in the previous example, to the next page to be placed in the VRMLSpec2 web.

First select the area of the image you want to use for this link. In the Create Link dialog box select the New Page tab and enter the required information, as shown in Figure 10-5.

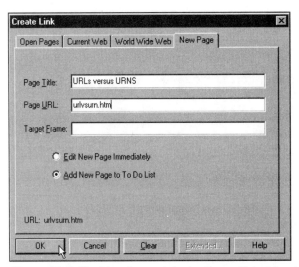

Figure 10-5: The New Page tab in the Create Link dialog box.

In this figure we have simply typed in the title we want for our new page, and then typed in the URL where this page can be found. When you choose OK, FrontPage then gives you the opportunity, as shown in Figure 10-6, to select what page template or wizard you wish to use for this new page.

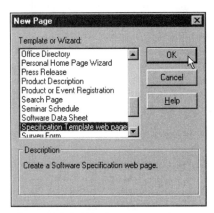

Figure 10-6: We chose to use the Specification Template web page.

We selected the Specification Template web page that we had created earlier. The Specification Template web page was created for use with the various protocol and specification pages that we have created on our site.

You'll find the Specification Template web page located in the page template subdirectory on the CD-ROM included with this book. We discuss this, and other templates and programs that are located on the CD-ROM, in Appendix C.

When you are linking to new pages in your web, keep in mind that you can identify a target frame on your new page which the new hyperlink is aimed towards. You also have the choice of editing the new page immediately, or adding the new page to your To Do List. In our example, as you can see from Figure 10-6, we added our new page to our To Do List.

Using Content Created Outside of FrontPage

There are many HTML tools available and perhaps you are already using some of them. These tools range from HoTMetaL Pro and HotDog to the range of Internet Assistants created by Microsoft for use with their Office products. In this section of the chapter, we're going to look at importing webs and pages created with other tools into a FrontPage web. The web and pages can then be edited and maintained using FrontPage.

Importing webs and pages

It is possible, using FrontPage, to copy whole web and page structures created outside of FrontPage into a web maintained by FrontPage. There are two basic methods of doing this. Interestingly enough, the first method occurs automatically if you are installing FrontPage Server Extensions on an existing web server. FrontPage will import any pre-existing web content for use with FrontPage.

The second method allows you to copy web page layout and structure from pages throughout the Web. What this means is that if, while cruising the web, you come across a format and layout for a web that you are particularly taken with, you have the capability of copying that page or web layout into FrontPage and using it for your own pages and webs.

Keep in mind that graphics and certain content is copyrighted and using it without permission is an infringement of the copyright owner's rights.

If you want to copy webs and pages in order to examine how your favorite web pages and webs are put together, follow these steps:

1. **Using the Windows Explorer, create a new empty web under your FrontPage Web subdirectory.**

   Give it whatever name you want. Under this new subdirectory create an /**images**/ subdirectory.

2. **Open Microsoft Internet Explorer and go to the pages on the Web you wish to copy. Using the Save As command in the File menu of Microsoft Internet Explorer, save the HTML files of the web you want to copy into this new subdirectory.**

3. **You'll have to save every graphic image one at a time. Click the right mouse button on each and every graphic used in the pages being saved.**

   Save each of the graphics to the /**images**/ subdirectory under the new web you created. You'll also want to do this with the background files for all of the pages you're saving.

4. **Now, use FrontPage to open the new web you created in step 1 above.**

   FrontPage will read the files you copied and incorporate these into your new web. You will probably need to redirect the links for the graphic files.

You can also import pages one at a time by using the Open Location option in the FrontPage Editor File menu.

Using other tools to create content

As we suggested, you aren't required to use the FrontPage Editor to create your web pages. You can use a variety of other web page creation tools that you might be more familiar with. After you've created the pages, you can use the techniques described in the previous section to import these pages into the web that you've created with FrontPage.

Using Microsoft Internet Assistants

You can use any of the Microsoft Office add-on Internet Assistants to create pages using Word, Excel, Access, PowerPoint, or Schedule. As with FrontPage, you can create documents for a web using little or no HTML code or Internet experience, by using the tools you are familiar and feel comfortable with. With Office 97, the integration of the Internet Assistant capabilities will probably be complete. With Office 95, however, you must download the Internet Assistants from Microsoft's web pages.

Internet Assistant for Microsoft Word

There are four versions of Internet Assistant for Microsoft Word currently available:

➡ Internet Assistant Version 2.0 for Word 6.0.6 for Macintosh

➡ Internet Assistant Version 2.03 for Word for Windows 95 (You need this version if you are using Internet Explorer 3.0.)

➡ Internet Assistant Version 2.0z for Word for Windows 95

➡ Internet Assistant Version 1.0z for 16-bit Word for Windows 6.0

If you are using Windows 95, Word for Windows 95, and Internet Explorer 3.0, then you need to download Version 2.03 of Internet Assistant. If you are using a different web browser, you can use Internet Assistant Version 2.0z. If you are still using Windows 3.1x and Word for Windows 6.0, then Internet Assistant Version 1.0z is for you.

Whichever version you are using, this program add-on will allow you to create and view web pages in Word, a word processing program that you may have grown accustomed to. In addition, this Internet Assistant's built-in browser capability enables you to go online from inside Word for Windows.

Using this program, you won't have to learn (or even see) the HTML codes for the web page documents that you're creating. This is similar to using FrontPage. By using the built-in browser that uses Word as its viewing screen, you're able to surf the Web. While surfing you can cut material from any web page to which you're connected and paste that material in the document you are working on.

Any document you create with Word can be converted to HTML with ease. This includes documents that have OLE objects embedded in them, such as spreadsheets, tables, presentations, and art work. Background pictures and sounds can be inserted using the Format/Background and Links command. You can even designate not to scroll the background picture from within this dialog box.

The Insert Graphic dialog box allows you to insert both inline video and sensitive maps. The Internet Assistant for Word, however, is not as good as the FrontPage Editor for creating and editing image maps.

You can also create forms and HTML tables. For those who enjoy working with the straight HTML source code, Internet Assistant allows you to choose the option of using HTML Source from the View menu. This view is fully editable.

Internet Assistant for Microsoft Excel

The Internet Assistant for Microsoft Excel add-in wizard can be used with the following versions of Microsoft Excel:

➡ Microsoft Excel Version 7.0 for Microsoft Windows 95

➡ Microsoft Excel Version 5.0 for 32-bit Microsoft Windows NT 3.*x*

➡ Microsoft Excel Version 5.0 for 16-bit Microsoft Windows 3.*x*

Download the add-in file HTML.XLA from Microsoft's web site and copy it to the Microsoft Excel Library directory. When you run Excel, you will find the HTML wizard available through the Add-ins command of the Tools menu.

This add-in for Excel allows you to create an HTML web page from any Excel spreadsheet. This means your company's Monthly Sales Reports or Monthly Expenditures can be placed directly on your web for comment by visitors.

Internet Assistant for Microsoft Access

The Internet Assistant for Microsoft Access can work with any Access database or with any ODBC-compliant datasource. This add-in is available from Microsoft's web site and requires

➡ A 386DX or higher CPU in your personal computer

➡ The Windows 95 or Windows NT operating system

➡ A minimum of 12MB of RAM for Windows 95 and 16MB of RAM for Windows NT

➡ Microsoft Access for Windows 95

➡ An HTML browser that has support for tables (Microsoft Internet Explorer 3.0 is available on the CD-ROM included with this book.)

➡ At least 1MB of free hard drive space above your Microsoft Access for Windows 95 installation

Using this assistant is as simple as using any of the other assistants we've discussed. From within Microsoft Access, choose Internet Assistant in the Add-ins option of the Tools menu. Select the database object you want to use, and then choose if you want to use a template or not. Then, select the folder where you want the HTML document placed. It's as simple as that.

Internet Assistant for Microsoft PowerPoint

This Internet Assistant works only with Microsoft PowerPoint for Windows 95. It will not work with PowerPoint 4.0 or earlier versions. The assistant is available for free download from Microsoft's web site and from the MSDESKTOP forum on CompuServe. This product allows you to easily convert the design templates, clip art images, digitized photographs, textures, and formatted text you've included in your PowerPoint slides into HTML for publication on the World Wide Web.

Internet Assistant for Microsoft Schedule

This Internet Assistant allows you to use Microsoft Schedule+ for Windows 95 to create a calendar of events or even a free/busy schedule for publication on your web site. You'll see how you can create a simple calendar template for FrontPage in Chapter 11.

An Internet Assistant example

We'll walk through the process of converting a document from Word to HTML using Internet Assistant for Word, and then show how this document can be imported into a FrontPage web.

This example uses Word 7.0 for Windows 95 and the proper Internet Assistant for Word. First, load a file into Word (in our example, the file is named FACTOROT.DOC), as shown in Figure 10-7.

The next step is to save the document as HTML by choosing the Save As command in the Word File menu. You should save the file to the FrontPage web directory where you want it to be located. If the file contains graphics, as does FACTOROT.DOC, as you save it these graphics will be saved as separate files. The end result will be that you will have an HTML file and several new graphics in the web subdirectory you've designated.

At this point you can modify the HTML file, adding headings and formatting the content. Figure 10-8 shows the results after we did this to the FACTOROT.HTM file.

You can now load this file created with Internet Assistant for Word into FrontPage. As seen in Figure 10-9, our FACTOROT file is located in the web directory, but is not a part of the web yet.

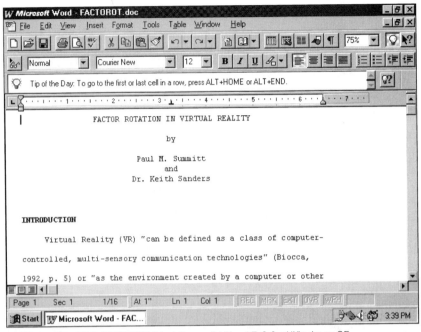

Figure 10-7: FACTOROT.DOC in Microsoft Word 7.0 for Windows 95.

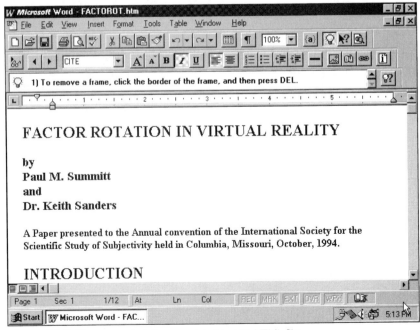

Figure 10-8: The converted document is now an HTML file.

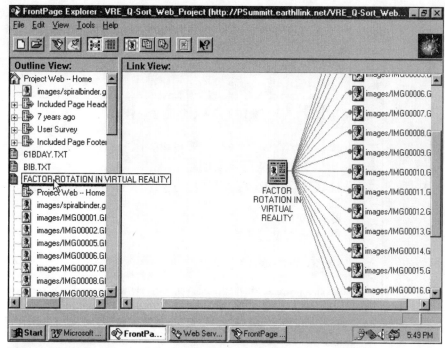

Figure 10-9: The converted file is now in the web directory, but not yet part of the web.

After loading the file into the FrontPage Editor, modify the page properties so that this page conforms to the graphic background and format of the rest of the pages in your web. After we did this, our file appeared as in Figure 10-10.

Using other products to create web content

Blue Sky Software is probably best known for their Windows Help products. Two of their products also provide you with the possibility of creating web page content for inclusion in your FrontPage webs. These two products are

➡ **WinHelp Office with HTML.** The new RoboHELP95 HTML Edition turns your Microsoft Word 7 program into a full-featured web page authoring tool. At the same time, using the same source code, you can create Windows help files. The WinHelp Office HTML Edition also includes an easy-to-use Help-to-HTML converter that allows you to convert any Windows 3.*x* or Windows 95 help file to HTML, no matter how that help file was created.

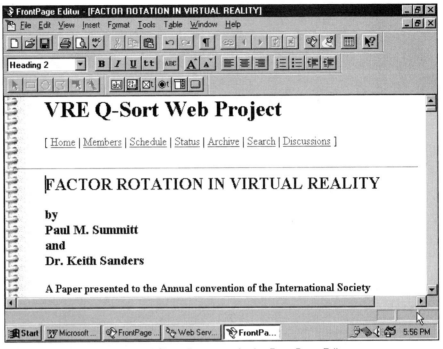

Figure 10-10: The completed file as it appears in the FrontPage Editor.

➥ **WEB Office.** WEB Office is a new product from Blue Sky that allows for easy HTML authoring from within Microsoft Word when using Microsoft Internet Assistant. As with their WinHelp Office product, any web or page created with this product can be easily imported into FrontPage.

If you're using Microsoft Word 6.0, you can use an add-on product, Quarterdeck's WebAuthor. Again, any page created from within this tool can be imported into FrontPage and edited with the FrontPage Editor.

Moving On

In this chapter we have looked more closely at the linking of your pages to other pages on the web. These links included those to pages within your own web, pages on other servers, pages open within the FrontPage Editor, and pages not yet created.

Finally, you learned that it was possible to create web page content with other web authoring tools and import this content into your FrontPage webs.

In the next chapter we examine how to use FrontPage with an intranet.

Using FrontPage with Intranets

In This Chapter

What is an intranet and how does it differ from a network or the Internet?

Understanding the benefits of an intranet

Seeing how companies are using intranets

Building your own intranet

Most of the attention paid to electronic communication, both in this book and in the rest of the media, has dealt with the Internet. Recently, however, the media has discovered the growth of something called intranets.

This chapter will examine what intranets are, reasons for creating your own intranet, and how FrontPage can be used to provide an interface and applications for your intranet. We'll also discuss common mistakes and pitfalls you should avoid as you create pages for both your intranet and the Internet.

What Is an Intranet?

Many organizations have their own computer networks. Are these networks intranets? Not necessarily. But, if the network is a company-wide system used for software and information distribution using HTTP and HTML protocols, the answer may be yes. An intranet would include everything from a simple HTML file linked to another file on a LAN to a sophisticated, full-blown system using a dedicated server. The key elements of an intranet are a TCP/IP-based network and complete separation from an external TCP/IP network (that is, the Internet). The latter can be accomplished through the use of firewalls.

An intranet refers to an organized set of applications built using Internet technologies on a private TCP/IP network. This TCP/IP network has all of the features and services found on the Internet, including hypertext page support for text, hyperlinks, images, and sounds, as well as other client/server applications, and, of course, database access. In fact, you could think of it as an internally focused Internet.

Why Intranets?

A study by the Georgia Institute of Technology, released in June 1996, reported that the demographics of the Web user were changing; for example, more women and minorities are beginning to go online. But the interesting fact from this survey for our purposes is that more than 80 percent of those surveyed said that they used the Web daily, and of those, almost half accessed the Web from their place of employment.

A study by Bluestone suggests that 80 percent of Web application development takes place on internal networks. Netscape suggests that over half of the server software they sell is being used for intranets. This means that the number of Web servers on the Internet is just the tip of the iceberg. The intranet business is exploding.

Now, some nay-sayers may be asking, "What is unique about an intranet over our proprietary software network?" We address this issue here.

Compared to a typical company network, with an intranet applications can be delivered across platforms. These applications can also be delivered across organizational structures (departments, subgroups, and so on). Intranet applications have the potential to be built at lower costs with higher degrees of internal control than proprietary systems.

Collaborative computer-based working environments via local area networks (LANs) and wide area networks (WANs), collectively called Groupware, have become an established solution allowing corporate users to communicate and share information. Lotus Notes is one of the software leaders in this arena, cornering over one third of the market.

Lotus Notes provides a graphical user interface, e-mail, templates for many common business applications, third party utilities, support for multiple platforms, and security of the network. Intranet technology provides these same facilities.

A big difference, however, is cost of operation. Lotus Notes licenses start at around $70 per user. The cost of a web browser ranges from being free to around $40 per user. Startup costs for an intranet server range from being free to around $1,000 compared with a minimum of $10,000 for Lotus Notes. Industry averages suggest that the average investment in a completed intranet installation will be less than $15,000, compared with an average investment of around $250,000 for Lotus Notes.

You should also take into account the costs of training your employees to use HTML tools as compared to training them to use proprietary software. Also, proprietary systems usually require skilled and expensive MIS departments to set up, maintain, and develop. The overall result is that companies like Lotus are converting their products to the Web to remain competitive.

Intranets offer many advantages to their corporate users. These advantages include

- Rapid prototyping

- The ability to start slow and grow at the company's own pace

- An easy navigation system

- The ability to integrate a distributed computing strategy

- Easy access to legacy information sources such as databases and existing word-processing documents

- Being extensible to other forms of multimedia such as audio, video, and other interactive media

- Being inexpensive to star

- Little investment in time, dollars, and infrastructure when compared with other alternatives

- Their distributed computing strategy utilizing company computing resources more effectively

- Using a familiar graphical user interface

- Open platform architecture which means a larger number of add-on applications are available

How Are Companies Using Intranets?

The advantages listed in the previous section mean that corporate intranets are doing more and more every day. We introduce you to some of these uses here.

Company internal communication

An intranet allows your company to communicate with your employees through a variety of different vehicles. Your intranet allows for software distribution via the FTP server capability. You can provide e-mail services, chat services, and every communication capability available on the Internet through your intranet. Newsletters can be provided over your intranet at a fraction of the cost of printed versions.

Some company presidents have taken to including a weekly audio or video message to their employees via their company's intranet. These methods provide easy-to-use mechanisms for presenting messages to your employees at their own pace.

Company internal technical support

As an intranet requires less support than other alternatives, your company's internal computing department can turn their attention to other MIS issues. This is possible due to the one-standard approach of the intranet. Your company can standardize on a web browser and employees can become their own self-service help desk. You can place Frequently Asked Questions (FAQ) lists on your server, providing employees with advice or answers to common problems and, using the HTML functionality, they can follow links to related information to help themselves get answers. FrontPage can be of great assistance in setting up this support web using the Product Support web template and the Frequently Asked Questions page template.

Human resources and research

Many corporate intranets are providing information on personnel policies, job benefits, and, in some cases, individual records in an interactive way on their intranet servers. Hospitals are using their intranets to share training materials with the staff and get feedback from them on common problems or issues of concern.

Some companies are using their intranets for communication between researchers concerning the various projects that they are working on. FrontPage assists in this research by providing a Project web template.

Sales force automation

By having a corporate intranet connected to the Internet, company sales people can connect to price lists, marketing materials, position papers, and product availability lists directly from a customer's site. At the same time, these documents are secure and available only to those having access to your company intranet. This means your sales force no longer is required to lug around price books, product manuals, and other sales documents.

One example of this is an insurance company that provides access to computing instant automobile insurance rates for their agents and can allow their agents to get a quote and sell a policy almost instantaneously.

FrontPage can be of assistance by providing the product description page and services page templates. We've also provided templates for sale item pages, programming examples pages, and specification pages on the CD-ROM included with this book.

Documents you could provide via your intranet

There are many types of documents that your company has that might possibly be better provided via your intranet than with your current media. This list of documents is not meant to be all inclusive, but rather is provided to get your own creative juices flowing.

➡ Company announcements

➡ Customer data

➡ Employee benefits programs

➡ Employee information

➡ Hardware manuals

➡ ISO 9000 work instructions

➡ Maps

➡ Marketing literature

➡ Meeting minutes

➡ Newsletters

➡ Online help

➡ Orientation materials

➡ Policy manuals

➡ Press releases

➡ Price lists

➡ Procedure manuals

➡ Product information

➡ Product catalogs

➡ Product demos

➡ Product specifications

➡ Programming tools

➡ Project white papers

➡ Quality manuals

➡ Quick reference guides

➡ Reports

➡ Sales figures

➡ Sales forecasts

➡ Sales literature

➡ Scheduling information

➡ Schematics

➡ Seminars

➡ Service information

➡ Software applications

➡ Software user guides

➡ Software utilities

➡ Specifications

➡ Spreadsheet templates

➡ Standards

➡ Style guides

➡ Surveys

➡ Templates

➡ Test data

➡ Training manuals

➡ Tutorials

Benefits of an Intranet

What would having an intranet mean to your company? There are several major reasons why your company should develop an intranet, including, (but not limited to)

➡ You obtain increased bandwidth.

➡ The cost is low.

➡ You gain cross-platform availability.

➡ Intranets are robust and reliable.

➡ The HTML capabilities are easy to learn.

We take a brief look at each of these major reasons for developing an intranet for your company, and then we look at some ideas on how you can use an intranet in the next section.

Increased bandwidth

One of the main strengths that an intranet has over the Internet is increased *bandwidth*. Bandwidth deals with the amount of information that can flow through a medium at any time. In other words, bandwidth implies the ability to serve more files to more users over the network in the same amount of time.

Most local area networks (LANs) are capable of bandwidths from 10 Megabits to 100 Megabits compared with the bandwidth of 28.8 kilobits for phone line connections.

What does greater bandwidth mean to you? It means that large graphics, fan-tastic forms, cool videos, outstanding audio, and other neat multimedia presentations load almost instantaneously on your screen via an intranet. At most, via an intranet, it takes seconds for these types of files to load as opposed to minutes over the Internet. This disparity is even greater if you are trying to download these files using a 14.4 Kbps modem, or even a 28.8 Kbps modem. Downloading a 1MB file over an intranet might take at most a minute; this same file downloaded over a 28.8 Kbps dial-in line can take 15 minutes or more.

Due to this increased bandwidth availability, intranets have greatly improved performance when compared with the Internet as a whole.

Low cost requirements to get an intranet going

Putting together an intranet using the computers you already possess within your company can be relatively inexpensive when compared with the costs involved in other more traditional methods of publishing company information. You already have the computers and, if they are already networked, your current system is capable of providing your intranet. Browser software is inexpensive or, in some cases, free. Server software is also inexpensive and in some cases this too is free. Microsoft has allowed us to provide their free Internet Information Server for Windows NT on the CD-ROM that comes with this book, for example. You've seen how to set up the Personal Web Server that comes with FrontPage and you can use that server as the basis for an intranet. Putting an intranet into place could be the most-cost effective business decision you make regarding the publication and distribution of company information for your company.

You can replace large and expensive proprietary software packages such as Lotus Notes with these less expensive, and in some cases free, alternatives. Even companies that don't already have installed computer networks can profit by installing an intranet. If your company has complex computer applications utilizing graphics and multimedia, and instant communication and delivery of information among employees is important to your success, an intranet could answer your need for speed and sophisticated file handling. Issues to consider when trying to make the decision to go with an intranet include

➡ What security features does your company really need?

➡ Will your system work with UNIX, IBM, and VMS systems if your company needs it to?

➡ Will your system work with a Novell network if necessary?

➡ Is the server easy to use?

➡ Is installation of the server easy and straightforward?

➡ Does the server manufacturer provide user support and application updates?

The minimum requirements your company would have to meet for an intranet server are remarkably simple:

➡ 486 CPU

➡ 16MB RAM

➡ Windows 95 (preferably Windows NT)

➡ 1 floppy disk drive

➡ 1 CD-ROM drive

➡ A hard drive with enough storage capacity for the software you are installing

In order to provide access to your intranet for your employees, they'll need computers meeting the following minimum requirements:

➡ 386 CPU

➡ 8MB RAM

➡ Windows 3.1x and DOS 5.0 (preferably Windows 95)

➡ 1 floppy disk drive

➡ A hard drive with enough storage capacity for the software needed on the employee's machine

➡ Web browsing software

Please remember that the above requirements are minimums. Performance of your intranet will be greatly improved with more up-to-date hardware and software.

Cross-platform availability

Don't worry about the fact that your company may have a mixture of PCs, Macs, and UNIX boxes. Don't worry about the mixture of operating systems either. It's all right if you have OS/2, Windows 3.1, Windows 3.11, Windows 95, and Windows NT. An intranet will enable every machine to speak the same language . . . . so to speak. This common language can then be used for sharing information. Rather than having to deal with a hodgepodge mixture of networks that may or may not work together, your intranet is a one-standard-based, broad bandwidth network.

Robust and reliable

Despite the fact that the Web is less than ten years old, the technology that makes it work has been around since the beginnings of the Cold War. These technologies are built around Internet tools and applications that have been tested since the late 1970s and are as secure and as fast as your own propri-etary and more expensive internal network software. And, as your system will be relying on one standard rather than many to maintain operation, you have simplified your task right from the start.

Easy to learn

From an employee training perspective, HTML is extremely easy to learn overall when compared with other proprietary software. This means that your company training budget is not strained in educating your employees how to use software to publish to your intranet. As you've seen in this book, using tools such as FrontPage, or one of the Microsoft Internet Assistant series tools, your employees don't even have to learn HTML. The majority of your company's employees will be accessing, and some will be creating, content for the new company intranet almost the minute your intranet goes online.

Top Ten Uses of an Intranet

In the tradition of late night talks shows, we've come up with a list of specific ways your company can use its own intranet. They range from employee nice-to-haves to uses that will help your company succeed in its basic business goals.

Use #10: Provide individual employee home pages where they can let the rest of the company know of the special events that have happened in their lives.

This may seem like a rather trivial reason for having an intranet from a corporate perspective, but it's not. Providing personal web pages as a creative outlet for company employees allows them to tell people about themselves and their families. Here they can let people know about recent family events, such as births or anniversaries, and current projects and hobbies. This can be a great morale booster. By the way, FrontPage provides an easy-to-use template just for this purpose. You can use either the Personal Web template in the FrontPage Explorer or the Personal Home Page Wizard in the FrontPage Editor. You'll also find the Resume/Vita template that we have included on the CD-ROM included with this book will be of value in providing documentation of employee credentials. The tools to create and view these pages are inexpensive. What small costs a company may put forth here, will reap great rewards in personnel morale.

> Use #9: Provide departmental home pages where departments can toot their own horns and let the rest of the company know what's going on in their area.

Departmental pages give a department the chance to demonstrate how important they are to the overall objectives of the company. The Corporate Presence Web Wizard could be used in the creation of these departmental pages. The departmental web page is a place where the department members can crow about their brilliance and provide information about how the department fits into the daily operation of the company. A department, using FrontPage and the Project Web template, can also create a project web for a given project and solicit input from other people in the company. Again, tools for creating and maintaining these pages, such as Microsoft FrontPage and Microsoft Internet Assistants, are relatively inexpensive. The tools for browsing these pages are also relatively inexpensive, especially when compared with the costs of proprietary network software and networking applications. The ease of information dissemination within the company more than compensates the company for the expense of the system.

> Use #8: Provide access to company databases such as the company phone book.

Although it would probably not be a good idea to place your company's entire phone tree and e-mail address book on an Internet page, an intranet-based company phone book might be a very good idea. This intranet-based phone book can provide more than information about employee phone extensions. Information about employees and links to their personal web pages, departmental web pages, and e-mail addresses can be made available here. Imagine the ease of doing a search on your company's home page for an employee's last name and having all of the important information you need appear instantly.

The cost of keeping an up-to-date hard copy publication of this nature would be exorbitant, while using the company intranet for this purpose won't add any costs to that of the intranet itself. This directory could also include pictures and audio and video clips, all maintained in the personnel database. (Keep in mind that this would require the use of CGI or some other form of database accessing programming in addition to the use of FrontPage.)

Use #7: Publish company documents, such as the company newsletter, annual reports, maps of company facilities, employee handbooks, company policy handbooks, and news items of importance to the company and its employees.

Intranets solve the problem often referred to as information overload. Often new employees are simply overwhelmed with information when they start a new job. They are handed a copy of the last annual report, an employee handbook, policy handbooks, and newsletters. Trying to wade through all this information to find out how to get a parking permit in the company parking lot, or to find out where the restroom is on their floor of the building can be extremely frustrating. Having an intranet with searchable versions of this information available makes things easier (not to mention the fact that it helps save trees). Allowing employees to follow links from facts in one publication to facts in a related publication may help them to more easily find the answers they need. Keep in mind that much of this information will be valuable to employees, but that you want it secure from the global Internet community; therefore an intranet is the perfect solution.

Use #6: Software distribution

Internet technology provides a wonderful architecture for both inter- and intra-company client/server applications. This technology is cross-platform, making your company's intranet cross-platform. HTML allows for the use of a single user interface, the web browser, to a broad range of applications. Databases, text, spreadsheet, video, and audio data are all available via this one easy-to-use user interface. This interface is so easy to use that many people are currently accessing huge amounts of data via the World Wide Web with little or no training.

Use #5: Training via HTML form support

Much of your company's employee training can be accomplished via an intranet. Using HTML form support, even employee advancement testing could be performed. Consider the savings in time and resources if your employee training program, at least that part not requiring hands-on applications, were placed on web pages on your company's intranet. Much education and learning consists of repetitive behavior. Your intranet provides you with the training tool that can be used over and over, and yet, can be updated with relative ease.

Use #4: Event registration

The same form support that allows online intranet employee training also allows your company to provide employee event and software registration via your intranet. Use your company's intranet to provide registration forms for every type of event from training conferences to the Labor Day picnic. And if you can register for events via your intranet, how about. . .

Use #3: Scheduling

One of the most difficult aspects of any activity is the scheduling of events. Posting a calendar on your intranet is a great way to keep the entire company informed as to what is going on.

Here's an idea for how you can create a calendar similar to the one shown in Figure 11-1 with FrontPage and post it on your company intranet to keep people up to date on upcoming events. You can do this using the Calendar Wizard which can be found in the FrontPage Development Kit (FDK). The FDK is available for free download from the Microsoft web site.

After you have downloaded the FDK, copy the Calendar subdirectory into the FrontPage subdirectory that contains the other wizards. On our system, for example, the full directory listing would be

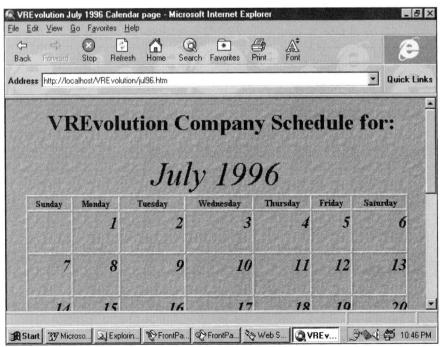

Figure 11-1: A calendar created with the FrontPage Calendar Wizard.

C:\Program Files\Microsoft FrontPage\Pages\Calendar.wiz

Open the FrontPage Editor and select the New command in the File menu. Select Calendar Page Wizard from the list in the New Page dialog box and follow its screens to create your calendar which will be based on an HTML table.

Use #2: Surveys

Another valuable use of the form capabilities of HTML is the ability to perform surveys via your intranet. This is a great way to get valuable information in regard to employee perceptions of company policy, obtain opinions about future directions, and gain insight about contributions your employees feel they can make to the company.

Use #1: Communication

This is the number one reason for having an intranet from both the company and the employee perspective. From the company's perspective, it increases the capabilities to communicate with all members of the corporate culture. An intranet decentralizes control over the management and distribution of company information. This information ranges from employee personal information on individual home pages to corporate annual reports. Responsibility for updating this information is spread over the entire corporate structure and is not placed on any one subgroup; therefore that subgroup does not become a bottleneck to the effective transmission and distribution of company information. Communication means more effective corporate management which makes your company more competitive. At the same time, communication can mean happier, better-informed employees.

Building Your Own Intranet

For all of it's positives, your new company intranet will have plenty of naysayers. While some corporate dinosaurs will refuse to use the new system and publish information on your intranet, other individuals will embrace the intranet and help produce a positive shift in corporate culture in a relatively short period of time.

The physical setup of your intranet can be relatively inexpensive considering the overall value obtained. Begin with a low-cost pilot project. This will enable you to recognize the value of an intranet. This experience will help you see creative ways to expand your system. Keep in mind that you already have the FrontPage Personal Web Server which is capable of performing the job of installing, creating, and maintaining an intranet.

Moving On

We discussed what an intranet is and why your company may need one.

You learned some of the beneficial uses of an intranet, and learned some guidelines to making the transition to an intranet in your organization using FrontPage.

In the next and final chapter, we look at things that make bad pages and bad webs on both the Internet and on intranets, and provide a few tips and tricks that will make your use of FrontPage easier.

Getting the Most from FrontPage

Avoiding common mistakes in designing your web pages

Learning some tips and tricks to add value to your FrontPage-created web site

This book is now coming to a close. Given the understanding of FrontPage that you now have, we want to end with some advice that you can use with FrontPage to achieve better and quicker results.

The first section of this chapter warns of some frequent mistakes people make in designing and using pages on the Web. The second section offers some interesting work arounds and tricks that might help you get even more out of FrontPage and its features.

Common Web Page Mistakes to Avoid

This portion of the chapter is important regardless of whether your pages are going to be seen only on your intranet, or on the Internet itself. These are common mistakes that people make on their pages, either in layout or content. We'll use the time-honored late night talk show method of the top ten list to present them.

Mistake #10: No discernible goal for the page

Too many times, both for individuals and for companies, the apparent goal for a given web page is simply for the person or company to be on the Web. Being on the Web should not be your goal in creating a page. You should take the time, before you begin page construction, to carefully define what your presence on the Web will accomplish for you or your organization.

For each page in your web you should ask yourself, why is this page here? What do I hope to accomplish with this page? Do I want to get and keep more customers or educate the Internet/intranet community? Take the time to define goals for your pages and your web and then strive to make sure that the pages and web meet those goals.

Mistake #9: No discernible purpose for the page

Closely allied with the goal of the page is the purpose of the page. Ask yourself what the purpose for each of your pages is. As we have suggested before, a web page is a method of communication and all communication has a purpose. Do you want to get customer feedback or keep employees up-to-date on training seminars available? .

If your goals and purposes for your pages and webs are confused and ill-defined it's likely the people who visit your pages and webs are going to be confused. If this happens, chances are they won't be back.

Mistake #8: Purposeless graphics

Don't add graphics to your page just so you can say you have graphics on your page. Use the graphics, whenever possible, for a purpose other than simple visual appeal. For instance, in Paul's web, there are many small graphics and icons in his biographical material; in addition to an effort toward visual appeal, these graphics are used as hyperlinks to the company, institution, or organization being discussed. The point here is that if you're going to put graphics on your page, try to make them be of use to your visitors.

Mistake #7: Bandwidth-hogging graphics and multimedia

Have you ever heard of JPEG graphics being referred to as *J-pigs*? Or how about *non-jiffy GIFs*? The term J-pigs refers to those hefty graphics that some people place on their pages. Non-jiffy GIFs refers to the fact that sometimes these graphics are slow to load. Here are some tips to avoid these bandwidth-hogging graphics and multimedia on your pages.

➥ Create your web graphics in the lowest pixelation and color depth that is acceptable to you.

➥ Warn your web visitors of the size of large graphics before they download them, as a courtesy. The minutes required to load graphics can sometimes seem like hours on an extra busy day.

➥ Save your graphics as both GIF and JPEG and compare the size of the two files. Use the smaller of the two.

➥ Don't use large image maps. Many times, well-chosen content and navigation buttons are far superior to unwieldy image maps.

➥ Keep your multimedia to a minimum. Try using smaller MIDI files, rather than bloated WAV files, when possible.

➥ Use Java, JavaScript, VRML, VBScript, and inline AVIs only when they add meaningful content to a page.

➥ Don't use frames when a table will do, or forms when e-mail will do. Frames are slow and forms can be difficult to use.

Probably the most valuable piece of advice anyone can give you concerning graphics and multimedia is that you shouldn't add something to your page that could impair its delivery simply for the sake of making it cool.

While this is probably more specific to those pages aimed at the Internet than pages on an intranet (because of an intranet's greater bandwidth), you should still pay attention to the total relative size of your page and its download time. Total relative size can be approximated by adding the total size of all graphics, components, and the page itself together. If it combines to 50 to 75K or more, you may want to reexamine the page's contents.

Mistake #6: Recycled content

Every medium of communication has value. Some media are better at communicating certain points and information than others. Provide information that is best suited to your web and that can't be obtained elsewhere. Using material that visitors have already seen is one sure way to guarantee that your visitors won't visit your site again.

Mistake #5: Bigoted pages

In the recent past, and even today to a certain extent, it has been somewhat the fad to optimize web pages to specific browsers. This, in some cases, has the effect of locking out certain potential visitors to your site because their browsers may not support certain extensions present in your prescribed browser. This approach can make your pages bigoted against those visitors.

Some web developers forget that many people access the Web, not via ISDN or T1 lines, but via modems at 14.4 Kbps and 28.8 Kbps over an often-slow Internet. The result can seem like Chinese water torture.

Some visitors to your site might be using text-based browsers. These are useful for the visually impaired who sometimes couple the text-based browser with a text-to-speech synthesizer. Don't lock these people out of your site.

Don't despair: This doesn't mean you have to create your web content for the lowest common denominator. You can use the tricks you learn here, and in other places, if you follow a few simple procedures. Your best bet, although it does require more work on your part, is to create multiples of the same page, configured for the various probabilities in browsers that visitors to your site may use. That is, you may have three pages all with the same content, but each configured for a different browser.

Unless there is a specific reason for doing so, it is best to avoid add-in components for browsers. These require that your visitors first go elsewhere, download and install the component, and return to your site before they can view the content. Some of your visitors won't come back if you send them away in this manner. It's all right to include these cool aspects of web programming. Just warn your visitors and give them a choice.

Mistake #4: Lack of navigation aids

Search engines on the Web are one of the most popular and most visited sites according to recent studies. This means that people are probably reaching your site, and parts of your site, in ways other than through your home page. The result is that you need to make sure that you make navigation aids a part of each and every page within your webs. Your visitors should be able to move about the hierarchy of your web with relative ease, moving up or down through the structure as the whim strikes them.

Mistake #3: Untested pages

Errors are the bane of your web page's existence. Your visitors are not guinea pigs. Don't test your pages out on them. Test them yourself.

When we say errors, we're not talking about the extensions to the HTML standard that are being proposed by Netscape and Microsoft. We are talking about plain and simple mistakes that are placed in pages because some web designers haven't taken the time to check their pages. These errors include, but are not limited to

➥ Character-set errors

➥ Header errors

➥ List-indenting errors

➥ Formatting errors

You may have the best monitor and the fastest access but your visitors could be accessing at 14.4 Kbps and using LCD laptop screens or 14-inch VGA monitors. Watch for things that will make your pages hard to read. These things include

➥ Extremely small type that becomes impossible to read on less than perfect monitors

➥ Not enough contrast between foreground and background objects

➥ Competing backgrounds that make it hard to read the type

➥ Nonstandard types, fonts, and color palettes

You should test your pages with a variety of browsers, screen resolutions, and access modes. A good guide is that your index page should show something immediately and should completely load on your visitors' machines in 20 seconds or less. Flush your cache to your browser before accessing your pages. This, combined with accessing at 14.4 Kbps will allow you to see your site pretty much the same way people around the country (or company intranet) will see it.

Mistake #2: Pages under construction

If your pages are so full of holes that you need to place under construction graphics all over them, then they shouldn't be up on the Web. Nothing frustrates a visitor so much, so fast, as not being able to access the information you've promised on your web. There's a good chance these visitors will not be back.

Mistake #1: Lack of content

Content is the holiday ham, and presentation is the pineapple and glaze. Never lose site of that fact. Make sure you have something to say with your pages and webs before you ever put them on the Web. Too many pages today are filled with under construction graphics, guest books, hit counters, feedback forms, and awards that should be on the web author's "I love me" wall, rather than on their web site. Pineapple and glaze is nice but you'd better make sure you place some ham on the page too, if you want your visitors to take you seriously and visit your site again.

FrontPage Tips and Tricks

FrontPage itself can do a great many of the things you're likely to want to do with your web pages. However, there are some less-than-obvious FrontPage procedures and some ways to use FrontPage with other products to do even cooler things. Most of these aren't hard to do at all. This section is intended to give you some interesting ideas about how to take FrontPage beyond the basics.

Adding a Java script to a page in FrontPage

You can add a Java script to your web pages as a method of increasing the interactivity available there. To do so, you can use the HTML Markup WebBot. From the FrontPage Editor, select the Insert menu and choose the Bot command. You'll find an example page called Java.htm on the CD-ROM included with this book that demonstrates how this is accomplished.

Adding a Visual Basic script to a page

You can also add Visual Basic scripts to your web pages as a method of increasing the interactivity available. From within the FrontPage Editor, use the HTML Markup WebBot available through the Bot command in the Insert menu. You'll find an example page called VBS.htm on the CD-ROM in this book that demonstrates how this is accomplished.

Adding color to the lines of frames and tables

Go to the Frame or Table Properties dialog box and choose the button labeled Extended. Now add **bgcolor=#xxxxxx** where #xxxxxx stands for the color's actual representation.

Creating customized horizontal lines

FrontPage allows two methods of creating a customized horizontal line. The first method lets you use a graphic as the horizontal line. We've included some public domain horizontal line graphics for your use on the CD-ROM in this book. You'll find them in the **\images\pd\lines** subdirectory.

The second method of customizing the horizontal line is to create it with the Horizontal Line command in the Insert menu of the FrontPage Editor. Using the right button on your mouse, click on the line and then choose Properties from the shortcut menu. You can now modify the line's appearance.

Creating drag and drop links

In order to do this, you'll need to size both the FrontPage Explorer and the FrontPage Editor to share the screen. Now, select the page for which you want to create the hyperlink in the FrontPage Explorer (it doesn't matter if you select it in the Outline, Summary, or Link View). Drag this page to the desired location on your page in the FrontPage Editor and release the mouse button. You now have a hyperlink for the desired document in the page you're working on.

Creating floating images

Insert your image at the start of a line and then, using the right mouse button, right-click on the image and choose Properties from the shortcut menu that appears. You can now choose to set the layout alignment as either left or right.

Creating interlaced images

This is one of the simplest tricks we have to share here. With the right mouse button, click on an image and choose Properties from the shortcut menu. Now choose type: Interlaced. That's all there is to it.

Using FrontPage pages on a server without FrontPage Server Extensions

If your service provider doesn't have the FrontPage Server Extensions installed on the server hosting your web site you can still use FrontPage to create your web and pages. You simply need to avoid certain FrontPage features, discussed in the following sections.

WebBot browse-time components

Most WebBot components affect your web pages only at the time you are authoring and creating a page. However, there are some, especially those used with forms, that rely on the FrontPage Server Extensions at browse time for their operation. You'll therefore need to avoid these bots:

➡ Confirmation WebBot

➡ Discussion WebBot

➡ Registration WebBot

➡ Save Results WebBot

➡ Search WebBot

These components will cause your users to receive the "HTTP 404" error when they access a page containing them.

FrontPage image maps

If you create image maps using the facilities available in FrontPage, these image maps rely on the FrontPage Server Extensions at browse time. The way to get around this problem is to create your image maps with the image map facilities that are specific to your target server and import them to your FrontPage pages.

Server incompatibilities

Whenever possible, develop your pages and webs on the type of web server that will be running on your target machine. If you must develop on another server (for instance, we develop on the FrontPage Personal Web Server and then transfer to Apache on a UNIX box) avoid incompatibilities between the servers. You'll find potential trouble areas in access control, filename extensions, and welcome filenames.

For access control, you'll need to re-enter any access control information for the new server because access control does not carry over between servers of different types. You may need to reconfigure some of the name extensions for MIME types as well. (An example of this is that UNIX-based servers recognize only the .html extension, while Windows-based servers recognize .htm.) Reconfigure your MIME mapping if possible so that the server recognizes the .htm extension. FrontPage creates and recognizes INDEX.HTM as the welcome page for your web. Some servers have different conventions in this area. Re-map your server to recognize INDEX.HTM if possible.

Transferring content

Don't transfer folders beginning with _vti_ to your target server. These folders contain files that are of no use to the server unless the Server Extensions are present. Access control files are of no general use without the Server Extensions, so you should remove all files beginning with a period, if transferring to a UNIX server, and all those beginning with the pound sign, if transferring files to a Windows-based server.

Deleting webs from FrontPage manually

While the preferred method of deleting a web from inside FrontPage is to use the Delete command in the File menu of the FrontPage Explorer, occasionally a web becomes damaged and cannot be deleted in this manner. On these rare occasions, you will need to delete the web manually by deleting the web name from the SERVICES.CNF file. This file is found in a default installation at the following location:

```
C:\Frontpage Webs\content\_vti_pvt\services.cnf
```

This file can be edited with Notepad. Simply delete the reference to the web you wish to delete and save the file.

Figuring out how big your web is

Some service providers only allow you a specific amount of space for your web. Figuring out how big your web is will be important to you in these situations. Select the root directory of your web with Windows Explorer, select the File menu and choose Properties. This will give you a total byte count for all files in all subfolders from the root directory of your web.

Including an AVI clip in FrontPage

Including video clips is relatively simple in FrontPage. Create a normal image in the FrontPage Editor. Select the image and choose Properties from the Edit menu. Choose the Extended button. Enter **DYNSRC="*name*"** where the name of your AVI file replaces the variable *name*.

Using borderless tables to control formatting

Choose the Insert Table command from the Table menu in the FrontPage Editor. You could also select any existing table using your right mouse button and simply choose Properties from the shortcut menu that appears. Choose a border size of zero.

Appendixes

In This Part

 A Resources

 B Installation Guide

 C What's on the CD-ROM

Resources

Our purpose in this appendix is to provide you with a list of the Internet Service Providers (ISP) that advertise that they are using Microsoft FrontPage. This list was correct and all URLs and phone numbers were verified as of July 9, 1996.

Where possible, we have attempted to determine and verify whether or not they provide FrontPage extensions on their server. With the exception of the first URL on the list, we've organized this list in geographical order to assist you in finding the ISP closest to your location. An updated version of this list is maintained at our web site at `http://vrevolution.pitton.com/frontpage/isplist.htm`.

Microsoft

➥ `http://www.microsoft.com/frontpage/ispinfo/isplist.htm`. This is the Microsoft listing of Internet Service Providers that support FrontPage. Many of the ISPs listed below also appear on the Microsoft list. In addition to listing the ISP's support for FrontPage, our list also provides a little information about the services the ISP provides.

National ISPs

➥ **AT&T.** `http://www.att.com/easycommerce/easywww/overview.html`. AT&T Easy World Wide Web (EW3) provides an easy-to-use, secure, reliable web site. EW3 is bundled with Microsoft FrontPage and AT&T provides a link to their Web Site Workshop from this page. The Web Site Workshop includes links to AT&T Creative Design Services, example web site applications, sample web sites, training seminars, and creative tips and ideas. For more information call 800-746-7846.

ISP Listing by State

This list is alphabetical by state. ISPs outside the United States are given at the end of the list. When we were aware of multiple offices for these companies, we listed all the branches.

Arizona

➤ **Sedona On-Line, Inc.** `http://fp.sedona.net/`. Located in Sedona, Arizona, the ISP sister company serves primarily the Verde Valley area of Arizona. Sedona On-Line provides web hosting, design, and maintenance services and operates FrontPage extensions using WebSite Pro server software running on a Windows NT platform. For more information call 520-204-2247.

California

➤ **CERFnet.** `http://cerfnet.com/frontpage/frontpage.html`. CERFnet provides Internet access and connections for over 600 organizations and individuals in California and nationally. Those customers already having a CERFnet account are able to install a FrontPage web on their account using an online form. For more information call 800-876-2373.

➤ **The Computer Shop Network (TCSN).** `http://www.tcsn.net/`. Located in Paso Robles, California, TCSN provides a form to fill out concerning posting your FrontPage web on their server. For more information call 805-227-7000.

➤ **Critical Mass Communications, LLC.** `http://www.criticalmass.com/`. Critical Mass Communications is located in Costa Mesa, California. For more information call 714-549-7689.

➤ **IMV Internet.** `http://www.imvi.com/frontpage.html`. IMV Internet has offices in San Jose, California and in Atlanta, Georgia. The company is a professional web hosting provider and offers both NT and UNIX FrontPage platforms, as well as other options. For more information call 408-574-0200.

➤ **Internet & Web Services Corp.** `http://www.iwsc.com/microsoft index.html`. IWSC is based in San Diego, California and specializes in hosting and designing World Wide Web sites. IWSC uses the industry-leading web technology on their sites. They also make FrontPage available to their customers for the creation and updating of customer sites. For more information call 800-701-6NET (638).

➤ **Internet Presence Providers.** `http://www.ipp.com/`. Internet Presence Providers is located in San Jose, California. This company provides web hosting and design services as well as marketing and consulting assistance in the creation of your web. For more information call 800-556-0131.

- **Sine Wave Solutions, LLC.** `http://www.sinewave.com/`. A small ISP located in El Sobrante, California, Sine Wave serves the San Francisco Bay area. For more information call 510-970-7448.

- **Sutter Yuba Internet Exchange (SYIX).** `http://www.syix.com/`. Serving Sutter and Yuba counties in California, SYIX's main office is in Yuba City. SYIX provides Internet access and web hosting services operating two UNIX systems and one Windows NT system. FrontPage is supported on the NT system running WebSite server software. For more information call 916-755-1751.

Connecticut

- **The Internet Access Company (TIAC).** `http://www.tiac.com/`. Billing itself as the largest Internet service provider in the Northeast, TIAC serves Connecticut, Maine, Massachusetts, New Hampshire, New Jersey, New York, Rhode Island, and Washington, D.C. In addition to providing Internet access services, TIAC also provides a variety of web hosting services. For more information call 202-822-6032.

- **NETAXIS, Inc.** `http://www.netaxis.com/`. NETAXIS is located in Stamford, Connecticut. This company specializes in interactive program development, creative and production services, Internet access, and network consulting. For more information call 203-969-0618.

- **Wing.Net.** `http://www.wing.net/`. With offices in East Berlin, Connecticut and Woburn, Massachusetts, Wing.Net provides a variety of web creation, design, hosting, linking, and maintenance services for their customers. For more information call 617-932-8500.

Delaware

- **Digiserve.** `http://www.digiserve.com/`. Digiserve is a full-service Internet service provider and web site design consulting company with offices in both the United Kingdom and the U.S. For more information send e-mail to `sales@digiserve.com`.

Florida

- **Creative Friendly Technologies.** `http://www.cftnet.com/`. Creative Friendly Technologies (CFT) is located in Tampa, Florida. CFT provides site hosting and other Internet services to the Tampa area. For more information call 813-980-1317.

- **Realacom.** `http://www.realacom.com/`. Realacom is located in Holly Hill, Florida. Realacom provides specialization in database connectivity to web sites. The company serves most of the Daytona Beach, Florida, area. For more information call 904-258-9500.

Georgia

➠ **Akorn Access, Inc.** `http://www.akorn.net/`. Akorn Access Inc. is a full-service Internet access provider located in Alpharetta, Georgia. Akorn specializes in virtual hosting and web design. FrontPage is used by their customers and by the company itself in the creation, design, and maintenance of webs on their servers. For more information call 770-569-1550.

➠ **IMV Internet.** `http://www.imvi.com/frontpage.html`. IMV Internet has offices in San Jose, California and in Atlanta, Georgia. The company is a professional web hosting provider and offers both NT and UNIX FrontPage platforms, as well as other options. For more information call 408-574-0200.

➠ **MindSpring Enterprises, Inc.** `http://web.mindspring.com/prod-svc/web/fp.virtual.html`. Located in Atlanta, Georgia, MindSpring Enterprises offers web site hosting, design, and maintenance. For more information call 800-719-4664.

➠ **Vivid.Net.** `http://fp.calamistrum.com/frontpage/`. Vivid.Net and the Calamistrum are located in Atlanta, Georgia. This partnership can host your FrontPage web and provide expert support for your FrontPage questions. For more information send email to `frontpage@vivid.net`.

Illinois

➠ **Glen Roberts Media.** `http://www.grm.com/`. The creator of the BizzNett Commerce Network, Glen Roberts Media specializes in creating and supporting effective business Web sites. Glen Roberts Media runs Microsoft Internet Information Server and supports a FrontPage support discussion forum. This discussion forum was created using FrontPage and is dedicated to answering questions about the use of FrontPage. Glen Roberts Media has offices in Chicago, Illinois and in Pittsburgh, Pennsylvania. For more information call 708-894-8893.

Kansas

➠ **Pittsburg Online.** `http://www.pitton.com/`. Located in Pittsburg, Kansas, Pittsburg Online offers Internet access and web site hosting to businesses and individuals in the southeastern area of Kansas. For more information call 316-231-0746.

Louisiana

➡ **Hiway Technologies, Inc.** `http://www.hway.net/`. Hiway Technologies is located in Boca Raton, Louisiana and provides state-of-the-art communications and marketing-related services to its customers. For more information call 800-339-4929.

Maine

➡ **The Internet Access Company (TIAC).** `http://www.tiac.com/`. Billing itself as the largest Internet service provider in the Northeast, TIAC serves Connecticut, Maine, Massachusetts, New Hampshire, New Jersey, New York, Rhode Island, and Washington, D.C. In addition to providing Internet access services, TIAC also provides a variety of web hosting services. For more information call 202-822-6032.

Maryland

➡ **Internet Express, Inc.** `http://www.x-press.net/`. Located in Damascus, Maryland, Internet Express provides a wide range of Internet access, web site hosting, and web authoring services. For more information call 301-253-1500.

Massachusetts

➡ **HarvardNet.** `http://www.harvard.net/`. Located in Harvard, Massachusetts, this Internet service provider provides dedicated Internet access, high-performance web hosting, and Internet planning services for organizations. For more information call 800-772-6771.

➡ **The Internet Access Company.** `http://www.tiac.com/`. Billing itself as the largest Internet service provider in the Northeast, TIAC serves Connecticut, Maine, Massachusetts, New Hampshire, New Jersey, New York, Rhode Island, and Washington, D.C. In addition to providing Internet access services, TIAC also provides a variety of web hosting services. For more information call 202-822-6032.

➡ **shore.net.** `http://www.shore.net/`. Serving most of Eastern Massachusetts with Internet service, shore.net is based in the community of Lynn, Massachusetts. The company provides a wide range of web hosting services and operates a UNIX system. For more information call 617-593-3110.

➡ **Wing.Net.** `http://www.wing.net/`. With offices in East Berlin, Connecticut and Woburn, Massachusetts, Wing.Net provides a variety of web creation, design, hosting, linking, and maintenance services for their customers. For more information call 617-932-8500.

Minnesota

➡ **Coron.** `http://www.coron.com/`. Located in Minnetonka, Minnesota, the Coron Company is an international full-service solution provider and developer of interactive multimedia web sites. The Coron Company believes that FrontPage will become the standard in the industry, due to its ease of use and low learning curve. For more information call 800-626-6727.

New Hampshire

➡ **The Internet Access Company (TIAC).** `http://www.tiac.com/`. Billing itself as the largest Internet service provider in the Northeast, TIAC serves Connecticut, Maine, Massachusetts, New Hampshire, New Jersey, New York, Rhode Island, and Washington, D.C. In addition to providing Internet access services, TIAC also provides a variety of web hosting services. For more information call 202-822-6032.

New Jersey

➡ **The Internet Acess Company (TIAC).** `http://www.tiac.com/`. Billing itself as the largest Internet service provider in the Northeast, TIAC serves Connecticut, Maine, Massachusetts, New Hampshire, New Jersey, New York, Rhode Island, and Washington, D.C. In addition to providing Internet access services, TIAC also provides a variety of web hosting services. For more information call 202-822-6032.

➡ **Internet Images Worldwide.** `http://www.inet-images.com/`. Internet Images Worldwide is located in Hoboken, New Jersey and offers site production, server setup and maintenance, web hosting, online market research and promotion, and other site-related training and services. For more information call 201-420-9191.

➡ **WebWorld, Inc.** `http://www.terradom.net/`. WebWorld, Inc. does business as Terradom Corporation in Cherry Hill, New Jersey. Running off an NT operating system, WebWorld, Inc. provides hosting services for FrontPage webs, online database development, training in the use of FrontPage, web page consulting and analysis, and site creation. For more information call 609-216-0800.

New York

➥ **The Internet Access Company (TIAC).** http://www.tiac.com/. Billing itself as the largest Internet service provider in the Northeast, TIAC serves Connecticut, Maine, Massachusetts, New Hampshire, New Jersey, New York, Rhode Island, and Washington, D.C. In addition to providing Internet access services, TIAC also provides a variety of web hosting services. For more information call 202-822-6032.

Ohio

➥ **CSD Internetworks.** http://www.kenton.com/. CSD Internetworks is located in Kenton, Ohio and serves Hardin County. There is considerable advertising on their home pages and their support forum was created using the FrontPage Discussion Web Wizard. For more information send e-mail to csdi@kenton.com.

Pennsylvania

➥ **Glen Roberts Media.** http://www.grm.com/. The creator of the BizzNett Commerce Network, Glen Roberts Media specializes in creating and supporting effective business Web sites. Glen Roberts Media runs Microsoft Internet Information Server and supports a FrontPage support discussion forum. This discussion forum was created using FrontPage and is dedicated to answering questions about the use of FrontPage. Glen Roberts Media has offices in Chicago, Illinois and in Pittsburgh, Pennsylvania. For more information call 708-894-8893.

Rhode Island

➥ **The Internet Access Company (TIAC).** http://www.tiac.com/. Billing itself as the largest Internet service provider in the Northeast, TIAC serves Connecticut, Maine, Massachusetts, New Hampshire, New Jersey, New York, Rhode Island, and Washington, D.C. In addition to providing Internet access services, TIAC also provides a variety of web hosting services. For more information call 202-822-6032.

South Carolina

➡ **CETLink.Net.** http://www.cetlink.net. Computer Enhancement Technologies, Inc. is located in Rockhill, South Carolina. The services provided by this company include Internet access, web creation, maintenance, and hosting, and network configuration and support. For more information call 803-327-2754.

Texas

➡ **Chrysalis Online Services.** http://www.chrysalis.org/. Chrysalis is located in Plano, Texas and serves the Dallas-Fort Worth metroplex. Having begun as a BBS in 1979, Chrysalis offers to its members a large library of files to browse. For more information send e-mail to garry.grosse@chrysalis.org.

➡ **FLEXnet,Inc.** http://frontpage.flex.net/. Serving the Southwest, FLEXnet fully supports FrontPage. They have a dedicated server for hosting FrontPage webs and have an online FrontPage specialist to answer your technical questions. FLEXnet is located in The Woodlands, Texas. For more information call 713-364-6500.

➡ **National Knowledge Networks, Inc. (nkn).** http://www.nkn.net/nkn/ms/nknfront.htm. nkn is located in Dallas, Texas and has supplied North Texas with Internet service for over two years. nkn specializes in Internet access and web creation, hosting, and maintenance services. For more information call 214-880-0700.

Virginia

➡ **AERA.** http://www.aera.com/. Advanced Engineering and Research Associates (AERA) is located in Arlington, Virginia. AERA's primary services are interactive, computer-based training and electronic documentation products and services, support services, and engineering support. For more information call 703-486-1993.

➡ **Judds, Inc.** http://www.judds.com/online/frontpage.htm. Founded in 1868, in Washington, D.C., Judds, Inc. is a major publishing and printing concern based in Virginia. The company prints over 140 popular magazines and periodicals. Judds offers online services that include magazine database hosting and web services. For more information call 800-368-3492 x 623.

Washington, D.C.

➡ **The Internet Access Company (TIAC).** `http://www.tiac.com/`. Billing itself as the largest Internet service provider in the Northeast, TIAC serves Connecticut, Maine, Massachusetts, New Hampshire, New Jersey, New York, Rhode Island, and Washington, D.C. In addition to providing Internet access services, TIAC also provides a variety of web hosting services. For more information call 202-822-6032.

Wisconsin

➡ **CyFi.** `http://www.cyfi.com/frontpge.htm`. Cyberspace Financial (CyFi) is located in Madison, Wisconsin. CyFi provides a range of services for corporations, financial institutions, trade associations, and processors. One interesting aspect of their web site is a white paper titled "The Evolution of Web Site Authoring." For more information call 608-223-2674.

International ISPs

Following is a list of some providers in other countries. This list is not nearly as finely researched as the U.S. state-by-state listing that precedes it. You may want to do a little extra research to really compare what's available in your country before you sign up.

Canada

➡ **CanLinks.com, Inc.** `http://www.canlinks.com/`. CanLinks.com Inc. is located in Mississauga, Canada. This company provides Internet access and web site hosting services. They fully support FrontPage sites and run the Microsoft Internet Information Server. For more information call 905-602-6721.

Ireland

➡ **Infomatique.** `http://infomatique.iol.ie/WEBHOST.htm`. Infomatique is located in Dublin, Ireland and employs both O'Reilly's WebSite server software and the Microsoft Internet Information Server software. For more information send e-mail to `williamm@infomatique.iol.ie`.

Taiwan

➡ **WonderNet.** `http://www.wonder.net.tw/`. Located in Taiwan, WonderNet provides Internet access and web site hosting services. For more information send e-mail to `webmaster@wonder.net.tw`.

United Kingdom

➡ **Digiserve.** `http://www.digiserve.com/`. Digiserve is a full-service Internet service provider and web site design consulting company with offices in both the United Kingdom and the U.S. For more information send e-mail to `sales@digiserve.com`.

Installation Guide

Appendix B

I n this appendix we show you how to install the FrontPage software with the Windows 95 and Windows NT Server Extensions. You also learn how to install Internet Information Server on the Windows NT platform. Finally, you learn how to install Internet Explorer on your computer.

Microsoft FrontPage

In this part of the appendix, we explain the system requirements and the installation process for the Microsoft FrontPage software. This section should enable you to install FrontPage without difficulty.

System requirements

To install FrontPage, you need the following configuration for your system:

➡ Windows 95 or Windows NT 3.51 or higher

➡ 16MB RAM minimum

➡ 20MB free hard drive space

➡ WinSock-compliant TCP/IP stack installed and properly configured

Installing FrontPage

In the following instructions we are assuming a normal and typical first-time installation on a Windows 95 operating system. We've placed notes concerning what will happen if you are installing over a previous installation where appropriate.

When you open the FrontPage package you find a set of six 3.5" floppy disks. On Disk #1 you find an installation program called Setup.exe.

The first thing you should do is to save all work you might currently have open in other programs and close these other applications. The reason for saving your work is that the installation process may require that the setup program restart your computer after installing FrontPage.

Insert Disk #1 into your 3.5" floppy disk drive. Choose the Start button on the Windows 95 toolbar and choose the Run option. Type in the name of the disk drive where you placed Disk #1 and the name of the installation program. For example, with the disk in drive A, it should read

```
A:/SETUP.EXE
```

Choose OK and, after a splash screen, you see a welcome screen. Choose the Next button.

You are now confronted with the Destination Path dialog box. This is where you choose the directory and subdirectories to install FrontPage into. Using Windows 95, FrontPage will be installed into the \Program Files\Microsoft FrontPage\ folder on your C: drive by default.

You can change the default by choosing the Browse button.

This option isn't available if you are installing over an existing version of FrontPage, as can be seen in Figure B-1.

Choosing the Browse button brings up the Choose Directory dialog box. The Path field in this dialog box displays the destination directory. Click in the Drive field to change drives. Change folders by browsing through your file system and selecting a different folder. You can connect to a new drive by choosing the Network button. After you've made all the changes you need to make, choose OK to accept the changes. If you've entered a folder in the Path field that doesn't exist, the installation program creates the new folder for you.

After the destination directory is set, choose the Next button again. You now see the Setup Type dialog box on your screen, as in Figure B-2.

Here you can choose what type of installation you want. You have two options: a typical installation or a custom installation.

There are three major components of FrontPage. These components are the FrontPage Personal Web Server and FrontPage Server Extensions, the FrontPage Explorer, and the FrontPage Editor. A typical installation installs all

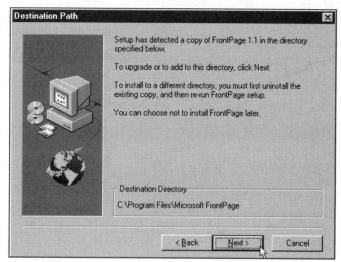

Figure B-1: If you're installing over an existing copy of FrontPage, you must use the previous directory or uninstall FrontPage first.

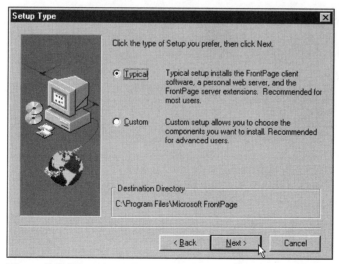

Figure B-2: What kind of installation do you want to perform?

the major FrontPage components and utilities on your system. You'll find this to be a fast, easy, and efficient method of installing or upgrading your FrontPage product on your system.

You can use the custom installation to install or upgrade any individual component of the FrontPage product.

When you first install FrontPage, we recommend that you use the typical installation
on your system. Choose the Typical button. The installation program now begins
installing the FrontPage Personal Web Server on your system. If this is the first
time that FrontPage has been installed on this system, FrontPage installs the
Personal Web Server in the \Frontpage Webs\ Server\ folder by default. Your
content will be installed in the \FrontPage Webs\Content\ folder by default.

If you want to designate different folders for these items, choose Browse and
name the folder in the Choose Directory dialog box.

If you have a previously installed version of the Personal Web Server on your
computer already, as in Figure B-3, then the Personal Web Server will be
installed over the previous installation.

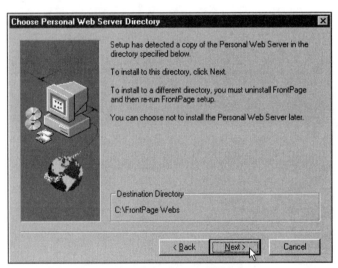

Figure B-3: Where to install the Personal Web Server.

In this case, the Browse button will not be displayed and you will not be given
the opportunity to change the installation directory.

The Personal Web Server dialog box will be displayed. This dialog box offers
you two options: Upgrade or Install.

The Upgrade option installs the new version of the FrontPage Personal Web Server
over the top of the previously installed version. If the previous version of the
Personal Web Server is not in the \FrontPage Webs\Server\ folder, it will be moved
there before being upgraded. The existing \Content\ folder will be maintained.

The Install option installs a new version of the FrontPage Personal Web Server in a different directory from that of the previously installed version. In this case, the installation program installs a new \Server\ and \Content\ directory separate from the original installation.

When you install a second copy of the Personal Web Server on your system, the original Personal Web Server maintains the TCP/IP port 80 configuration and the new server installation is assigned to TCP/IP port 8080.

After making your selection, choose the Next button. You now see the Select Program Folder dialog box, as in Figure B-4.

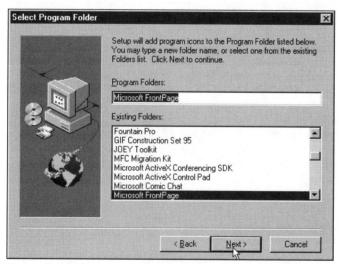

Figure B-4: Tell your computer what folder you want the FrontPage icons to be kept in.

This dialog box is used to select the program folder where you want the Microsoft FrontPage icons to be added. The default folder name for these icons is the Microsoft FrontPage program folder. You can accept the default or, by selecting a different folder from the Existing Folders list field or entering a new folder name in the Program Folders field, choose a different folder. Choose the Next button when you've made your selection.

The Start Copying Files dialog box is now displayed on your screen. This dialog box displays the settings you've made so far. If you want to change any of these settings, choose the Back button until you reach the appropriate dialog box. Once there, make your changes and then choose the Next button until you come back to the Start Copying Files dialog box. Choose the Next button and FrontPage will be installed. While this is happening you'll be treated to a graphical representation of the progress of the installation program on your screen. At the end of this, you may be prompted to restart your computer.

You need to register as the administrator of the server if this is a new installation. The installation program will prompt you to input the necessary information in the Administrator Setup for Personal Web Server dialog box. This information includes the user name you want to use for this server and the password to use with the user name. You'll be prompted to enter the password twice for confirmation. There's no limit on the length of the name or the password, but it is more secure to use a password of at least eight letters. Choose the OK button to register your name and password.

Make sure you write down your user name and password somewhere safe. You need to supply this name and password to create or open a web on the server.

This completes the installation. Choose the Finish button to exit the setup program. You can now start the FrontPage Explorer from your Start/Programs menu.

Microsoft Internet Information Server

Internet Information Server ships with Windows NT Server 4.0. In this part of the appendix, we explain the system requirements and the installation process for the Microsoft Internet Information Server for the Windows NT platform. This section should allow you to install the Internet Information Server quickly and without difficulty.

System requirements

In order to install Microsoft Internet Information Server for Windows NT you need

➡ Windows NT Server version 4.0.

➡ A computer with a minimum configuration necessary to support the Windows NT Server.

➡ Enough free disk space for both the installation and your information content. It is recommended that all drives used with Internet Information Server be formatted with the Windows NT File System (NTFS).

➡ WinSock-compliant TCP/IP stack installed and properly configured. This is included with Windows NT. You can use the Network applet in the NT Control Panel to install and configure the TCP/IP protocol and related components.

Internet publishing requirements

In order to publish a web to the Internet you need the following:

➡ An Internet connection

➡ A static Internet Protocol (IP) address from your Internet Service Provider (ISP)

➡ Domain Name System (DNS) registration for that IP address (Although this requirement is considered optional, we highly recommend it.)

➡ A network adapter card suitable for your connection to the Internet

Intranet publishing requirements

Publishing a web on your organization's intranet requires the following:

➡ A local area network (LAN) connection

➡ A network adapter card suitable for your connection to the LAN

➡ Either the Windows Internet Name Service (WINS) Server or the Domain Name System (DNS) service installed on a computer in your intranet (Although this requirement is considered optional, we highly recommend it.)

Installing Internet Information Server

There are four basic steps to installing the Internet Information Server. These four steps are simple and straightforward, and are detailed in the sections that follow.

1. **Configure Windows NT before installing the Internet Information Server.**
2. **Run the Internet Information Server Setup program.**
3. **Set up the HTML and other files you wish published on the Internet or your intranet.**
4. **Test your installation.**

Windows NT configuration

Before you install the Internet Information Server, it is best if you configure the Windows NT Server networking component. This ensures that your server will be able to operate either on the Internet or on your intranet. This also gives you the opportunity to enhance the Windows NT Server default security settings and implement other security measures to prevent users from tampering with your network.

You use the Network applet in the Windows NT Control Panel for all configuration tasks discussed in the steps given here.

1. **Obtain an Internet connection.** In order to publish on the Internet, you're going to need a connection to the Internet from an ISP. We've listed ISPs who support the FrontPage Server Extensions in Appendix A. This might be a good place to start. Also, you might look in the phone book under Computers/Networking, or in your local newspaper's business or technology section.

2. **Install Windows NT Server software.** If you're installing Windows NT Server 3.51, you need to install Service Pack 3. This is included on the CD-ROM with the Internet Information Server package. Internet Information Server is one of the options for installation with Windows NT Server 4.0, Beta 2.

3. **Configure your TCP/IP protocol.** Install the Windows NT TCP/IP Protocol and Connectivity Utilities. If you have already installed the FTP Service that comes with Windows NT, remove it.

4. **Obtain your server's IP address.** Your ISP must provide you with your server's IP address, subnet mask, and default gateway's IP address.

5. **Configure your server's domain name.** The domain name is sometimes referred to as the host name. An IP address, such as http://206.53.99.200/index.htm, can always be used to contact your server. However, if you register your domain name in the DNS, your server can be contacted using a user-friendly domain name, such as http://vrevolution.pitton.com/index.com. Your ISP will usually be able to assist you with domain name registration.

6. **Configure name resolution.** You must have a DNS server's IP address in order to use its friendly name when browsing other servers on the Internet. If your server is on a TCP/IP LAN with WINS servers, you need to obtain the name of the WINS server to use.

Internet Information Server setup

Inside the directory of the Internet Information Server, you find the subdirectories listed in Table B-1.

Table B-1	Internet Information Server Subdirectories
Subdirectory	**Contents**
\IIS\	Use the Setup.exe in the root directory to install the Internet Information Server and all of its components.
\Admin	Use the Setup.exe in this subdirectory to install only the Internet Service Manager.

Subdirectory	Contents
\Alpha	This subdirectory contains the files necessary to install the Internet Information Server on an Alpha AXP-based platform.
\Clients	Use the Setup.exe located in this subdirectory to install only the Windows NT-based Internet Explorer client.
\Help	This subdirectory contains all of the WinHelp files.
\I386	This subdirectory contains all files necessary to install the Internet Information Server on an Intel-based plat form.
\MIPS	This subdirectory contains all files necessary to install the Internet Information Server on a MIPS-based plat form.
\Ppc	This subdirectory contains all of the files necessary to install the Internet Information Server on a PowerPC-based platform.
\Samples	This subdirectory contains sample HTML content files that come with the Internet Information Server software.
\Sdk	This subdirectory contains some of the header files for the Internet Extensions for Win32 and Internet Server Application Programming Interface (ISAPI). A complete ISAPI software development kit is available from Microsoft.
\Winnt351.qfe	Run the file Update.exe in this subdirectory to install Service Pack 3.

After you have your Internet connection and have Windows NT Server configured, you're ready to install Internet Information Server. The first thing you need to make sure of is that you are logged on to the system with administrator privileges. If you are going to configure the server using the Internet Service Manager, your user account must be a member of the Administrators group on the target computer. Follow these instructions to install Internet Information Server:

1. **Start Setup.**

    This is accomplished in one of two ways: from the File Manager you can double-click on the file named Setup.exe in the \IIS\ directory on your hard drive; or, from the command prompt change to the \IIS\ directory on your hard drive and then type **setup**.

2. **A welcome dialog box appears. Choose the OK button to proceed.**

3. **In the next dialog box, several options for installation appear and all are selected by default.**

   The options are

   - **Internet Service Manager** is the administration program for managing services.

   - **World Wide Web Service** creates the WWW publishing server.

   - **Gopher Service** creates Gopher publishing server.

   - **FTP Service** creates the FTP publishing server.

   - **ODBC Drivers and Administration** installs Open Data Base Connectivity (ODBC) drivers. These ODBC drivers are required for logging to ODBC files and for enabling ODBC access from the WWW service. If you want to provide access to databases through the Internet Information Server, you need to set up the ODBC drivers and data sources by using the ODBC applet in the Control Panel.

   - **Help and sample files** installs online Help and sample HTML files.

   - **Internet Explorer** installs the Windows NT version of Microsoft Internet Explorer.

   If you do not want to install a specific component, click on the box next to the option to clear it. You can also use this Setup program later to add or remove any or all of these components.

4. **Accept the default installation directory (C:\Inetsrv), or choose the Change Directory button and enter a new directory.**

5. **Choose the OK button. The Publishing Directories dialog box appears. Either accept the default directories for the publishing services or change the directories.**

6. **Choose the OK button. When prompted to create the service directories (Wwwroot, Gophroot, and Ftproot by default), choose yes.**

7. **The Create Internet Account dialog box appears on your screen. Enter a password and then type the password again for confirmation. Choose OK.**

   Setup now copies all remaining Internet Information Server files onto your hard drive.

8. If you selected the ODBC Drivers and Administration option earlier, the Install Drivers dialog box appears. Select the SQL Server driver from the list of available ODBC Drivers list box and choose OK.

9. Setup finishes copying files to your hard drive.

You're now ready to publish either on the Internet, or your intranet, or both. However, in order to take full advantage of the advanced publishing features of FrontPage, you need to install the FrontPage Server Extensions for the Internet

Microsoft Internet Explorer

In this third part, we explain the system requirements and the installation process for the Microsoft Internet Explorer browser. This section should allow you to install FrontPage without difficulty.

System requirements

There are several versions of Microsoft Internet Explorer available now. There are versions for Windows 3.1, for the Macintosh, for Windows 95, and for Windows NT.

The Microsoft Internet Explorer 3.0 for Windows 95 and Windows NT only works with Windows NT Build 1381 or later.

Installing Internet Explorer

If you installed the Internet Information Server and did not remove the check next to the Internet Explorer option, this version of Internet Explorer was installed along with the Internet Information Server.

You'll want to check in at http://www.microsoft.com for upgrades of this browser software.

What's on the CD-ROM

Appendix C

Table C-1 contains a listing of the directories on the CD-ROM included with this book and the contents of those directories.

Table C-1	CD-ROM Contents
Directory	**Contents**
\images\	Various subdirectories containing graphics and other image files
\images\anartist\	Graphic files supplied by An Artist, Inc.
\images\imagfarm\	Graphic files supplied by the Image Farm
\images\pd\	Graphic files that are in the public domain
\VRE\	A mirror image of the VREvolution web as created for this book. This reflects the web as it appeared when this book was being completed in July and August of 1996.

In addition to those directories listed in the preceding table, **\template** is a subdirectory that contains the page and web templates we've created for you to use with FrontPage. These templates include

- Adopt-a-Pet page template
- Business "Store Front" page template
- Collectibles page template
- Collectibles Discussion web template
- Government Office "Store Front" page template
- Humane Society page template
- Humane Society web template
- Item For Sale page template
- Missing Child page template
- Missing Child Help web template
- "Our Town" web template
- Programming Examples page template
- Programming Specification page template
- Programming Specification web template
- Resume/Vita page template
- Utilities "Store Front" page template

(continued)

(continued)

(continued)

(continued)

WEB DESIGN WITH IMAGE FARM™ IMAGES

The Source for Photographic Textures & Backgrounds on CD-ROM.

Regularly **$99** each

"For a different approach to texture and background images, turn to Image Farm." - PC Magazine, May 1996

In a black-and-white ad, we can't *possibly* show you the incredible range of high-quality, 24-bit color images we have, but there are *other* places where we can.

For a free full-color brochure, call 1-800-GET-FARM.

To see a sample of our images, check out **www.imagefarm.com** or view some of the tiles created from our images on the **CD-ROM supplied with this book**.

Image Farm has **5 unique CD-ROMs, each with 100 photographic textures and backgrounds**. Photographed in captivating regions throughout the world, they are ideal for web page design, graphic design, multimedia, advertisements, 3-D texture mapping, video and television graphics, desktop publishing and more.

- **Full 24-bit color images.**
- **5 unique volumes, each with 100 images.**
- **Royalty-free, without any hidden costs or locked files.**
- **Original photos, not found in other image libraries.**
- **Mac, PC and UNIX compatible CD-ROMs.**
- **5 resolutions per image, from 72K to 18MB (up to 2048 x 3072 pixels).**
- **$99 for each volume, and greater savings when buying 2 or more.**

1-800-438-3276
www.imagefarm.com

Order Now and Save 10%

Present this coupon to Image Farm and receive 10% off the regular price* of volumes 1 through 5. Discount only applies to orders placed directly with Image Farm and can be redeemed through mail, fax or phone orders.

Offer valid through 6/30/97

*Regular Prices: 1 Disc - $99   2 Discs - $189   3 Discs - $269   4 Discs - $339   5 Discs - $399

Image Farm™ Inc. - 110 Spadina Ave., #309, Toronto, ON M5V 2K4 Tel: (416) 504-4161 Fax: (416) 504-4163
All prices quoted in approximate U.S. funds. Payments must be in Canadian funds. Prices subject to change without notice.

IDG BOOKS WORLDWIDE, INC.

END-USER LICENSE AGREEMENT

Read This. You should carefully read these terms and conditions before opening the software packet(s) included with this book ("Book"). This is a license agreement ("Agreement") between you and IDG Books Worldwide, Inc. ("IDGB"). By opening the accompanying software packet(s), you acknowledge that you have read and accept the following terms and conditions. If you do not agree and do not want to be bound by such terms and conditions, promptly return the Book and the unopened software packet(s) to the place you obtained them for a full refund.

License Grant. IDGB grants to you (either an individual or entity) a nonexclusive license to use one copy of the enclosed software program(s) (collectively, the "Software") solely for your own personal or business purposes on a single computer (whether a standard computer or a work-station component of a multi-user network). The Software is in use on a computer when it is loaded into temporary memory (i.e., RAM) or installed into permanent memory (e.g., hard disk, CD-ROM or other storage device). IDGB reserves all rights not expressly granted herein.

Ownership. IDGB is the owner of all right, title and interest, including copyright, in and to the compilation of the Software recorded on the disk(s)/CD-ROM. Copyright to the individual programs on the disk(s)/CD-ROM is owned by the author or other authorized copyright owner of each program. Ownership of the Software and all proprietary rights relating thereto remain with IDGB and its licensors.

Restrictions On Use and Transfer.

You may only (i) make one copy of the Software for backup or archival purposes, or (ii) transfer the Software to a single hard disk, provided that you keep the original for backup or archival purposes. You may not (i) rent or lease the Software, (ii) copy or reproduce the Software through a LAN or other network system or through any computer subscriber system or bulletin-board system, or (iii) modify, adapt or create derivative works based on the Software.

You may not reverse engineer, decompile, or disassemble the Software. You may transfer the Software and user documentation on a permanent basis, provided that the transferee agrees to accept the terms and conditions of this Agreement and you retain no copies. If the Software is an update or has been updated, any transfer must include the most recent update and all prior versions.

Restrictions on Use of Individual Programs. You must follow the individual requirements and restrictions detailed for each individual program. These limitations are contained in the individual license agreements recorded on the disk(s)/CD-ROM. These restrictions include a requirement that after using the program for the period of time specified in its text, the user must pay a registration fee or discontinue use. By opening the Software packet(s), you will be agreeing to abide by the licenses and restrictions for these individual programs. None of the material on this disk(s) or listed in this Book may ever be distributed, in original or modified form, for commercial purposes.

<u>Limited Warranty</u>.

IDGB warrants that the Software and disk(s)/CD-ROM are free from defects in materials and workmanship under normal use for a period of sixty (60) days from the date of purchase of this Book. If IDGB receives notification within the warranty period of defects in materials or workmanship, IDGB will replace the defective disk(s)/CD-ROM.

IDGB AND THE AUTHOR OF THE BOOK DISCLAIM ALL OTHER WARRANTIES, EXPRESS OR IMPLIED, INCLUDING WITHOUT LIMITATION IMPLIED WARRANTIES OF MERCHANTABILITY AND FITNESS FOR A PARTICULAR PURPOSE, WITH RESPECT TO THE SOFTWARE, THE PROGRAMS, THE SOURCE CODE CONTAINED THEREIN, AND/OR THE TECHNIQUES DESCRIBED IN THIS BOOK. IDGB DOES NOT WARRANT THAT THE FUNCTIONS CONTAINED IN THE SOFTWARE WILL MEET YOUR REQUIREMENTS OR THAT THE OPERATION OF THE SOFTWARE WILL BE ERROR FREE.

This limited warranty gives you specific legal rights, and you may have other rights which vary from jurisdiction to jurisdiction.

<u>Remedies</u>.

IDGB's entire liability and your exclusive remedy for defects in materials and workmanship shall be limited to replacement of the Software, which is returned to IDGB at the address set forth below with a copy of your receipt. This Limited Warranty is void if failure of the Software has resulted from accident, abuse, or misapplication. Any replacement Software will be warranted for the remainder of the original warranty period or thirty (30) days, whichever is longer.

In no event shall IDGB or the author be liable for any damages whatsoever (including without limitation damages for loss of business profits, business interruption, loss of business information, or any other pecuniary loss) arising out of the use of or inability to use the Book or the Software, even if IDGB has been advised of the possibility of such damages.

Because some jurisdictions do not allow the exclusion or limitation of liability for consequential or incidental damages, the above limitation or exclusion may not apply to you.

<u>U.S. Government Restricted Rights</u>. Use, duplication, or disclosure of the Software by the U.S. Government is subject to restrictions stated in paragraph (c) (1) (ii) of the Rights in Technical Data and Computer Software clause of DFARS 252.227-7013, and in subparagraphs (a) through (d) of the Commercial Computer—Restricted Rights clause at FAR 52.227-19, and in similar clauses in the NASA FAR supplement, when applicable.

<u>General</u>. This Agreement constitutes the entire understanding of the parties, and revokes and supersedes all prior agreements, oral or written, between them and may not be modified or amended except in a writing signed by both parties hereto which specifically refers to this Agreement. This Agreement shall take precedence over any other documents that may be in conflict herewith. If any one or more provisions contained in this Agreement are held by any court or tribunal to be invalid, illegal or otherwise unenforceable, each and every other provision shall remain in full force and effect.

Installation Instructions

For information about how to install the programs on the CD, please see
Appendix B. For further, in-depth information about each program on the CD,
please see Appendix C.

IDG BOOKS WORLDWIDE REGISTRATION CARD

RETURN THIS REGISTRATION CARD FOR FREE CATALOG

Title of this book: **Creating Cool™ FrontPage™ Web Sites**

My overall rating of this book: ❏ Very good [1] ❏ Good [2] ❏ Satisfactory [3] ❏ Fair [4] ❏ Poor [5]

How I first heard about this book:

❏ Found in bookstore; name: [6] _____   ❏ Book review: [7] _____

❏ Advertisement: [8] _____   ❏ Catalog: [9] _____

❏ Word of mouth; heard about book from friend, co-worker, etc.: [10] ____   ❏ Other: [11] _____

What I liked most about this book:

_____

_____

_____

What I would change, add, delete, etc., in future editions of this book:

_____

_____

Other comments:

_____

Number of computer books I purchase in a year: ❏ 1 [12] ❏ 2-5 [13] ❏ 6-10 [14] ❏ More than 10 [15]

I would characterize my computer skills as: ❏ Beginner [16] ❏ Intermediate [17] ❏ Advanced [18] ❏ Professional [19]

I use ❏ DOS [20] ❏ Windows [21] ❏ OS/2 [22] ❏ Unix [23] ❏ Macintosh [24] ❏ Other: [25]_____
(please specify)

I would be interested in new books on the following subjects:
(please check all that apply, and use the spaces provided to identify specific software)

❏ Word processing: [26] _____   ❏ Spreadsheets: [27] _____

❏ Data bases: [28] _____   ❏ Desktop publishing: [29] _____

❏ File Utilities: [30] _____   ❏ Money management: [31] _____

❏ Networking: [32] _____   ❏ Programming languages: [33] _____

❏ Other: [34] _____

I use a PC at (please check all that apply): ❏ home [35] ❏ work [36] ❏ school [37] ❏ other: [38] _____

The disks I prefer to use are ❏ 5.25 [39] ❏ 3.5 [40] ❏ other: [41] _____

I have a CD ROM: ❏ yes [42] ❏ no [43]

I plan to buy or upgrade computer hardware this year: ❏ yes [44] ❏ no [45]

I plan to buy or upgrade computer software this year: ❏ yes [46] ❏ no [47]

Name: _____   Business title: [48] _____   Type of Business: [49] _____

Address (❏ home [50] ❏ work [51]/Company name: _____)

Street/Suite# _____

City [52]/State [53]/Zipcode [54]: _____   Country [55] _____

❏ **I liked this book!** You may quote me by name in future
IDG Books Worldwide promotional materials.

My daytime phone number is _____

IDG BOOKS

THE WORLD OF
COMPUTER
KNOWLEDGE

☐ YES!

Please keep me informed about IDG's World of Computer Knowledge.
Send me the latest IDG Books catalog.

COMPUTER
BOOK SERIES
FROM IDG